THE WINES OF NORTHERN

THE INFINITE IDEAS
CLASSIC WINE LIBRARY

Editorial board: Sarah Jane Evans MW and Richard Mayson

There is something uniquely satisfying about a good wine book, preferably read with a glass of the said wine in hand. The Infinite Ideas Classic Wine Library is a series of wine books written by authors who are both knowledgeable and passionate about their subject. Each title in The Infinite Ideas Classic Wine Library covers a wine region, country or type and together the books are designed to form a comprehensive guide to the world of wine as well as an enjoyable read, appealing to wine professionals, wine lovers, tourists, armchair travellers and wine trade students alike.

The series:

THE WINES OF NORTHERN
SPAIN

From Galicia to the Pyrenees
and Rioja to the Basque Country

SARAH JANE EVANS MW

infiniteideas

Sarah Jane Evans MW is an award-winning wine-writer, journalist and speaker at conferences worldwide, and is co-Chairman of the Decanter World Wine Awards. She became a Master of Wine in 2006, winning the Robert Mondavi Winery Award for the highest marks in the theory papers, and is a past Chairman of the Institute of Masters of Wine. She was the winner of the WSET Outstanding Alumni Award in 2017. To recognize her expertise in Spanish wines, she was made a member of the Gran Orden de Caballeros de Vino in 2010; she is also a Dama de Albariño in Rías Baixas, a Dama de Solear (Manzanilla Sherry), and was awarded the Premio de Honra by DO Ribeiro.

The right of Sarah Jane Evans to be identified as the author of this book has been asserted in accordance with the Copyright, Designs and Patents Act 1988.

First published in 2018 by
Infinite Ideas Limited
www.infideas.com

A CIP catalogue record for this book is available from the British Library

ISBN 978–1–908984–96–8

Front cover photo showing vineyard and church at Leza with the Sierra de Cantabria beyond, Alava, Spain © Mick Rock/Cephas Picture Library.

Maps created by Darren Lingard. Map on page 201 showing proposal for Rioja subzones created from an original © José Hidalgo.

All colour plates © Sarah Jane Evans except plate 1 © CVNE; plate 2 (bottom) courtesy James Sturcke; plate 5 (top) courtesy of Norrel Robertson; plate 5 (bottom) courtesy of Fernando Mora; plate 6 (top) by kind permission of Spanish Wine Lover; www.spanishwinelover.com

Typeset by DigiTrans Media, India

Printed in Britain by 4edge Limited

CONTENTS

INTRODUCTION

Spain is the most exciting country in Europe for wine lovers, and one of the most exciting in the world. In the last 30 years it has lived through an exceptional period of change – cultural, social and political, as well as vinous. It now offers us wine styles of every kind. This is the country where you can find wines of glorious maturity, polished in oak barrels to a fine complexity, where people talk fondly about '45, '64 and '70, through to 2001, '04 and '05. It is also home to the new reds, the fresh, zesty Atlantic styles; the aromatic whites; the pale-coloured *rosados*; the 'traditional method' sparklings; the sweet Moscatels; the wines aged under *flor*; and the wines from vines grown on slate, clay, limestone or sand, all expressing their origins. Amongst these wines I have highlighted examples of heroic viticulture, on steep, steep slopes; of continental climates with extremes of temperature; and of vineyards with their toes more or less in the sea.

This mosaic of wines comes just from northern Spain. I had originally intended this to be a book on the whole of Spain, in part to replace and update those that had been published in English back in 1999 and 2004. A book on the wines of Spain is very much overdue. But it quickly became clear that Spain has become so diverse and so interesting that it needed two separate books to manage the story. This book therefore draws a line from the Pyrenees to Aragón and Navarra, and turns west to Rioja, Ribera del Duero, Castilla y León, and Galicia, also taking in Txakoli country, and Asturias. It remains for the next book to cover Catalunya, the Levant, Southern Spain and Andalucía, not forgetting the islands.

Within the boundaries of this book, Rioja, Navarra and Ribera del Duero are long established, as is the Tempranillo grape. Ribeiro too has a

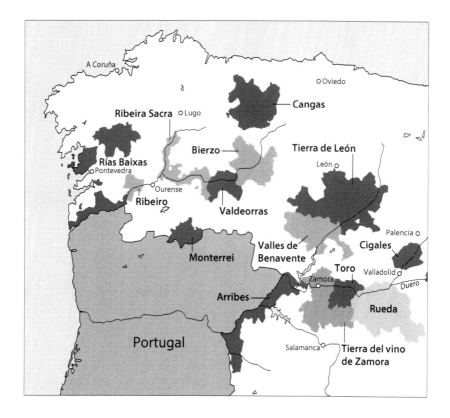

venerable history, as a region that traded with the English before the Port trade began. Yet there is so much more than this. Northern Spain has so many new stories to contribute to the world of contemporary Spanish wine, so many new enterprises, so many growers launching their own businesses, all in addition to the established names. One case in point is Galicia, and especially Rías Baixas, which has grown rapidly, as is reflected in the number of pages devoted to it here. Another is Ribera del Duero, which again has greatly increased space assigned to it. A third is Castilla y León, which now has a fascinating and varied collection of wineries.

In terms of grape varieties, Spain has plenty to celebrate, with its renewed confidence in its own heritage. Garnacha is a big story, and not just in its home territory of Aragón. So too are Mencía, and Galicia's reds. The transformation of Spain's white wines has also been

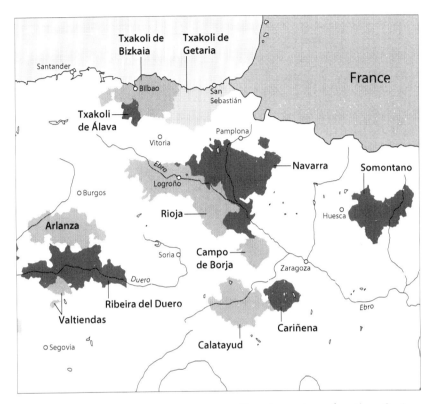

The wine regions of northern Spain

remarkable. As I highlight in these pages, the best of these wines can be thrillingly pure and complex.

Until as little as five years ago, Spain had a deserved reputation in export markets for overuse of oak. Not content with delivering bold fruit, too many wines were loaded with high-toast oak and drying tannin. What a difference a few years make! I discuss the different approaches to winemaking in the Ribera del Duero chapter. Meanwhile in Rioja, I explore the various current debates, on single vineyard and village wines, on the benefits of classifying wines in terms of their time in oak barrels, and how best to define the quality differences between wines from the same zone.

From technically correct wines, many producers are now choosing to move back to the old ways, and some are farming organically or biodynamically. This book gives me the chance to highlight growers and producers who are choosing a different path from the anonymous wines. What has always fascinated me are the people behind the wines, and their role in interpreting the soil and vine. This, then, is a personal selection. I have included all or nearly all of the well-known or established producers, to assist readers who want to discover more about Spain, and build their knowledge. I have also included others who particularly interest me, and who make fine wines. Where the project is very new, or is yet to prove itself, the information is listed briefly at the end of the section under the heading 'On the radar'. These are wineries and regions to watch.

Above all, my intention is that you should discover and enjoy these wines for yourself, and that they should give you as much pleasure as they have given me. Visit the producers, take time to linger in the countryside, and enjoy the fine regional foods, some of which I highlight in the final chapter of the book, starting on page 301.

USING THE BOOK

Finding a winery
If you are looking for information on individual wineries or facts about DOs, then use the Index or search alphabetically in each chapter. In general, the prefix bodega or adega has been removed, so search under the brand or family name of the winery. Wineries are listed under their commonly used names, thus 'Pérez Pascuas' rather than 'Hermanos Pérez Pascuas'. I have used 'winery' and 'bodega' interchangeably.

Addresses
I have removed all the *calle* (street) prefixes, leaving only the street name and number. Other words are abbreviated: Ctra is *Carretera* (highway), Avda is *Avenida* (avenue), Pza is *Plaza*, s/n means *sin numero*, which indicates that the property does not have an assigned number and will *probably* be obvious from the road.

Grape varieties
Different areas have different names for the same variety. Tempranillo, as Chapter 2 shows, is the most obvious case, as it is a nationally known

variety but comes under many names and guises. In general, I use the name of the variety that the winery prefers. In Ribera del Duero, for instance, many producers speak of Tempranillo. Some do this to emphasize their credentials to export markets familiar with Tempranillo. Others, often wishing to highlight their old clones and their adaptation to the terroir, use the local Tinto Fino. Galicia offers a riot of names especially where red varieties are concerned.

'Old vines'

This is a much-argued term. However Spain has old vines without a doubt. In some regions, such as Toro and Rueda, the sandy soils are such that the phylloxera louse could not survive. These vines are on their own rootstocks, very low yielding, and well over 100 years old. In many other places there are vines that were planted after phylloxera, on resistant American rootstocks. These will be 90–100 years old. In general I have accepted that anything older than 60 years is 'old' but have specified in most cases where the vines are exceptionally old.

Fact boxes

Every DO featured here has an 'at a glance' box which gives systematic information on permitted and experimental grape varieties, specific aspects of winemaking legislation, and data on the vineyard area, the number of growers, and the number of wineries. These last three items are particularly useful for comparing the size and style of the different zones. Look at Rías Baixas, for instance, and the structure of *minifundia* is apparent, with many growers and few wineries. The information is correct at the time of writing, although some of the data supplied by the regulatory bodies may not be as up-to-date as one might wish.

Richard Ford

I have used occasional extracts from the writer Richard Ford. He remains an irresistible companion for any lover of Spain. His observations from his time in Spain in the 1830s are pointed, and often surprisingly accurate and relevant, though written almost two centuries ago.

April 2018

1

THREE THOUSAND YEARS OF HISTORY

Spanish wine is coming full circle. The Phoenicians who traded across the Mediterranean around 1100 BC brought wine to Spain in amphorae, or clay pots. Today, more than 3,000 years later, some of Spain's winemakers are turning back to amphorae, albeit with the addition of temperature controls and other gadgetry. It is perhaps a natural reaction to the recent years of technological winemaking, with its cultivated yeasts, and cultivated flavours.

The Phoenicians were in due course supplanted by the Romans, who left a substantial footprint on wines and winemaking in Spain. They planted vines, for the production of wines to sustain their soldiers and their settlements. They hollowed out stone troughs to ferment their wines, and improved the quality of the amphorae. The fermentation troughs have survived the centuries and are still to be found.

There is plenty of archaeological evidence of winemaking across the peninsula. Outside Jerez, there are traces of Phoenician *lagares*, for treading and pressing grapes. Utiel-Requena has an extensive settlement at Las Pillas dating back to the seventh century BC, where archaeologists have found grape seeds, *lagares* and stones clearly used for winemaking. Across Spain from Tarragona to Navarra and Ribera del Duero there are plenty of Roman remains, including impressive mosaics of the god of wine, Bacchus, in Roman villas. Monterrei, on the Galicia/Bierzo border, has a number of *lagares* hollowed out of the rock.

After the Romans came successive northern invaders, the Vandals, the Alani and the Visigoths. The most significant invasion, however, came from Africa. For almost 700 years there was Moorish rule in many parts of Spain. Wine may not have flourished under the Moors, but evidence shows that it continued to be made. Over the centuries Moorish rule weakened and the north Africans were driven back slowly from their virtual dominance. The shrinking of the Moors' territories made way for the arrival of the Church from France. The Christians established monasteries and brought with them enhanced vine growing practices. The production of wine increased significantly and the Ribeiro region began exporting to England.

'A GLASS OF GOOD WINE'

The monasteries in Ribeiro were significant in developing viticulture and winemaking. *O Ribeiro*, the DO's history of the region, quotes the historian A. Huetz de Lemps: 'the monasteries were the real creators of the vineyards of Ribadavia [Ribeiro], incentivizing plantings through innumerable contracts, and thus they transformed the valley of the River Avia almost exclusively into a vinegrowing region'. Similarly the history of wine in Rioja starts with a monk, and a monastery. The first record of a region named Rioja (or Rioxa, as it was then written) is from 1092, although there are records earlier than this that refer to the (unnamed) vineyard region. The story relates to the monk, Gonzalo de Berceo, at the Rioja monastery of San Millán. De Berceo is commonly regarded as the father of the Spanish language. In the first ever poem in Spanish, from the early thirteenth century, he writes of '*un vaso de buen vino*'.

The wine story then moves to Aragón. Aragón's history had begun with Luis the Pious, when the region became an independent kingdom between Navarra and Catalunya. In the eleventh century Aragón merged with Navarra. In 1469 Prince Ferdinand of Aragón married the single-minded Isabella of Castile, becoming King of Aragón ten years later. Thus Castile, Aragón and Catalunya were united in one Kingdom, opening the way for the creation of a united Spain with the eventual end of the *Reconquista* – the banishment of the last remaining Moors. In 1492 came the endlessly chronicled *annus mirabilis* when the Moors were finally driven from the Iberian peninsula and Columbus 'sailed the ocean blue' to America.

The *Reconquista* has suffered from reinterpretation by subsequent historiographers, especially in the twentieth century. After all, in one sense this was not a 'reconquering' of Spain. The north Africans had occupied much of the peninsula for seven centuries. Many parts of it could be regarded as a settled satellite country of North Africa where many Christians had become Moors and some Moors had become Christians. Historiographers have also made much of celebrating the *Reyes Católicos*, the 'Catholic Kings', Ferdinand and Isabella. In fact, they were no more Catholic than any other of Spain's kings, who were and remain Catholics. The important fact is that in a history book written in the middle years of the twentieth century, under a dictatorship, these were the Catholic kings who had opposed Islam, Judaism and other heretical organizations.

Under the newly united Spain winemaking returned, as did exports. In the cellar, producers had turned from amphorae to cleaned and cured animal skins, but near the end of the fifteenth century oak butts appeared. When Francis Drake attacked the Spanish armada in Cádiz, his booty was 2,900 casks of fortified wine from Jerez.

The first regulations to control production and trading were set in Ribera del Duero as early as the fifteenth century. By 1635, Logroño had banned wagons and horses from roads next to the ageing cellars, to prevent the vibrations disturbing the wines. Logroño also figures in public records at this time because the town was the regional Tribunal for the Office of the Spanish Inquisition, introduced by Isabella in 1478, covering the whole of the Spanish Basque country. In 1610, the Logroño Inquisition held one of its gruesome public rituals, known as an *auto-da-fé*, or act of faith. In *The Basque History of the World*, Mark Kurlansky reports that this particular event was famous for the number of witches burned, eleven in all, part of the frenzy of accusations of witchcraft at the time. At the same event, twenty-five heretics were also sentenced, six of whom were found guilty of Judaism, one of Islam, one of Lutheranism, twelve of heretical utterances and two of impersonating agents of the Inquisition.

THE BEGINNINGS OF RIOJA

One hundred and fifty years after that event the name of Rioja appears for the first time. The Real Sociedad Económica de Cosecheros de Rioja ('the Rioja Wine Growers' Royal Economic Society), established in 1787, enabled members to identify the region and the industry collectively.

The next step forward in Rioja came in winemaking itself. In the late eighteenth century Manuel Quintana y Quintana travelled from Rioja to Bordeaux to learn how producers there had mastered the art of cooperage and wine quality. He brought home some of the new-fangled Bordeaux casks he encountered but it wasn't easy to convince his neighbours that the new methods were better. However, when he shipped his wine to Cuba in well-sealed oak barrels this also conditioned the young wine well and he found he could charge more because of the wine's better quality after the voyage, compared with the other wines. This was the first indication that oak barrels would be so important in the quality and style of Rioja.

Back home Quintana y Quintana was not popular. The Real Sociedad argued that there should be no price differential, even if his purchase of barrels did mean that his wine cost more to make than that of his neighbours. Although this proved a false start for oak in Rioja, life brought higher rewards for Quintana y Quintana, who was promoted to a senior position at Burgos Cathedral.

During the nineteenth century Spain was riven by civil wars. Known as the Carlist Wars, these conflicts were nominally wars over the succession to the throne between two brothers, and their descendants. Effectively they became civil wars between, on one side, the Church, the army generals, the state and the liberals, and on the other, the Carlists (followers of Carlos), who were small farmers, and the conservative lower nobility. The Carlists had strong support in the Basque country and Navarra. The three wars ran intermittently between 1830 and 1876. From a wine perspective the wars had an upside, since a number of people spent time in exile in Bordeaux. Luciano de Murrieta, who eventually became Marqués de Murrieta, studied winemaking in Bordeaux while in exile and returned to make wine in Bordeaux casks in Rioja. Bodegas Murrieta date the first wine made in this way to 1852. Meanwhile the Marqués de Riscal returned from exile in Bordeaux, with a similar interest in making wine, bringing back Bordeaux vines, and later hiring a consultant. Who produced the first wine in the modern style in Rioja? It would seem that Riscal bottled his first wine a little later than Murrieta, but this is a debate between friends that has been going on for the best part of two centuries. The important point is that both producers were there at the beginning, and both remain today. Murrieta and Riscal may have brought Bordelais practices to Rioja, but over the last 150 years these have gone native, and become part of the complex terroir of Rioja.

EXPORT, EXPORT, EXPORT

Just two decades later, in the 1870s, Rioja enjoyed a boom. Having survived oidium, or powdery mildew, the fungal disease which hit France first and then crossed the Pyrenees, Rioja was better prepared when the root-eating vineyard louse phylloxera appeared in Bordeaux's vineyards. French investment found Rioja conveniently over the border and a number of wineries were established, most notably in Haro beside the railway station, in the Barrio de la Estación, or Station Quarter. The key concern was shipping wine in bulk back to France, so that the hearty Rioja could bulk up the weedy remnants of the Bordeaux vineyards.

However, at the start of the twentieth century phylloxera eventually reached Rioja. Table 1 shows the devastating social and economic impact of phylloxera to growers who depended on their vines. The official history of La Rioja Alta S.A. notes that between 1902 and 1904 'the phylloxera crisis led to considerable social conflict', and as a result there were up to eighteen strikes by agricultural workers in the Haro area. For many of the workers the only solution was emigration, with the abandonment of their former livelihoods.

During those turn of the century years, France eventually regained the use of its vineyards, and no longer needed Rioja's supplies. Markets in the Americas dried up with the loss of Spain's last colonies, known as 'The Disaster', but gradually confidence was restored. The Rioja Wine Exporters' Syndicate was founded in 1907 to guarantee the authenticity of Rioja wines in export markets. Not surprisingly eleven of the sixteen producer members came from that convenient centre of export to the outside world, Haro. The region's confidence in defending its identity and quality continued to grow, and in 1926 Spain's first ever regulatory council, or Consejo Regulador, was created.

Table 1. The impact of phylloxera on grape production in Rioja 1906
(Source: Three Centuries of La Rioja Alta, S.A.).

Municipality	Average harvest pre-1900 (in *cántaras**)	Harvest 1906 (in *cántaras**)	Percentage loss
Aldeanueva de Ebro	300,000	20,000	93
Alfaro	250,000	20,000	92
Arnedo	150,000	130,000	13
Briñas	70,000	20,000	72
Briones	350,000	70,000	80
Cenicero	350,000	100,000	72
Elciego	110,000	20,000	82
Haro	240,000	35,000	85
Lapuebla	100,000	28,000	72
Oyón	80,000	8,000	90
Páganos	20,000	1,000	95
Rodezno	150,000	36,000	76
Tudelilla	120,000	60,000	50

cántara = container of c.18 litres

Just a decade later in 1936, Spain was torn apart by the Civil War. Commenting on the Rioja region, Antony Beevor records that 'over 2,000 people were executed and buried in mass graves outside Logroño. There was practically no village in the Rioja which did not have inhabitants buried in the mass grave of La Barranca'. Paul Preston in his magisterial *The Spanish Holocaust* documents atrocities on both sides during the Civil War and in the run-up to it. He says, 'Logroño was a small, tranquil city at the centre of the Rioja wine trade. As Civil Governor, [the Nationalist General] Mola appointed an artilleryman, Captain Emilio Bellod Gómez, telling him, "Be harsh, be very harsh", to which he replied: "Don't worry, General, That is exactly what I will do".' Preston goes on to detail the executions and maltreatment. He concludes: 'In the course of the war, 1 per cent of the total population [of the province] was executed'. To preserve the memory of what happened in La Barranca and in Rioja during the Civil War an Association was established in 2008; its website records the dates of death of citizens by village.

THE LONG ROAD TO RECOVERY

The outcome of the Civil War was a ruined country. Recovery was long and slow. Yet for wine lovers there were some exceptional years despite the horrors of war and recovery, notably 1945, and some exceptional vineyards were also planted at the time. In the years after the Civil and Second World Wars Spain was isolated. When exports resumed, consumers were purchasing Spanish Burgundy and Spanish Chablis rather than Rioja. (Producing copycat wines wasn't a uniquely Spanish habit, of course; at that time all the world was imitating the classic originals, and went on doing so until quite recently.) A significant pioneer at this time was Miguel Torres, who introduced stainless steel and temperature control into winemaking, and started on a long path of research and development.

Taking a narrow view, focusing just on the implications for wine, the years of dictatorship brought government which did not foster careful management of vines in the best places. In Ribeira Sacra, as elsewhere, land and homes were lost to hydroelectric power. Cooperatives, as commentators have noted, were instruments of state control. Those years are thankfully past. In rapid succession after Franco's death in 1975 democratic government was installed, Spain joined the European Union and winemakers were able to travel the world in large numbers to live and learn. On their return they also discovered a pride in their own terroir, its diversity and its potential for making great wine.

There is one dark cloud overshadowing the Spanish wine industry and that is the fact that Spain is the largest exporter of bulk wine in the world. Fifty-seven per cent of Spain's wine exports are in bulk. Some of that bulk wine goes to France to be packaged and shipped on, giving value to the French producer, rather than the original grower. Managing this is a structural issue. However, the focus has to be on turning the industry towards quality, following the model of the terrific producers in the following pages. Spain has never been at a more exciting place for wine lovers than it is today.

2

A GUIDE TO THE GRAPES: ALBARÍN TO VIDADILLO

The fame of Rioja and Ribera del Duero can make it seem that Spain *is* Tempranillo. A quick look at this introduction to northern Spain's varieties will show that this is firmly not the case. What makes the country's wines so exciting now is the work that is being done to recuperate the country's viticultural heritage. Miguel Torres Sr started the work with his now very extensive collection in Penedès. Growers sent and still send cuttings of old vines or varieties they don't recognize in their vineyards. From those 'old' cuttings some successful 'new' varieties are being grown on and made into wine.

Many varieties were almost lost during phylloxera, at the turn of the nineteenth century. Afterwards most growers replanted with easy-to-grow, disease resistant varieties, even if they lacked interest. This explains the presence of Palomino in so many parts of the country. However, not all was lost. There are areas, particularly those with sandy soils, where phylloxera could not survive. This accounts for some of the exceptionally old vines profiled in this book. Rioja is one case where *viticultors* talk of the 100 varieties and more that used to be grown before phylloxera. There are some old vines still to be found, and there is a gradual process of renovation.

Perhaps the most exciting region in recent times has been Galicia (and by extension Bierzo, its neighbour). Tucked in the top left-hand corner of the peninsula, it has been isolated politically and economically for many parts of history. The benefit of that isolation has been that many of its varieties have not travelled. To enjoy them, you need to discover them in their purity. Try Mencía from Ribeira Sacra; you won't find it in Navarra. Or look to Cangas in Asturias, and the crisp, light Carrasquín.

Anyone writing about grape varieties today owes a debt to the work of Robinson, Harding and Vouillamoz and their majestic *Wine Grapes*. I have written these grape profiles below on the basis of my own experience, and my interviews with *viticultors*. *Wine Grapes* has been invaluable for cross-checking synonyms, although on occasion – and especially in Galicia – there is still debate on which is related to which and under what name.

WHITE VARIETIES

Albarín Blanco

Not to be confused with Albariño or Albillo Real, this rare variety is found in the north-west. In Tierra de León, it makes a bright, aromatic white for Leyenda del Páramo. In Vino de la Tierra de Cangas, it is a crisp, floral wine.

Albariño

Which came first: Albariño or Portugal's Alvarinho? Portugal has a strong case, but either way this is an old variety in north-west Spain. Every wine region proudly claims to have its old vines, even though some of them may be no more than 30 years old. If you are looking for really old vines, then there are a few Albariño vines in Galicia that may be as much as 300 years old. Do Ferreiro's Cepas Vellas in Rías Baixas is made from the fruit of a 200-year-old vineyard.

It is *the* great variety of Rías Baixas, distinguished by its elegant floral aromatics – lime blossom, honeysuckle with citrus – together with a full body. It can sometimes also show a note of bitterness on the finish. The benefit for the grower, especially in rainy Rías Baixas, is that while it is sensitive to oidium it is resistant to botrytis, and nowadays has a good sugar production capacity, with the ability to reach 12–13% abv. In the Rías Baixas DO it is usually made straightforwardly in stainless steel but the examples which are lees-aged, even for just a few months, are much more interesting. More interesting still, though scarce, are the aged Albariños. The most famous is Pazo de Señoráns Selección de Añada which is sold with a minimum of 30 months on lees and reveals superb complexity. There are also a few Albariños which are partially or totally barrel-fermented, with some barrel age. These can work if sensitively handled.

Albariño was Spain's first commercially successful fresh white with international appeal. It is suffering from its success, with supermarkets driving prices down, and requiring ever larger yields, opening it to the risk of travelling the same journey as Verdejo. A dilute Albariño is not a lovely thing. The variety is found elsewhere: in addition to Portugal's Alvarinho, there are Albariños over the border in the south of France, and more recently it has appeared in coastal Uruguay, California and New Zealand. Most growers have taken the lead from Rías Baixas and planted in maritime sites. Australian farmers also planted Albariño, only to discover in 2009 that they had been in fact been sold Savagnin.

Albilla, Albillo Mayor

Albilla was cited as far back as the sixteenth century. Since that time the records have become somewhat confused, with the DOs listing these varieties and ones with similar names almost interchangeably. Albilla turns up in the lists for Ribeiro, while in Ribera Duero it is typically Albillo Mayor or Pardina (and it is also Rioja's Torrontés Riojana). It was traditionally used in field blends with Tinto Fino, and continues to be co-fermented by some producers. It is cultivated in small quantities but remains the variety with greatest potential to be claimed by Ribera del Duero as its own white. In general it produces rich, fleshy wines.

Albillo, Albillo Real

Albillo Real is frequently confused with other varieties. It is an early ripening variety with average yields and moderate sweetness. The bunches are medium-sized with golden berries when ripe, and thin skins. It makes pale coloured, aromatic wines with stone fruit aromas. The traditional interplanting of white varieties with red to be fermented together has the technical advantage of fixing or stabilizing the colour; it can also be combined with the aromatic Albillo Real and Tinto Fino – as with Viognier added to Shiraz – to bring some welcome floral, fruity aromatics to a red variety. Importantly the white variety can raise acidity. This is important both for providing a sensation of freshness and to ensure the ageability of the wines.

Alcañón

A fairly rare native of Somontano, producing bright, fresh whites.

Blanca de Monterrei

From Monterrei, as its name suggests, this rare, early ripening variety has a distinctive note of bitterness on the palate.

Caíño Blanco, Caíño Branco

This Galician variety found in Monterrei and Rías Baixas still covers few hectares but its popularity is growing. It has been confused with Albariño and Portugal's Alvarinho, and certainly displays many Albariño characteristics, alongside a linear acidity. Terras Gauda makes a distinctive example, La Mar, blended with a dash of Loureiro and Albariño for a fresh, zesty and saline wine.

Chardonnay

Chardonnay appears occasionally in the vineyards covered by this book. There's a little in Txakoli de Getaria, for instance, and Somontano, with its international profile, also has Chardonnay. Chivite's Colección 125 is the notably successful example. The great Bordeaux oenologist, the late Professor Denis Dubourdieu, consulted for Chivite and the Colección series is his legacy to them.

Chenin Blanc

There is some Chenin in Catalunya, but not a great deal. Tierra de León has a small quantity registered.

Doña Blanca

Originating in the north-west of the Iberian peninsula, this variety goes by a number of aliases, including Síria, and is known as Valenciana in Valdeorras. The 'white lady' has been another of the candidates for development as a promising indigenous white variety for the north-west of Spain. However it has hitherto been a frequently boring, workhorse variety. The work in the vineyards, in clonal selection and in the winery is all serving to improve its aromatic character and charm.

Garnacha Blanca

Here's a variety, a mutation of Garnacha, that has undergone a transformation in reputation in the last decade. It did not even appear in *The New Spain* and has travelled a long way, from making oxidative, flabby whites, to making wines with fascinating textures and richness. As a variety it stars in Catalunya but is gradually coming into its own again in Rioja, if still only in a small way. Abel Mendoza's single varietal is the one to look for in Rioja.

Garnacha Gris

This is a pale almost pink Garnacha.

Gewürztraminer

Gewürztraminer has established itself comfortably in Somontano. The Viñas del Vero and Enate versions speak clearly of the variety. They are pleasant, polished wines, but one cannot help wondering why anyone would import this variety, with its distinctly foreign character, into Spain in the first place.

Godello

In the 1970s Godello was close to extinction. What a reversal! Its very best expression is surely in Valdeorras. It reaches its summit in the vineyards of Rafael Palacios, and above all with O Soro, his top wine. In terms of wine trends, if not actual plantings, Godello is taking over from Albariño as Galicia's most highly regarded white. This may be more a function of Albariño's slump in overall quality, but nevertheless the best Godellos have an elegant richness, and an underlying minerality. It is more productive than Albariño and flourishes in dry climates. Barrel fermentation can add an extra level of interest. As a variety it is much more adaptable to oak than Albariño. Though as happens here occasionally, and elsewhere, allowing wines to go through malolactic fermentation is a pity – turning crunchy freshness into something flabby. It is perhaps not as aromatic as Albariño, which is why it is often found in blends across Galicia, with some or all of Loureiro, Albariño and Treixadura. It is known as Verdello in Monterrei and is the main white variety in Bierzo.

Gros Manseng

Although much better known in south-west France, this variety is permitted in Txakoli de Álava and Txakoli de Getaria.

Hondarribi Zuri, Hondarribi Zuri Zerratia

The ampelography of this variety is as unusual as its spelling is to non-Euskera (the Basque language) speakers. Effectively this, the white grape of the Txakoli DOs, is the name given to the three grape varieties Courbu Blanc, Crouchen and Noah (the latter is a hybrid). Petit Courbu may be the synonym of Hondarribi Zuri Zerratia.

Izkiriot Tipia

South-west France's Petit Manseng, this is permitted in Txakoli de Álava and Bizkaya. Although only grown in tiny quantities it has strong potential for sweet wines.

Lado

This very rare variety is found in Ribeiro. Given its scarcity it is usually to be found in multi-varietal blends. Its distinct freshness and vivacity make it a good candidate for development in the future.

Loureiro/Loureira

In a blind tasting of Atlantic whites, I noted that the Loureiro wines were lower in alcohol, and had a very appealing aromatic style. The name suggests that you may notice laurel, or bay, aromas, though it also has a sweet spice – nutmeg or cinnamon – character. A later ripening variety, sensitive to botrytis, it can be high yielding. It can deliver vivid acidity. It's found in Ribeiro and Monterrei, above all, plus some in Rías Baixas, to where it almost certainly travelled from northern Portugal, where it is typical of Vinho Verde. Generally it is used in blends for its sumptuous peach and floral aromas.

Malvasía Riojana

When wine growers talk about Malvasía in Rioja, listen carefully, for Malvasía Riojana is not one of the Malvasía family at all. Strictly speaking it is Alarije, and it is partly related to Pedro Ximénez. In Catalunya it is known as Subirat Parent, and under that name makes a charming sweet Cava for

Freixenet. Abel Mendoza in Rioja makes a single varietal Malvasía Riojana, and the style of the wine proves the difference from mainstream Malvasía. It is rich, golden, almost honeyed. Brian MacRobert at Laventura in Rioja makes a Malvasía which is fermented on skins, more in the orange wine style, to build the texture.

Maturana Blanca

This is a more recent arrival to the permitted varieties in Rioja. Diego Pinilla, Director of Winemaking at the Codorníu group, who has a single varietal Maturana Blanca in the Bilbaínas range in Rioja, says it is very mineral and citric: 'its most important characteristic is its intensity. It's a bit like Chablis in that respect. That's why we are fermenting it in barrel to give it a little more weight and texture in the mouth.'

Moscatel de Alejandría

This is the poor relation of the Moscatel family; less highly rated than Moscatel de Grano Menudo (à petits grains). Spain has some exceptional Moscatels, though outside the geographical boundaries of this book, as they are in the south, near Málaga. The variety has many synonyms; as Moscatel Romano, for instance, it is found in Navarra and also Cariñena.

Moscatel de Grano Menudo

The hero of Moscatel à petits grains in Spain is surely Javier Ochoa, whose winery is in Navarra. He launched a delicate late harvest Moscatel in 1994, and has built its reputation since. His daughter Adriana subsequently created the delightful Moscato-ish fizz known as MdO. Other producers using the same variety for a sweet wine include Chivite in its Colección 125.

Mune Mahatsa

Also known as Folle Blanche, this variety is found in the Basque country and is one of the lesser ingredients of Txakoli.

Palomino

This variety is known in many parts of Spain as 'Jerez', which is where it has become famous for Sherry. It was widespread in Spain, particularly after phylloxera, mainly because of its productivity, and is used for making traditional fortified wines in a number of regions. High yield

Palomino does not make good table wine, and is disappearing from outside Jerez. However it is still to be found in Rueda and Bierzo and is also found in Ribeiro.

Parellada

One of three varieties best known for their role in Cava blends. Thus it is not surprising to find it just over the border from Catalunya in Cariñena as an authorized variety. It is rarely found as a single or dominant variety, as it doesn't have star quality.

Pedro Ximénez

The variety for making exceptionally sweet wine. It is rare in the north and north-west, though registered in Tierra de León.

Riesling

Although scarcely found in northern Spain there is just a little in Txakoli de Getaria.

Sauvignon Blanc

Planting Sauvignon Blanc in Rueda in addition to Verdejo was an obvious transference of ideas, given that the wines seem so similar. However when compared with the Loire or New Zealand, most of the Sauvignons in Rueda seem to have something missing. Perhaps it is a matter of waiting until the vineyards age, but it is currently hard to find a reason to buy Sauvignon Blanc from Rueda when you could buy it from New Zealand or the Loire – or more cheaply, from Gascony.

Tempranillo Blanco

Tempranillo Blanco is a genetic quirk, found one day in a vineyard. It is one of those varieties that has established itself rapidly in terms of wine-trade recognition because of its relationship to Tempranillo. In winemaking terms its identity is less clear. In general it looks to be made as a fresh, young wine, picked early to emphasize the acidity. One winemaker who has worked with it remarked that it is best to grow it 'on stony soils in a fresh region, and at higher altitudes; that way it keeps its freshness, with white flowers, citric and balsamic notes. It's an aromatic wine, vibrant and mineral, with the structure for cellaring.'

Treixadura

In Ribeiro the best wines from this variety offer a lovely complexity, with pear and tropical notes. It's known as Verdello Louro in Monterrei, and is also found in Valdeorras and Ribeira Sacra, mainly in blends. The grapes are elliptical in shape, sensitive to botrytis, and can deliver a white pepper flavour, like Grüner Veltliner. It is valuable for delivering roundness and balance to a blend.

Turruntés/Torrontés

There is a riot of possibilities with this variety. It seems that Turruntés in Rioja is the same as Albillo Mayor; while the Galician Torrontés is the same as Malvasía Fina. Within Galicia, the Torrontés from Ribeiro is different from that in other parts of the region. The key point to draw from the narrative is that none of these Spanish varieties has anything to do with the Argentine one of the same name.

Verdejo

Some producers in Rueda suggest that Verdejo goes back as far as the days of King Alfonso VI in the eleventh century, and that the variety had been brought from North Africa, or from earlier settlements in southern Spain. Plantings of Verdejo (see box, page 119) have boomed in recent years. It has a characteristic note of bitterness, which is often fleeting, but just enough to give the wine a memorable finish.

The contemporary story of Verdejo was launched by the Marqués de Riscal, who was seeking a reliable variety and region near Rioja for a white wine. Since then lovely wines in a quasi-Sauvignon Blanc style have been made, but latterly high-volume production and low-price demand have damaged its reputation. There are a few exceptional pre-phylloxera bush vines still extant.

Viognier

There is a really tiny amount in northern Spain (and hardly any more anywhere else in the country). Prieto Pariente has a partly barrel-fermented Viognier, from a parcel planted in 1999.

Viura

Poor Viura, it has had a very bad press. Too many white Riojas made from it have been tired and oxidized (not in a good way). Elsewhere in Spain it has lacked acidity and made frankly drab wines. One of the many offenders when it comes to damaging Viura's reputation has been Rueda. While a 100 per cent Verdejo in Rueda can be a lovely thing, if the back label does not say 'Rueda Verdejo', then it probably has Viura in it as well. While a Verdejo–Viura blend may be cheaper to produce, too often it is dilute. The point about Verdejo is its vivid expression; blending in Viura lessens the impact.

Also known in Rioja as Macabeo, Viura is undergoing a revival. Producers are learning to change picking time, be sensitive to the use of oak, and bring in texture and freshness. The finest white Riojas today are made with Viura, and are fascinating wines.

RED VARIETIES

Araúxa

Galician synonym for Tempranillo.

Bastardo

This has been somewhat overshadowed among collectors of rare grape varieties by its synonym Trousseau, given Trousseau's role in the eastern French region of Jura. However, though Jura is fashionable now, the crisp, fresh reds of north-west Spain are also gaining attention. Indeed Spain accounts for half the world's 3,400 hectares of Bastardo/Trousseau. Grape-naming is not an exact science, and it does not respect DOs or political boundaries, thus Bastardo is also known as María Ardoña in Monterrei, Merenzao in Ribeira Sacra and Bierzo, Estaladiña in Castilla y León, Verdejo Negro or Tinto in Asturías, as well as Maturana Tinta in Rioja. José Luis Mateo at Quinta de Muradella in Monterrei makes a rare single-varietal Bastardo, amongst many of the exciting blends and single varietal wines from indigenous varieties. It's typically fresh, with firm acidity and firm tannin, and moderately coloured. Also look for an excellent single varietal from Algueira.

Brancellao/Albarello

This Galician variety probably crossed the border from Portugal, where it is known as Alvarelhão. Found in very small quantities in Galicia, the variety has great potential. It shows at its best on Ribeira Sacra's steep slopes and on red schist in Rías Baixas.

Bruñal

Bruñal is the Baboso Negro of the Canary Islands, and the Albarín Negro of Asturías. It is better known as the Alfrocheiro of Dão in Portugal and is also part of an interconnected north-west Iberian family, joining up with Juan García, Bastardo and Prieto Picudo. Rich and dark-fruited, it is not especially tannic.

Cabernet Franc

Fundamental in the Loire and Bordeaux, DNA research shows that this variety is related to two Basque cultivars, Morenoa and Hondarribi Beltza. The church of Roncesvalles, established in the twelfth century, was a key stopping point on the French–Spanish border for pilgrims en route to Santiago de Compostela. The priests naturally had vineyards of local varieties, and one of these was Achéria, the Basque name for Cabernet Franc. Today there is only a scant amount in Spain. There is some in Tierras de León, and in occasional other vineyards, where it typically appears in Bordeaux blends. Catalunya has a good selection. A very fine example is Torres' Reserva Real, made from Cabernet Sauvignon, Cabernet Franc and Merlot grown on *llicorella*, slate soil. The 2010 won the Decanter World Wine Awards International trophy in 2015 for the best red Bordeaux blend in the world.

Cabernet Sauvignon

Cabernet Sauvignon is found in DOs that decided to build a reputation with international varieties, notably Navarra and Somontano, also turning up in blends elsewhere. Its history in Spain is much longer than this would suggest, as it arrived with the French experts who advised nineteenth-century producers. That's how it arrived at Vega Sicilia, and at Marqués de Riscal in Rioja. The Marqués de Riscal Reserva Médoc 1945 is one of the fabled wines of Rioja, 70 per cent Cabernet Sauvignon and 30 per cent Tempranillo. While Cabernet Sauvignon was regarded as 'experimental' in the region, it is so well adapted to the Riscal vineyards, with such a long history, that it can reasonably be regarded as native.

Caíño Tinto

Galicia is alive with rare and quirky grape varieties. Among the Galician DOs, it is most commonly found to the south in Monterrei and Ribeira Sacra. It is not especially widespread, probably because it is known for tart acidity and chewy tannins. Over the border it appears in Vinho Verde as Borraçal. One of the most interesting wines to try is the 100 per cent Caíño Tinto from Val do Salnés in Rías Baixas. It's made by Eulogio Pomares of Zárate, who is working to revive the almost forgotten traditions of local vines and winemaking.

Caladoc

Caladoc is quite widely found in southern France. It is a fairly modern crossing that dates back to 1958, of Garnacha with Cot, giving growers the great benefit of a variety that is resistant to *coulure*. It is mostly found in Catalunya, but is also permitted in Tierra de León.

Cariñena

See Mazuelo.

Carrasquín

An Asturian red variety that is gradually becoming more known, as the wines of Cangas themselves become more known. Pale coloured, it is typically used in blends.

Espadeiro

The vigorous Espadeiro is on the list of varieties in Rías Baixas, and is also found in south and east Galicia. There is a Portuguese variety of the same name, but they are not related. This is also known as Camaraou Noir.

Ferrón

A visitor from the Basque Country, Ferrón is known in France as Manseng Noir. It is found in blends in Ribeiro, where it gives firm structure and character to the wines.

Garnacha

The Sardinians would argue that theirs is the true home of Garnacha. However Spain, and particularly Aragón, strongly and reasonably claim the honour belongs to them. The evidence is in the fact that Garnacha in Spain has developed more variants (black, white, grey, as well as the hairy-leaved *peluda*), though it should not be confused with Garnacha Tintorera (which is Alicante Bouschet).

Garnacha has an upright habit, and buds early but is late to ripen. Vigorous, it is at its best grown as a bush vine. If there's one real disadvantage it is that it can deliver very high sugar levels in the grapes, which convert to high alcohol. Where that was once a selling point, today wines with 15% abv or more are falling out of favour. However it is resistant to drought and to the current plagues of vine wood diseases, which guarantees its continued usefulness.

In Spain, the variety leads a double life. At one extreme, it provides some of the cheapest red wines in Europe. At the other extreme, the old vines, some of which are centenarian and pre-phylloxeric, are part of Spain's proud viticultural heritage. Navarra, Priorat, Méntrida, Gredos, Aragón, Calatayud and parts of Catalunya, can make exceptional reds. In Navarra it was the most widely planted variety before phylloxera attacked Spain's vines, and after replanting continued to account for 90 per cent of the Navarra vineyard until the 1970s, when international varieties were introduced. By 2017 plantings of Garnacha in Navarra had slumped from 24,000 hectares two decades earlier to just 3,000 hectares.

The arrival to international fame of Priorat was the most important event in restoring Garnacha to the iconography of top grape varieties. When Garnacha appeared as an essential component of that region's internationally acclaimed wines, most notably Álvaro Palacios' L'Ermita, then it had to be taken seriously.

Given the grape's relatively low tannins and acidity it works in blends, and traditionally Rioja has always been about blends. Garnacha can provide the warmth, generosity and spiciness that Tempranillo often lacks. In Navarra, Garnacha was the basis for popular deeply coloured *rosados* which are falling out of fashion internationally.

Spain offers consumers some of the cheapest Garnachas in the world. Its Garnachas makes deliciously juicy, simple, fairly pale and not overly tannic reds and *rosados*, perfect for summer drinking and available globally at low, low prices. At the same time Garnacha has caught the imagination of a new generation of winemakers in Spain, who are making fine, original wines, many with a glorious purity. All of them would regard themselves as growers or *viticultors* first and winemakers second – their land and in particular their old bush vines are the key to their wines.

This new generation is making the wines in a Burgundian style, using whole bunches, foot treading and adding back stems. Priorat's Garnachas, grown on *llicorella*, brown schist, are the most dense and elegant, and the longest lived. They need subtle oak handling in order not to drown the drinker in tannin. Aragón, where it all began, and Calatayud should not be forgotten. Careful viticulture is reviving the old vines and managing new ones, to make wines with a sense of place.

Garnacha Peluda

This variant of Garnacha has leaves with hairy undersides. It typically produces wines that are lower in alcohol than Garnacha and is usually found in blends.

Garnacha Tintorera

Garnacha Tintorera is very common, especially in north-west Spain. However it is not Garnacha at all, but rather Alicante Bouschet. A distinctive feature is that it is one of the rare varieties to have coloured flesh, what is known as a *teinturier* for the way it stains the wine. Thus it delivers deeply coloured wines, very different from Garnacha itself. There are some 18,320 hectares in Spain, mainly in Castilla-La Mancha and Galicia. While it is usually used for boosting colour in blends, when well managed with lower yields it can make a wine with fine tannins.

Graciano

Graciano comes into its own in Rioja. There are still only a few single varietal versions: Contino's stands out as a single vineyard wine, while Ijalba has an organically farmed version. Other producers include Valdemar and Dinastía Vivanco. Many others use a small amount of Graciano to lift their blends. It is an aromatic variety, fresh, with a keynote liquorice and spice palate. It has a reputation for not being easy to grow. Anecdotally its name comes from growers disliking it and saying '*no, gracias*'.

In Andalucía, it's been suggested that it is a relative of Tintilla de Rota, the little black-berried grape from Rota town. González Byass makes a delightful fortified sweet red from it.

Gran Negro

Grand Noir is a cross made by M. Bouschet of Alicante Bouschet fame (it is Petit Bouschet x Aramon) in the nineteenth century. A *teinturier*, a red grape with red flesh, to add depth of colour to red wine, it is found in Valdeorras and elsewhere in Galicia where it is used instead of Alicante Bouschet, as it is more resistant to humidity.

Hondarribi Beltza

Beltza means black in Euskera, and Hondarribia is a town in Guipúzcoa. This is the red variety of the Txakolis of the Basque country. Despite its name it is not related to Hondarribi Zuri, the white grape. It is related to Cabernet Franc, and with its herbal aromatics, bright acidity and firm tannin certainly has similarities. Red Txakoli is scarce, however Doniene Gorrondona produces a fine version from pre-phylloxera vines.

Juan García

A native of Arribes del Duero, founded in the national park of the same name that crosses Spain and Portugal, it is being revived by a new generation of producers who are working to find its best expression. Among the newer producers is Beatriz Herranz of Barco del Corneta in Medina del Campo, who started work with it in Arribes. She makes an old vine Juan García called Prapetisco. Sara Groves-Raines and Patxi Martínez at La Setera, up against the Portuguese border, also make Juan García reds which match their goats' cheese.

Juan Ibáñez

Authorized in Cariñena, this is a synonym of its close neighbour Moristel in Somontano.

Malbec

Malbec in Spain means Vega Sicilia. It was one of the French varieties brought in at the outset.

Marselan

A fairly recent (1961) cross of Cabernet Sauvignon with Garnacha, this has been more successful than most despite its lack of history. There is some in Catalunya, and it has experimental status in Tierra de León.

Maturana Tinta, Merenzao

A synonym for Merenzao and Bastardo, and for the Jura's Trousseau.

Mazuelo, Mazuela, Cariñena

If Garnacha has had to travel a long way to reach international recognition, how much further has Mazuelo had to go? This was definitely a workhorse grape, delivering colour and acidity, tannin and plenty of yield. In Rioja, it is useful in small quantities for adding backbone. A notable *rosado* is Marques de Murrieta's stylish 100 per cent Mazuelo. Cariñena has come into its own in Priorat, not only in Garnacha blends but also in some exceptional single varietals. Mas Doix 1902 is an outstanding example, named after the age of the vineyard. Jorge Navascués, winemaker in Cariñena and elsewhere comments: 'It's one of the best varities we have for combatting climate change, as its high total acidity guarantees a slow evolution.'

Mencía

The reds of Bierzo, through the Mencías of Ricardo Pérez Palacios of Descendientes de J Palacios and Raúl Pérez (no relation), have become international favourites. That's particularly the case among sommeliers looking for gastronomic wines, wines that have the same elegance and freshness as Loire Cabernet Franc and Burgundy Pinot Noir. To be honest, Bierzo Mencía was never a lovely thing when made for home consumption. Furthermore, when producers started to use toasty new oak to 'modernize' the styles the wines were also unhappy. There is a geographical divide too. The higher altitude, less accessible vineyards so far produce the better wines. Thankfully there are now producers making juicy, likeable, unoaked Mencías, or handling them carefully in French oak, in larger sizes, for shorter times.

The fame of Mencía has encouraged wine buyers to look north over the border into Galicia and discover Mencía in Ribeira Sacra, Monterrei, Valdeorras, Rías Baixas and Ribeiro. In the process they have discovered the other Atlantic red varieties. Mencía is known as Jaen in Portugal. There are suggestions that it came to Bierzo with the pilgrims en route from Portugal to Santiago de Compostela.

Merlot

There's a trace of Merlot in Vega Sicilia's Valbuena 5, as it's a variety which came in early on with French advice. DOs looking for international varieties have Merlot: Navarra, for instance, and Somontano, as well as parts of Aragon. In Rioja, Antonio Palacios planted the variety, and his daughter Bárbara continues the business. She has named her golden retriever Merlot and makes a Tempranillo–Merlot blend called Barbarot.

Moristel

Despite the similarity in the name, Moristel is no relation of Monastrell, which stars further south in Mediterranean Spain. Lighter, and fresher in style, for drinking young, it is most widely found in Somontano, often in blends with international varieties.

Mouratón

A synonym for Juan García found in Ribeira Sacra and Rías Baixas.

Parraleta

Parraleta, no relation of the Parellada in Cava, is particularly found in Somontano and across Aragón. It has been overtaken by the international varieties popular in that DO, but makes aromatic reds that are quite intensely coloured.

Pedral

This promising, late-ripening variety is found only in tiny quantities (with 79 hectares in Galicia, and a mere handful in Portugal), typically in Rías Baixas. Both Attis and Señorío de Rubiós make fresh, medium bodied wines, with a light rasp of tannin.

Petit Verdot

This variety, most famously introduced to Spain by the Marqués de Griñón at the Dominio de Valdepusa at the end of the twentieth century, can be wonderfully aromatic when fully ripe, with firm, rounded tannins. It has been successfully established as a single varietal at Abadía Retuerta in Castilla y León as well as in many more southerly and Mediterranean vineyards, where the grapes can achieve full ripeness.

Prieto Picudo

A dark-skinned variety found in the area of León, notably in DO Tierras de León, and VC Valles de Benavente, this makes deeply coloured red wines, as well as *rosados*, and it is often blended with Tempranillo or Mencía. It is aromatic, with good tannins and fresh acidity, which means that it can make a vinous *rosado*, as opposed to a simple pink drink. It also takes well to some oak ageing.

Rufete

Rufete has a number of relatives in Iberia, suggesting that it is an old variety. It is close to Prieto Picudo in Spain, and Touriga Nacional in Portugal. Not the easiest variety to grow, it is pale with firm tannins, which probably accounts for its relative scarcity. In Spain it is found in Arribes, often in blends.

Sousón

This Galician variety, better known as the Portuguese Vinhão, particularly in Vinho Verde and the Douro, is a very deeply coloured, almost inky red, which is difficult to bring to ripeness. Thus it typically has a marked acidity, and is found as part of a blend. Quinta de Muradella in Monterrei is one of the producers of a single varietal.

Syrah

Syrah has been in Spain's vineyards for a number of years, though it still has something of the status of a surprise. The first producers to use it became well known for their innovation. Plus, of course, they had to work in a region that allowed for this experimental variety. Not all the early Syrahs were a great success, planted in the wrong places they made syrupy wines. Some are still like that. But in the right places, they work.

FLOR ON TOUR

The influence of Sherry is popping up all over the place in Spain. The production of Sherry itself may be confined to the strict territory, but that doesn't stop the butts and the wine from travelling. Olivier Rivière's Mirando al Sur is a case in point. The name of this Rioja producer's Viura is a play on 'south-facing', since these wines are also 'southward-looking' to Andalucía and Jerez. Initially the wine is aged in French oak for just six months, but it then goes into two Sherry butts for another year. Rivière has one that formerly contained Manzanilla and another that once held Amontillado. It's a clever way to introduce the Sherry feel, giving the wine a mysterious complexity, which tones down the fruit.

In Bierzo, Grégory Pérez has done something similar, ageing his Godello in Sherry butts. Over the border to Galicia, in Valdeorras, with Rafael Palacios, I spotted a couple of large barriques of Godello with some carefully tended *flor*. Not far away in Monterrei at Quinta de Muradella, José Luis Mateo has been working with the local Doña Blanca variety, aiming to develop a layer of *flor*-type yeast across the top of the wine. Complicated, and unexpected, the wine – called Crianza Oxidativa – is undoubtedly fascinating but can't take the local appellation as it's definitely not made to the rules.

There has long been a tradition of growing Palomino all across Spain and some of the islands. Being super-productive made it an easy option, no matter that the wines from it were dull, flabby and dilute. No wonder Rueda and so many other regions turned cheerfully to the freshness of Verdejo and other varieties made in stainless steel. What's exciting now is that a new generation is coming back to the old Palominos, planted after phylloxera. One example is Barco del Corneta – although in Rueda, the winemaker has chosen to make Palominos under *flor*, thus putting herself outside the DO regulations.

The traditional oxidative wines of Rueda were Dorados, 'golden'. It's still possible to locate them; Rueda producer De Alberto has a lovely Verdejo made the old way, in a *solera* and with oxidative ageing. Felix Lorenzo Cachazo has released Carrasviñas Dorado, a Palomino–Verdejo blend.

Blending the Sherry culture with the Riojan culture is not new. CVNE was doing it in 1915, when they created a wine finished with a small amount of Manzanilla from Sanlúcar de Barrameda. There was no DO when that was created, and so the wine continued to be made for years. In 2016, CVNE relaunched Monopole Clásico with the 2014 vintage, calling in their former winemaker Ezequiel García to take them through the process. It's a mainly Viura-based wine, but contains small amounts of Calagraño, Garnacha Blanca and Malvasía. CVNE went back to the Hidalgo family for the Manzanilla. The wine is aged in barrels and butts (the ones used to ship the Sherry), and has a dash of Manzanilla to top it up. It's a lovely tradition, and great to see a large Rioja bodega rediscovering its old wisdom rather than just consigning it to some dusty shelves. The second vintage was not perhaps as good as the first. But these wines are young, and it will be good to see how they develop.

Tempranillo

Tempranillo deserves a book to itself. Spain's hero grape variety appears in a number of guises as Tinto Fino, Tinta de Toro, Tinto del País, Cencibel, Ull de Llebre, Araúxa – and plenty more. This should not be taken to mean that Spanish wine is 'all Tempranillo'.

DNA analysis indicates that Tempranillo probably developed rapidly in Navarra and La Rioja, and spread out rapidly from there. The vines then adapted themselves to their own environments. At Vega Sicilia they have identified eight different Tinto Finos in their vineyards. RODA, in Rioja, has a project with 500 different morphotypes for its Tempranillo Seed Bank.

In Ribera del Duero, Aalto's Mariano García loves the character of the grape saying, 'even St Emilion doesn't have the subtlety of Tempranillo'. He works with 100 per cent Tempranillos. Isn't it a risk with the extreme weather not to have other varieties for blending? Not at all, he says: 'The Tempranillos in Rioja, Ribera, Toro, are all the same genotype. But they are very different – ours in Ribera has adapted to our different climate.'

What *is* distinctive about Tempranillo, with black cherry and red plum fruit, and moderate to low acidity, is that it is not stylistically dominant like Cabernet Sauvignon or Syrah. It lends itself well to blends, and also to careful oak ageing. The risk with Tempranillo is that vast tracts of the variety have been planted with the same two or three clones. If Rioja wants to recognize its village wines and their different flavours it will take time for the vines to mature and adapt to their terroir.

Vidadillo

A very rare red variety found in Aragón.

3

GALICIA: PILGRIMS, *PARRALES, PAZOS*

In 1845, Richard Ford, author of *A hand-book for travellers in Spain*, compared the green meadows of north-west Spain to Switzerland's pastures. He recognized the quality of the wines and their potential, but was altogether less complimentary about the winemaking saying, 'Rich wines are produced; of these the best are those of Valdeorras, Amandi [Ribeira Sacra], Rivero [Ribeiro], and the Tostado of Orense [Ribeiro], and they would rival the vintages of Portugal, were the commonest pains taken in the making; but here, as on the eastern coast, everything is managed in the rudest and most wasteful manner.'

Almost two hundred years later, how things have changed! Galicia's wines have undergone a remarkable transformation. There are wines produced here that rank with the world's best. It would be enough to explore the wines of Galicia without travelling further into Spain. Possibly the new 'traditional method' sparklings do not measure up to the best Cavas, and sweet wines are scarce, but there are wines, both white and red, to charm, to cellar and to enjoy. What's more, Galicia is a wonderful region for the visitor. For centuries Galicia was the forgotten corner of Spain. As a result there are still kilometres of unspoilt beaches, and lovely walking country. This is not tower-block tourism. As for the food, the seafood is of the freshest, and the Galician beef is exceptional.

Santiago de Compostela is the magnet for tourism, perhaps explaining why there are more airports per square kilometre here than anywhere else in Spain. If you want a budget flight, then there are plenty on offer. The religious significance of the city for pilgrims following the historic *camino* to the Cathedral of St James also means that you are very likely to come across senior clerics – I once spotted the Archbishop of Canterbury in the queue for boarding.

RÍAS BAIXAS

The Albariños of Rías Baixas are the wines that alerted the world to the fact that Spain could produce fine white wines. These fresh, unoaked whites, made for drinking young, and with seafood, captured a new audience. What's more, the grape was a local variety, and therefore more interesting than Sauvignon Blanc or Chardonnay.

Since then other Spanish grapes have gained international acclaim: Verdejo, Viura, Garnacha Blanca, Xarel·lo and Godello, among others. More are demanding our attention: Treixadura, Albillo, Listán, Palomino, Merseguera. Spain has entered a phase of real excitement where its winemakers are recovering old varieties, and working hard in the vineyard. However Albariño is still head and shoulders above the rest.

Yet there is a risk to this international acclaim. Retailers require ever lower prices, and producers increase their yields to satisfy demand. More vineyards are planted, not always in the best places. The young vines lack character. When the wines are quickly and cleanly fermented with reliable yeasts in stainless steel, the result is too often anonymity, often with an element of residual sugar thrown in. This is what has happened to Rueda, and Rías Baixas is teetering on the edge of that same precipice. Increasingly there is a division of reputation, with a selection of wineries at the top which are outstanding and an increasing number outside producing 'commercial' wines. Furthermore, the DO is dedicated to the single varietal; 96 per cent is Albariño. Some of the most fascinating wines in Rías Baixas are blends. Yet at the moment they are still regarded as poor relations. The DO has a future with creative blends.

Rías Baixas can never be a source of cheap wine. This is not a region for economies of scale. What defines Rías Baixas is *minifundia*; it's a land of very many small growers with tiny plots. The large estates with expansive vineyard holdings common elsewhere in Spain are scarce here. Only six companies produce more than 500,000 litres. The average land ownership per grower is just 0.6 hectares, divided up into 3.7 parcels. You will see farmers on tiny tractors beetling up and down the roads.

Few of them have any use for hefty tractors, especially where the vines are trained into *parral* or pergola canopies.

Rías Baixas first became a denomination in the 1980s and was then called DO Albariño. However upon Spain's entry into the European Union, it had to change to a non-varietal name and in 1988 chose Rías Baixas. This was much more accurate, clearly describing the style of the terrain, with its 'low inlets/firths'. The growth since then has been remarkable: in 1987 there were just 14 bodegas and 492 growers, with a vineyard area of 237 hectares, making 5,850 litres of wine. Fast forward thirty years and, as the box below shows, Rías Baixas has changed beyond all recognition.

Rías Baixas at a glance

Grape varieties

White: Albariño, Loureira Blanca, Treixadura, Caíño Blanco, Torrontés, Godello
Red: Caíño Tinto, Espadeiro, Loureira Tinta, Sousón, Tempranillo, Mouratón, Garnacha Tintorera, Mencía, Brancellao.

Size

Vineyard: 4,077 hectares
Growers: 6,031
Wineries: 181

The sub-zones

Rías Baixas is not a typical denomination in that it is divided up into five sub-zones, some of which are not contiguous. Visit the DO and it is soon clear why they are separated, with each sub-zone following different river valleys, and inlets from the sea. The soils here are mainly granitic, some with clay, limestone, sand or alluvial gravels as well as gravels formed from the decomposition of iron-rich red schist. The decomposed granite is known as *xabre*. The soils are very poor in organic matter, and the wines have a resulting minerality.

Ribeiro do Ulla
The youngest of the five sub-zones, created in 2000, this lies along the Ulla river, bringing the DO almost up to the borders of the city of Santiago de Compostela. Currently it accounts for less than five per cent of total production.

Val do Salnés

This is the original and largest sub-zone, with more than 50 per cent of the vineyard area, and 70 per cent of the growers. The best wines are said to show a savoury, marine, almost salty character.

Soutomaior

The smallest of the sub-zones, created in 1996, this has only 30 growers and supplies just 0.1 per cent of total production.

O Rosal

O Rosal, like Salnés, faces out to sea, and runs along the River Miño, the boundary with Portugal. There are some particularly attractive hillside vineyards here. One such belongs to Altos de Torona. O Rosal's soils are alluvial over granite. The wines here generally have an aromatic richness and are proving popular in wine competitions because of their easy charm with a punch of acidity.

Condado de Tea

The most southerly and inland of the sub-zones, Condado is the warmest and driest, with granitic and slate soils. Hence its dominance in red wine production – no less than 60 per cent, compared to 23 per cent in O Rosal and 12 per cent in Salnés. The Albariño here is often blended with Treixadura, giving a richer, less overtly fruity style.

The small print

Rías Baixas Albariño is 100 per cent Albariño and may be from a blend of sub-zones. White wines that carry the name of a sub-zone must be 70 per cent Albariño (with the following exceptions). Rías Baixas O Rosal must be 70 per cent Albariño and Loureira. Rías Baixas Condado do Tea must be 70 per cent Albariño and Treixadura (although in both these sub-regions many producers prefer 100 per cent Albariño). Rías Baixas Barrica has a minimum of three months oak ageing, and may be red or white. Espumosos – sparklings – are made according to the traditional (Champagne) method.

Viticulture and winemaking

There's a continuing debate about pruning. The traditional system of viticulture is the *parral*, with vines grown up granite posts (often now scaffolding poles) with crossbars. This protects the fruit from inclement weather, and also has the advantage of allowing some vegetable gardening underneath for the family. In the late twentieth century, the cordon canopy came in. It allowed for more mechanical handling for those who had large enough plots of land to enable machinery. Which produces the better fruit? The jury is out. However the new investors are using a version of the *parral*, just as elsewhere many are going back to bush vines.

Similarly, in the 1980s change came to winemaking in Rías Baixas. Albariño had formerly been fermented in large, old wooden vats, but then fibreglass was introduced – easy to clean, no running repairs needed – followed by stainless steel, with the additional advantage of temperature control, for limpid, functional wines. Intentionally oaked wines were a later project. At the time buying barrels wasn't always straightforward. Winemaker Cris Mantilla, who consults across the region, remembers: 'the tonnelleries would sell you red wine barrels. That's where American oak barrels came to be used. Veigadares [from Galegas] was launched with 30 per cent American oak, because that's what they had.'

Fortunately the DO now also permits 500 litre barrels, as the typical 225 litre barrel is altogether too dominant for many Albariños. In the early days of the DO, recalls one winemaker, 'we fought to get as high as 11.5% abv. The wines were so acid that we had to do malolactic fermentation.' Today with more work in the vineyard, malolactic has become a stylistic choice.

Red winemaking in Rías Baixas

Just twenty-six wineries work with red varieties, and eleven of them are in Salnés. The total production is just 0.74 per cent of the total 33 million kilogrammes annual average production of the DO. The largest producer is Forjas de Salnés, where winemaker Raúl Pérez introduced Rodrigo Méndez to red winemaking. Eulogio Pomares of Zárate followed on in 2009. Neither man could have anticipated the critical and commercial success of these wines. In this part of the world the reds mature at least three weeks later than Albariño and producers admit that it is particularly nerve-wracking to hang on to the right moment for harvest. Yield is an issue: a typical yield of Albariño might be 12,000 kilogrammes per hectare; whereas the ideal for a red vineyard is as little as 4,000 kilogrammes per hectare.

Climate

The climate is clearly Atlantic with average annual rainfall of 1,300 millimetres. From north to south the climate varies, with Condado de Tea the warmest of all the sub-zones. Within the last decade, it is heat rather than rain that has been a distinctive feature of the climate, notably the exceptionally hot weather in summer. This resulted in extreme and intense forest fires raging in Galicia and Portugal. As Neves in Rías Baixas suffered the brunt of the fire on 16 October 2017. Jorge Hevella, a consultant winemaker in the region, reported that in the area of As Neves close to the border, 'Over 90% of the agricultural land has been burnt and somewhere between 15–20% of that is vineyards.' But climate change brings its benefits, according to a leading producer: 'Talk to the older growers and they will remember that 30 years ago wines scarcely reached 11 degrees at harvest. It always rained at harvest, and mildew was rampant. The climate has changed since then, though Rías Baixas has so far avoided the weather extremes that have led to the severe frosts and hail elsewhere.'

Producers

Albamar

Aldea o Adro 11, 36639 Cambados
Tel.: +34 660 292 750

The Alba family owns 2.5 hectares near the mouth of the River Ulmia, and works with another 10 hectares. Xurxo Alba's parents made and sold their wine in their bar; in 2006 it was Xurxo who started bottling the wine. His interest is in farming organically and sustainably, as well as whole bunch ferments and native yeasts without malolactic fermentation. Albamar is his entry level Albariño, made in stainless steel. The Pepe Luis bottling, named after his brother who died in a car accident, is aged in large, old oak. His Sesenta e Nove Arrobas is a tiny production (the name means 69 *arrobas*, which is equivalent to 1,000 litres) of vividly fresh Albariño from

60–100 year old vines. In addition to growing, making and marketing his Albariños he also makes a red blend in Rías Baixas, a Mencía – Fusco – in Ribeira Sacra and a Godello – Ceibo – in Valdeorras. This multitasker is one to watch.

Altos de Torona

Ctra Tui-Laguardia 45, 36760 As Eiras
Tel.: +34 986 288 212
www.altosdetorona.com

This winery in O Rosal occupies a glorious setting overlooking the water. Founded in 2003, it has come to attention recently for its award-winning, polished, likeable whites, and lays claim to the largest single planting of Albariño in one block in private ownership in the DO, at over 100 hectares. It also makes some wines under the Salnés sub-zone, including Pazo de Villarei. It belongs to the HGA Group which also has projects in Ribeira Sacra, Ribeiro, Rioja and Ribera del Duero.

Ángel Sequeiros

Quinta Gaviñeira 1, 36450 Salvaterra de Miño
Tel.: +34 607 779 578
www.angelsequeiros.es

Like so many Spaniards who left home at the time of the Civil War, Sequeiros eventually returned, and in 1960 he purchased Quinta A Gaviñeira, a 7.4 hectare estate, in Condado de Tea. It is run by his son Clement, who released the first wines in 2009. His Foudre quickly came to international attention, winning the international trophy for best single varietal white at the Decanter World Wine Awards in 2013. The wine is fermented in stainless steel and then aged on its fine lees in a French oak foudre, adding texture, complexity and biscuit notes, but not oakiness. Very subtly handled, this is a wine to drink or keep. In addition there is a 'regular' Albariño, one *sobre lías* and limited edition wines that are cross-vintage blends.

Attis

Morouzos 16D, Dena, 36967 Meaño
Tel.: +34 986 744 790
www.attisbyv.es

This was founded in 2000 by the third generation of the Fariñas, a family of growers who own 12.3 hectares across 30 plots. In 2011 they opened a new bodega and took on French consultant Jean-François Hébrard. A great source of reds; here one has the chance to taste the varieties and discover their expression.

VISITING SANTIAGO DE COMPOSTELA

Every visitor to Galicia must visit Santiago at least once. The only problem is that in addition to the pilgrims there are so many tourists. Two suggestions: first, consider spending a night or two in the Hostal de Los Reyes Católicos in the cathedral square, now a luxurious Parador rather than a hospital for ill or dying pilgrims as it was in past centuries. By sleeping there, you can be sure to enjoy the cathedral late at night or first thing in the morning before the coach parties arrive. Second, if you want to see the Botafumeiro, the huge censer, swinging down the aisle of the cathedral, visit the cathedral website (www.catedraldesantiago.es) to check the days and times it is in operation before you book your trip.

Cabana das Bolboretas

Piñeiro 9, Valiñas, 36190 Barro
Tel.: +34 676 142 435
www.cabanadasbolboretas.com

'Traditional method' sparkling from Albariño seemed – to me at least – an impossibility. The variety is too aromatic, surely, and not quite acid enough. Then I met Natalia Canal (the business manager) and her husband Pablo Bermúdez (the winemaker) and their fine sparkling Gorgola, and discovered how wrong I was. In addition they have a young Albariño named after the winery, and Esquiza, which is matured in acacia wood. They are very hospitable, and let out rooms for visitors in their traditional Galician home.

Condes de Albarei

Lagar a Bouza 1, 36639 Cambados
Tel.: +34 986 543 535
www.condesdealbarei.com

This cooperative, one of the founding members of the DO, controls over 300 hectares of Salnés vineyard from which are produced bright, mineral Albariños.

Eidos

Padriñan 65, 36960 Sanxenxo
Tel.: +34 986 690 009
www.adegaeidos.com

The treasure here is the old Albariño, some ungrafted, grown on granite in plots overlooking Sanxenxo in the south of the Salnés valley. Eidos is made from the younger vines, while Veigas de Padriñán comes from the older ones. Contraaparede is a selection from the oldest, ungrafted vines, matured for some three to four years in large stainless steel vats.

Fillaboa

Lugar de Fillaboa s/n, 36450 Salvaterra do Miño
Tel.: +34 986 658 132
www.bodegasfillaboa.com

The Masaveu family purchased this glorious 70-hectare estate in 2000. Tucked away behind granite walls, it overlooks Portugal from the slopes on the north side of the river. The Masaveus also own Murúa in Rioja Alavesa and Pagos de Aráiz in Navarra, and have shares in Leda (Castilla y León) and Aalto (Ribera del Duero). In Asturias they make a Canadian-style ice cider – Valverán 20 Manzanas. Their substantial investment has transformed the house, which is decorated with a fine collection of paintings and sculptures. In the vineyard, the soils have been analysed and the land divided into eleven parcels. Winemaker Isabel Salgado's top wine is from the Monte Alto parcel: fine, fresh, well balanced. An innovation was the Fillaboa 1898 – a special release of their 2010 vintage aged for six years on lees in stainless steel. It celebrates the shipping of a Fillaboa wine to Cuba in 1898. Isabel choose 2010 because of the quality of the vintage; if Fillaboa continues with this style it will join the small group of wineries to release aged Albariño.

Forjas de Salnés/Rodrigo Méndez

Pol. de las Siete Pías, Nave 35 bajo, 36630 Cambados
Tel.: +34 986 744 426

Rodrigo Méndez is one of Galicia's cult producers, from a strong pedigree as nephew of Do Ferreiro's Gerardo Méndez. The winery is named after his father's forge. He has the heritage of vines dating back to 1912, and as a local has access to a number of the old vineyards, including the 150–200 year old vines used for the foudre-aged Finca Genoveva. He's perhaps best known for his elegant, Burgundy-style red wines and is the largest producer of red wines in Salnés, which includes 15,000 bottles of Goliardo. He started making reds with Raúl Pérez, and is making Albariños in the old style. The rich, spicy, firm and textured Cos Pés was one of the early white wines to be made like a red, with foot treading (from the lightest people around) and a number of months on skins.

Rodrigo Méndez has other separate projects; under his own name he makes two wines named after local islands. Cies is mostly fermented in old wooden tanks, and then aged partly in a selection of different sizes of oak, and partly in stainless steel, creating a fascinating combination of apricot fruit and penetrating freshness. Salvora is made from vines planted in 1905, and fermented and aged in 600-litre oak vats for 12 months. This is old style Albariño in the making, delivering a crisp, dense, linear wine. The grapes originally went into his Forjas de Salnés Leirana. He has another project making reds and whites from local varieties, as well as a Bierzo, Barredo Pinot Noir, with Raúl Pérez. One to keep on watching.

Fulcro

Ctra de Rouxique, 36690 Sanxenxo

Manuel 'Chicho' Moldes is an engaging, genuine garagiste. In a quiet country lane, not far from the glamorous holiday fleshpots of Isla La Toja and Sanxenxo, you will find this bespectacled ex-economist at work behind the roll-down door. The production is low-tech, and very high quality. Moldes started out as a winemaker in 2009 and his progress has been rapid. He draws on Albariño from different terroirs – granite and schist. Fulcro from the schist has a laser-like intensity. Finca A Pedreira, aged for five months on lees in stainless steel and with 10 per cent of barrel aged wine, comes from granitic soils with plenty of quartz and mica. It has an appealing austerity, with none of the tropical fleshiness of more commercial styles. I'm indebted to Xoan Cannas for introducing us when I spoke at an Atlantic wine conference at the Instituto Galego do Vino (www. institutogalegodovino.com). Xoan knows his wines; he is the co-owner of the Michelin-starred Pepe Vieira restaurant (see Where to Eat, p. 303) and a former best sommelier of Spain.

Galegas

Pazo de Almuiña, Almuiña 9 y 10, 36430 Aarbo
Tel.: +34 986 657 143
www.adegasgalegas.es

Galegas draws on grapes from O Rosal and Condado de Tea. It was founded in 1995 and became particularly well known for Veigadares which was one of the early barrel-fermented Albariños (a blend with 10 per cent Treixadura and 10 per cent Loureira). They are still not especially common, or well done elsewhere. The grapes come from Pazo de Almuiña, which is a classic Galician estate with an old manor house or *pazo* at its heart, a *hórreo*, the traditional granary on stilts, and a Roman road running past. Gran Veigadares is the big brother wine, fermented in oak, and aged in French and American oak barrels and stainless steel, it is altogether bolder and richer. The rest of the range is lively and well-packaged, including Danza, a 'traditional method' sparkling Albariño.

Gerardo Méndez

Galiñanes 10, Lores, 36968 Meaño
Tel.: +34 986 747 046
www.bodegasgerardomendez.com

Old vines (*cepas vellas*) and Gerardo Méndez are practically synonymous. Here there's none of the New World debate about whether an 'old' vine is 30 or 70 years old. Méndez is working with some vines that are over 200 years old, grown on the traditional pergolas. He's the third generation of the family, and as a young man, way back in 1973, created Do Ferreiro, farming 10 hectares of family vineyard, as well as buying in grapes from longstanding suppliers. His son Manu also now works in the business. He produces a 'regular' Do Ferreiro Albariño, a Do Ferreiro Cepas Vellas from the old vines, and a Barrica, fermented in 500-litre barrels, and aged in barrel for eight months. Rebisaca is his blend of Albariño with Treixadura and Loureiro. While Méndez protects his heritage, he is also continuing to develop his insights in Albariño with a range of 'limited edition' wines. Adina is grown on red slate very close to the sea, a rare terroir in Salnés, which is also found in Portugal. Following cold maceration it is lees aged in stainless steel, giving a distinctly mineral wine. The website says frankly that Do Ferreiro is all about 'Charismatic Albariños de Autor'. A bold statement, but it's hard to argue with it.

Granbazán

Lugar de Tremoedo 46, 36628 Vilanova de Arousa
Tel.: +34 986 555 662
www.agrodebazan.com

Founded in 1980 by Manuel Otero y Otero, a fine foods and conserves entrepreneur, this winery, with distinctively ornate labels, now owns 15 hectares and controls another 45. The Ambar is from the oldest vines on the property, the Verde is a younger crunchier style. Limousin, aged for six months in French oak, is a successful version of the oaked style. It was purchased in 2017 by the owner of Baigorri in Rioja, the businessman Pedro Martínez Hernández.

Lagar de Cervera

Estrada de Loureza 86, 36770 O Rosal
Tel.: +34 986 625 875
www.lagardecervera.com

White Rioja spent a number of years in the doldrums. No wonder that in 1988 La Rioja Alta took the decision to look beyond Rioja for a fine white. They lit upon O Rosal and have now assembled the largest vineyard in the zone, an impressive extension of vines. There's a limit to the interest in visiting stainless steel wineries; engagingly the towering tanks have been transformed into a literal forest, each one wrapped in monochrome photographs of trees. There are two wines – Albariño and Pazo de Seoane, a blend with some Loureiro, Caíño Blanco and Treixadura. Look out for the traditional *orujo*, Viña Armenteira de Hierbas.

La Val

Barrio Muguiña-Arantei, 36458 Salvaterra de Miño
Tel.: +34 986 610 728
www.bodegaslaval.com

One of the DO's early wineries, founded in 1985, this has grown substantially over the last decade and acquired new investment in 2010 with a management buyout. La Val originated in O Rosal and now has 60 hectares of vineyards across Salvaterra de Miño, As Neves and Tui. The regular La Val Albariño has always been reliable, but there has been a step up in quality in recent times. The Crianza Sobre Lías (lees-aged) from pergola-grown vines, has an appetizingly creamy, citric minerality. Its three years on the lees once again prove Albariño's capacity to age and develop.

Maior de Mendoza

Rúa Xiabre 58, Trabanca-Sardiñeira, Carril, 36618 Vilagarcia de Arousa
Tel.: +34 986 508 896
www.maiordemendoza.com

The Barros family have been growers since the 1970s. Today they own some 10 hectares and work with another 19. From this they produce a two-tier range. In the lower tier, there's the unforgettably named off-dry Sex Appeal. Of the upper tier, the most interesting are the Sobre Lías, which spends three months on lees, and is full of aromatic charm; and the 3 Crianzas. This comes from a single vineyard; the three *crianzas* referring to the three different ageing processes: nine months on lees, five months in tank, and then five months in bottle. The palate is complex and is carried by a vivid line of acidity, and an impressively long finish.

Mar de Frades

Finca Valiñas, Lugar Arosa 16, 36637 Meis
Tel.: +34 986 680 911
www.mardefrades.es

This is the wine in the blue bottles. You either love them or hate them: while I'm in the latter camp when it comes to the packaging, the good news is that the quality of the liquid in the bottle is so much better than the blue colour suggests. (There's also a thermographic label, that reveals a galleon on the high seas when the wine is at the right temperature.) Winemaker Paula Fandiño joined Mar de Frades in 2007 and continues to be busy experimenting with fermentation, yeasts, batonnage and single vineyards. Of the DO's 'commercial', mainstream Albariños, Mar de Frades is reliably one of the best. Fandiño's research has led her to produce the elegant single vineyard Finca Valiñas, fermented in new French oak with six months on lees. The 'traditional method' sparkling Albariño is very good. I was a doubter – thinking the Albariño would be too dominant, a bit like sparkling Sauvignon Blanc from New Zealand – but it is beautifully balanced and I am a convert. Mar de Frades is part of the Zamora group led by Ramón Bilbao (Rioja).

'FOREIGN' INVESTORS

Rías Baixas has been the favourite choice of large producers from elsewhere in Spain looking for a prestige white wine for their portfolio. This is not an exhaustive list.
- Avante Selecta, Viña Nora
- Freixenet, Vionta
- González Byass, Pazos de Lusco
- The HGA Group, Altos de Torona
- Marques de Vargas, Pazo de San Mauro
- The Masaveu family, Fillaboa
- Orowines, Lagar da Condesa
- La Rioja Alta, Lagar de Cervera
- Torres, Pazo das Bruixas
- The Zamora group, Mar de Frades

Martín Códax
Burgáns 91, 36633 Vilariño, Cambados
Tel.: +34 986 526 040
www.martincodax.com

It seems as if Martin Códax cannot put a foot wrong. The very model of a modern cooperative, this is named after the famed Galician troubadour, and was founded in 1985 by fifty growers with 30 hectares between them. The winery opened in 1986 and the first vintage was launched that year. Today the co-op has 270 shareholders, and works with another 200 families as long-term contractors. The figures reveal the complexity of co-op management in Rías Baixas: in Salnés they manage 440 hectares in 2,385 plots; in Condado de Tea, 35 hectares in 7 plots; in O Rosal 20 hectares in 8 plots. It's not surprising that the winery's director general Juan Vázquez was awarded Personality of the Year at the IWC's Spanish Merchant Awards 2017. The judges said, 'he has been a pioneer in driving quality wines in north-west Spain … particularly noteworthy is his role as a leader in cooperatives, given that cooperatives account for 65 per cent of Spain's wine production.'

The winery is on an exceptional site, overlooking the bay and the mussel beds. Though strongly export oriented there is a lively visitor programme. In the summer the area on the hilltop outside the winery is put to good use with music and informal tastings. Visits are strictly controlled – one of the rare times you will see me in a lab coat – but they are well worth it for the discovery of what is new in the research and development department.

The classic Albariño is named after Martin Códax himself. Lías has ten months on lees with batonnage in stainless steel to build richness. Moving through the range Organistrum undergoes malolactic fermentation in Allier oak barrels; and Gallaecia is a rare late-harvest Albariño. Of their top wines, my preferred is undoubtedly Vindel. It comes from an old low-yielding vineyard that produces pink-tinged grapes. Fermented partly in stainless steel and partly in lightly toasted French oak barrels, it is then aged for a year in stainless steel. Complex and textured, it shows what Albariño can achieve and is well worth seeking out. They also produce wines in Valdeorras in Bierzo. The Bierzo winery, Cuatro Pasos, produces a *rosado* and a series of reds, all from Mencía.

Nanclares & Prieto

Castriño 13, 36639 Castrelo
Tel.: +34 986 520 763
www.nanclaresyprieto.com

Bearded and beetle-browed, with an intense gaze, Alberto Nanclares is one of Rías Baixas' distinctive figures. A one-time economist he began a new life making Albariño in the 1990s, first of all in tiny amounts. His approach to wine is considered and unshowy. He gradually accumulated land, and now has some 2.5 hectares, which he farms organically. Each of his vineyard plots is fermented with its own wild yeasts. There's nothing soft about these wines; they have all their natural acidity. He has been in partnership since 2015 with winemaker Silvia Prieto and together they produce a growing range of wines. These include Dandelion, from parcels around Cambados, and Alberto Nanclares Albariño from 30–60 year old vines. There are some single vineyard selections including a foot-trodden, skin-fermented Albariño called Crisopa Branco Tradicional. They also make two foot-trodden, whole-cluster reds in Ribeira Sacra, and another in Ribeiro.

Paco & Lola

Valdamor 18, Xil, 36968 Meaño
Tel.: +34 986 747 779
www.pacolola.com

This winery with its stylish polka dot label is Rías Baixas' largest cooperative. It tends to be looked down upon when wine tasters don't taste blind, first for its size, second for its fun packaging and perhaps third for its brand name. However Paco & Lola continues to improve and the 'regular' Paco & Lola Albariño is bursting with stone fruit and has a mouthwatering finish. The winery was founded in 2005 and has 400 members managing 200 hectares spread over 1,800 plots in Salnés. From these grapes a range of fresh young Albariños is produced, some with long lees-ageing. There is also a Tempranillo–Garnacha red made in Valdizarbe in Navarra.

Palacio de Fefiñanes

Plaza de Fefiñanes s/n, 36630 Cambados
Tel.: +34 986 542 204
fefinanes@fefinanes.com

Palacio de Fefiñanes is one of Rías Baixas' great wineries. It is made all the more glorious by the fact that it *is* indeed a glorious palace. The L-shaped building forms two sides of the main square of Cambados, which is itself the headquarters of Val do Salnés; it's the place where all the Albariño partying is held. I was made a Dama de Albariño here so I must admit that I have a special affection for it, and the events in the garden.

The building of the palace was started in the sixteenth century and finished in the 1620s by the first Viscount of Fefiñanes. The front is ornate with distinctive balconies on the corners. Behind there's an old vineyard, with Albariño growing up short granite poles. As always in Rías Baixas, the message is 'watch out, don't bang your head!'

The winery was founded in 1904, and winemaking has changed radically over the years, though it's still possible to see the old wooden vats from bygone days. With consummate skill, winemaker Cris Mantilla works around the physical difficulties of a historic property, and the many tourists keen to take a look. She has had a career as a consultant working across Galicia and also works with Valmiñor and Castro Brey in Rías Baixas, Valdesil in Valdeorras, Pazo de Rivas and Vitheras in Cangas del Narcea in Asturias.

The owner is Juan Gil de Araujo who is also President of the CRDO (the Consejo Regulador). With Palacio de Fefiñanes he offers a very distinct, carefully considered range of wines, a clear ladder of quality and style which some of the more confused ranges elsewhere could take as a model. Albariño de Fefiñanes is just that – an absolutely textbook Albariño, youthful and clearly of its place. The 1583 Albariño de Fefiñanes dates back to the year the first Viscount was born. Different in style and more textured, it has spent just three months in barrel on lees. Decide which style you prefer. Outstanding is Albariño de Fefiñanes III Año, a wine that is in its third year having spent 28 months on lees in stainless steel. The glory of fine aged Albariño is once again revealed in this wine.

Pazo Baion

Lugar de Abelleira 4-6, 36614 Vilanova de Arousa
Tel.: +34 986 543 535
www.pazobaion.com

A terrific property, and one with a pretty terrific history too, closely connected with a very famous drug dealer in these parts. It's old history now but the murky stories keep being repeated. Perhaps it's the contrast with the beauty of the estate now and the dark days in the past. Whatever it once was, Pazo Baion is a special place. The property was built by a Galician who had made his money in Argentina and returned at the beginning of the twentieth century to build a suitably grand home with a crenellated tower. The 75-hectare estate, with a lovely large manor house in the centre, has overall some 22 hectares of vineyards. These have been assessed and divided into different parcels to assist the blending. After some years of uncertainty following the departure of the owner, Condes de Albarei took the business on, making a very fine Albariño from the estate grapes.

Pazo de Barrantes

Pazo Barrantes, 36636 Ribadumia
Tel.: +34 986 718 211
www.pazodebarrantes.com

This is a rare estate in Rías Baixas with a grand, granite *pazo* dating back to 1511 within a large vineyard – for Rías Baixas – of 12 hectares. Even rarer is the fact that it remains in the same hands – the Condes de Creixell, owners of Marqués de Murrieta in Rioja. The winery was launched in the 1990s. The vineyard has been returned to the traditional pergola from the modern canopy and the wines seem all the better for it. Pazo Barrantes is the stainless steel Albariño with two months on lees. La Comtesse, launched in 2009, is the flagship: destemmed before pressing, fermented in 3,000 litre French Allier vats, followed by six months on lees. A further year in vat puts it in the specialist category of Albariños with age.

Pazo de Lusco

Lugar Grixo-Alxen s/n, 36458 Salvaterra do Miño
Tel.: +34 986 659 102
www.lusco.es

The new name for Lusco do Miño, which was acquired by González Byass in 2016.

The *pazo* is a manor house with 5 hectares of vineyards, which lies very close to the Portuguese border, in Condado de Tea. There are currently two wines, Pazo de Lusco Albariño with all the peachy ripe fruit of sub-zone overlaying the freshness, and Pazo Piñeiro, the name of the estate.

Pazo de San Mauro

Porto, 36458 Salvatierra de Miño
Tel.: +34 986 658 285

The Rioja estate Marqués de Vargas purchased the *pazo* and its 30 hectares in 2003, although the original winery was established in 1988, and there is evidence that wine was made in the *pazo* back in the sixteenth century. The property is in the tiny zone of Condado de Tea. There are two wines: Pazo de San Mauro, and the top wine Sanamaro, which spends four months on lees and six months in bottle before release.

Pazo de Señoráns

Lugar Vilanoviña s/n, 36616 Meis
Tel.: +34 986 715 373
www.pazodesenorans.com

If you ever think of getting married in Spain, then Pazo de Señoráns is the place to go. I've visited several times for parties or when the house is laid out before a wedding and it has been beautiful, bright with flowers and candles. It's even possible to dream for a few hours that this might be your own home, right down to its swimming pool and robotic lawnmower. In fact it is easy to forget the Señoráns is a very significant winery, in terms both of its role in the history of Rías Baixas and of the quality of the wines. Marisol Bueno, the mistress of the house, was also the first president of the CRDO, a post she held for twenty-one years, and was vital in driving the formation of the Rías Baixas we have today. She kept the O Rosal and Salnés together when they were ready to launch on their own: 'Can you imagine what it would have been like with two DOs just two steps apart fighting each other?'

In terms of wine Señoráns has been a pioneer, developing wines with long ageing on lees. There was no recipe, just consistent experimentation between Bueno and her winemaker, Ana Quintela, who has been with her since 1991. Pazo Señoráns Colección has five months in tank and then 35 months in bottle. Pazo Señoráns Selección de Añada is the star of the set with 30 months in tank on lees and then six months in bottle. Both of these wines have maturity; my personal preference is for Selección de Añada, a complete original with its silky, persistent, layered style. The grapes come from their own vineyards within a 10 kilometre radius of the sea, and are grown on pergolas. Don't miss the *orujos* here, and a visit to the distillery, as well as the impressive *hórreo*.

Pedralonga

Cruceiro de Santiago 17, 36615 Caldas de Reis
Tel.: +34 986 535 201
www.pedralonga.es

The Alfonso family have been growers and producers for several generations; they founded their winery in 1997, and work their vines biodynamically. Their classic Albariño is Pedralonga, Barrica has six months in French oak and Vendetta is the tiny production from the free-run juice prepressing. DoUmia is their red, from Mencía with Caíño and Espadeiro.

Pombal A Lanzada

Pombal 1, 36990 Noalla
Tel.: +34 986 743 078
adegapombal@gmail.com

A young and promising winery with its toes in the ocean: that is to say, the vines aren't far from the sea, and there's a parallel family business – mussel farming in the Ría de Arousa. The Rodríguez family works with seven plots across 0.85 hectares of decomposed schist and granitic sand. Consultant Dominique Roujou de Boubée and his wife Laura Montero, of Terroir en Botella (www.terroirenbotella.com) are working with them to produce seriously saline Albariño, as well as introducing biodynamic farming. Mytilus has four months in stainless steel, and Arcan nine months. As Bateas (the name of the mussel farmers' floats) has nine months ageing in stainless steel and then three years in bottle. They also now produce a Mytilus red from Sousón and Pedral. Burbullas das Bateas is their 'traditional method' sparkling. That wine is made by expert hands as Montero worked at Raventós i Blanc for a number of years and still consults there.

Quinta de Couselo

Couselo 13, 36770 O Rosal
Tel.: +34 986 625 051
www.quintacouselo.com

Quinta de Couselo's history dates back to the Cistercians, who built a beautifully sited monastery at the head of a bay, apparently the only one of their properties built on the Atlantic coast. What is now Quinta de Couselo was one of their farms, sold off at the time of the dissolution of the monasteries. It remained in the same family until 2013 when it was sold to the present owners, Grandes Pagos Gallegos de Viticultura Tradicional. Two days after the sale, a devastating fire swept through O Rosal. It just missed their vineyards, meaning the new owners were still able to make some award winning wines. The 6 hectares of vineyard are on decomposed granite, mainly Albariño with some other local white varieties. Turonia sees four months on the lees, and has bright stone fruit, with fresh acidity. The flagship Quinta de Couselo has a little Caíño Blanco, Treixadura and Loureiro in the blend, and is aged for six months on lees to produce a wine that is much more aromatic and complex than the 'average' Albariño. The top wine, Quinta de Couselo Selección, is 100 per cent Albariño with several years of ageing. The result is a powerful wine, with hints of evolution on the palate, and a vibrant, long finish. Grandes Pagos Gallegos de Viticultura Tradicional also make Fraga do Corvo Godello in Monterrei.

Santiago Ruiz

Rúa do Vinicultor Santiago Ruiz, 36760 San Miguel de Tabagón
Tel.: +34 986 614 083
www.bodegasantiagoruiz.com

Santiago Ruiz was a prime mover in creating Rías Baixas and the image of the DO. Later he became best known for the lively labels on his eponymous wine, with a sketch map of the region on the front. (The map was drawn by his daughter to show guests how to get to her wedding.) In fact though the wine was a great advertisement for Rías Baixas it was never just Albariño. It's a blend, with 10 per cent Loureiro, 7 per cent Godello, 5 per cent Treixadura and 4 per cent Caíño Blanco. In recent years other producers have overtaken Santiago Ruiz, but the label undoubtedly remains a very strong brand. In 2015, his daughter Rosa launched a 100 per cent Albariño under her own name. It's well-balanced, delicate and aromatic – and as ever with this family, nicely packaged.

Señorío de Rubiós

Bouza do Rato s/n, Rubiós, 36449 As Neves
Tel.: +34 986 667 212
www.bodegas-cotoredondo.com

This young cooperative in Condado de Tea, formed by 57 members in 2003, launched its first wine in 2006. The wines came to my attention when one of their reds scored 92 at a 2017 Decanter blind tasting. We praised the wine – Manuel d'Amaro Pedral – for its purity, persistent red berry character, elegance and clear, Atlantic freshness. It also showed us that Pedral is a promising variety in Rías Baixas; certainly the team at Rubiós thinks it's the cooperative's most distinctive red variety. There is a full range of reds to explore, Sousón, Espadeiro, Mencía and Caíño Tinto. In contrast to the rest of Rías Baixas, they have a more limited range of whites: two Albariños and a blend.

Sucesores de Benito Santos

Curras 46, 36629 Caleiro
Tel.: +34 654 182 684
www.benitosantos.com

Benito Santos founded the winery in 1979, and was one of the people involved in creating the new denomination in 1988. It's his heirs, or *sucesores*, who are in charge now. There are several well-packaged young wines. Top of the range is Pago de Xoan, made from old pergola vine Albariño grown on granitic sand, with plenty of floral charm and bright acidity. In Monterrei they also make a Benito Santos Godello and a Benito Santos Mencía.

Terras Gauda

Estrada Tui-A Guarda Km 55, 36760 O Rosal
Tel.: +34 986 621 001
www.terrasgauda.com

The 160-hectare estate stretches across O Rosal, though part of it has been carved up by one of Galicia's many highways. From these vineyards they produce 1.5 million bottles. But despite the volume, there are wines of quality, above all the Caíño Blanco. The longstanding research and development programme includes clonal selection of Albariños, work on mannoproteins released during fermentation, and isolation and patenting of a micro-organism in Caíño Blanco. The flagship Terras Gauda, a blend of Albariño with 20 per cent Caíño Blanco and 10 per cent Loureiro, is a typically full-bodied, fresh O Rosal wine. The black label Terras Gauda is a blend that is fermented in French oak and aged for five months on lees with batonnage. La Mar, their most interesting wine, is Caíño Blanco with 10 per cent Albariño and Loureiro. It has an underlying freshness revealing exotic notes over the top and ages well.

In 2002 they acquired Pittacum in Bierzo and in 2010 Quinta Sardonia in Ribera del Duero.

Tricó

Pombal-Porto s/n, 36450 Salvaterra de Miño
Tel.: +34 672 322 273
www.trico.es

Tricó means the youngest child in a family, the spoilt child, but also the unexpected one. For owner José Antonio López this was the unexpected arrival in his working life, and one that brought great satisfaction. His focus is on expressing the traditional character of Albariño, and the style of the different vineyard plots. The traditional approach is mirrored in the labels, which come from his mother's school notebooks. The first wine appeared in 2007. The portfolio has gradually grown, each wine expressing the vintage, with profound intensity. Dominique Roujou de Boubée and Laura Montero consult here. These are wines worth seeking out.

Valmiñor

Calle Portela s/n, 36770 O Rosal
Tel.: +34 986 609 060
www.adegasvalminor.com

The winery was founded in 1987 and today has 34 hectares. Winemaker Cris Mantilla focuses on bringing out the aromatic character of the wine by using Loureiro and Caíño Blanco, as in Davila M100. L100 is their 100 per cent Loureiro, showing the florality and ripeness of the variety in O Rosal. The 100 per cent Albariño is aromatic, with a fleshy, stone fruit palate and a mineral touch at the end. Valmiñor is a bodega that is useful if you want to discover more of the Atlantic reds. Mantilla makes one of the still rare Rías Baixas reds from the scarce Castañal; Davila C100 has a light palate with cherry freshness and a distinct tannic grip. The six months spent in French oak barrels do not mark the wine strongly. Torroxal, a blend of Sousón, Brancellao and Caíño Tinto is an energetic, rustic red, with notes of crab apples and rosehips.

Viña Nora

Bruñeiras 7, 36440 As Neves
34 986 667 210
www.vinanora.com

Viña Nora could not be in a drier, higher or warmer place anywhere else in Rías Baixas or Condado de Tea. It's a relatively young member of the DO, founded in 2002. The 16 hectares of estate vines are pergola grown and overlook the river Miño at altitude of around 600 metres. Three wines are made, all of them 100 per cent Albariño. Two are lees aged in stainless steel, while Nora da Neve is barrel fermented in 225- and 600-litre lightly-toasted French oak, with batonnage for five months. The bodega is now owned by the Avante Selecta group.

Vionta

Lugar Axis s/n, Parroquia de Simes, 36968 Meaño
Tel.: +34 986 747 566
www.vionta.com

The Ferrer family, of Cava producers Freixenet, owns Vionta. The modern winery on the hill has a glorious view over the valley and vineyards towards the sea. The main wine is Vionta, named after one of the offshore islands, and aged for between four and six months on lees. It is creamy and textured with notes of peach conserve and cinnamon.

Zárate

Sisangandara 22, 36636 Ribadumia
Tel.: +34 986 718 503
www.bodegas-zarate.com

Eulogio Pomares is a man of many parts, gifted and quietly thoughtful. Not only a member of the winning team in the Revue de Vin's World Blindtasting Championship in 2014, he also makes wine well outside his family vineyard. In 2016 he paired up with Susana Esteban in Alentejo, Portugal, in her Sidecar project for guest winemakers. Made from old vines fermented in white clay amphorae, Sidecar is – unsurprisingly – a treat: aromatic, sweetly spicy, with a pure taut freshness. In Rías Baixas Pomares can appear a person of seriousness, gowned up for the annual procession through Cambados of winery owners and dignitaries to celebrate Albariño. In the 1950s Ernesto Zárate was a pioneer of Albariño; today winemaker Pomares and his wife Rebecca Zárate, the third generation, manage a thrilling range of expressions of Albariño in granitic Salnés from 11 vineyards across 10 hectares. In addition to the 'regular' Zárate Albariño, there is El Palomar, from a single vineyard of 120-year-old ungrafted vines, fermented in French oak. El Balado is from an enclosed, granite-walled vineyard, aged with lees stirring for a full texture. Tras da Vinya, another single vineyard wine, has fine mineral acidity, and richness from its lees ageing. Under the Zárate label, Pomares also makes Loureiro, Espadeiro and Caíño reds.

His Grandes Vinos Desiguales project enables Pomares to make some (beautifully packaged) individual wines, which explore the boundaries of Albariño and Albariño winemaking. His Parcelarios project extends the concept. Fento Wines is his *négociant* business, with wines from what he calls the Garden of Eden: Salnés valley, Ribeira Sacra, Condado de Tea and Dão.

On the radar

Consultants **Terroir en Botella** (www.terroirenbotella.com) have other clients in Galicia, all worth keeping an eye on. **Torgo** (www.torgo.es) in Condado de Tea, is a small family business with a single hectare of vineyard. It does not belong to the DO and makes a wine that is a blend of Albariño with other varieties. In Salnés, they work with **Don Olegario** (www. donelgario.com) a 4-hectare family business. Also in Salnés, in Barrantes, is a lovely property, **Lagar de Pintos** (www.lagardepintos.com) run by the fourth generation of the family. The wines include 3000 Cepas, which is made from old vine Albariño on their own rootstock. With Franck Massard of **Epicure Wines** (www.epicure-wines.com), they make Alma in O Rosal and Audacia in Valdeorras. These two wines they make as a trio of friends calling themselves 'Les 3 Amis'.

PONTEVEDRA

The headquarters of the Consejo Regulador are here, and importantly there are plenty of good places to eat. Richard Ford, on visiting in the 1830s, liked it greatly, commenting that 'Pontevedra, Pons Vetus, with its long bridge, rises on a slope overhanging its beautiful ría and the estuary of the Lerez. It is a clean, well-built, well-paved town.' Ford was, however, harsh on the people of the time: 'The Pontevedrans are good haters, and regard their neighbours of Vigo as the men of Santiago do their brethren at La Coruña.' There are more bridges now, and the population has grown, but the overall impression of the heart of old Pontevedra is unchanged. Ford is a fierce critic of the Galicians, and I disagree with him over this. However when it comes to his impression of Pontevedra itself, he's quite right.

MONTERREI

Created in 1994, Monterrei is the youngest of Galicia's DOs but it has the oldest traces of winemaking, with Roman *lagares* carved out of the rock, still extant. Before the DO was created there was a cooperative that worked with Valdeorras nearby.

Monterrei is in the south-west of Ourense, by the Portuguese border. It is bisected north–south by the River Támega, the only one of the Galician rivers that doesn't finish in the Atlantic or the Miño – it flows into the Douro. Though Monterrei is Galician, it is the warmest of its DOs, and when it comes to viticulture and wine everything about Monterrei is different from the rest of the region – the Mencía here has the more 'meaty' characteristic of Bierzo. The climate is Atlantic, with continental influences, making for cold, dry winters, and very hot, dry summers. Thus the contrast in climate between inland Monterrei and coastal Rías Baixas is striking. The rainfall is four times higher in Rías Baixas. There are three main types of soil: slate and shale, which are good for aromatic reds; granitic, sandy soils, good for white wines; and sedimentary and clay soils, which are particularly good for reds. There are slopes at 300–400 metres, but also *mesetas* (plateaus), at 500–700 metres; it's the blend of these that give the wines added personality.

The average vineyard holding here is 1 hectare, and the *minifundia* seen elsewhere in Galicia are not so common in Monterrei. A function of the fact that Monterrei is in a time of transition is that I have selected only two wineries to feature here. Come back in five years and there will be more, in addition to the larger wineries from over the border, such as Martín Códax from Rías Baixas, who are adding Monterrei to their portfolio.

Monterrei at a glance

Grape varieties

White: Doña Blanca, Verdello (Godello), Treixadura, Albariño, Caíño Blanco, Loureira, Blanco de Monterrei
Red: Araúxa (Tempranillo), Caíño Tinto, Mencía, Bastardo (María Ardoña), Sousón

Size

Vineyard: 532 hectares
Growers: 446
Wineries: 25

Producers

Gargalo

Rúa do Castelo, 32600 Verín
Tel.: +34 988 590 023
www.gargalo.es

Gargalo was founded in 1998 by the fashion designer Roberto Verino, whose maternal grandparents were growers in Ribeira Sacra. The 8-hectare estate at the foot of the Castle of Monterrei has Godello, Albariño, Doña Branca and Loureira, with Mencía, Araúxa and Merenzao. There is a clear ladder of quality: at the top is Viña Verino, a Godello, fermented in new French oak barrels, with six months on lees followed by six months in bottle: creamy, plump, with a fine acidity. Beneath that there's a stainless steel fermented Godello/Treixadura Sobre Lías, with eight months on lees; and a 100 per cent Mencía, Terra do Gargalo Carballo. In addition to the other wines in the portfolio there is a classic range of flavoured liqueurs.

Quinta de Muradella

Avda Luis Espada 99, 32600 Verín
Tel.: +34 988 411 724
bodega@muradella.com

This is a treasure trove for those who enjoy discovering indigenous varieties. Across his 20 hectares (5 hectares are rented) of granite, quartz and sandy soils, in twenty-three different plots, José Luis Mateo tends and recuperates a great range of varieties, the list of which seems to keep growing as he works. He started out in 1991 and today he counts amongst the whites Doña Blanca, Treixadura and Verdello, and the reds Araúxa, Bastardo, Caíño Redondo, Garnacha Tintorera, Mencía, Caíño Longo, Souson and Zamarrica. The vineyards also contain some Monstruosa de Monterrei which, as the name might suggest, is a vigorous, mighty plant. Mateo has been developing it but still has only a tiny quantity. He currently blends it with the other white varieties. He admits that not all the varieties (including the Monstruosa) are within the DO permitted list. Since 2008 one of his projects has been to revive a pre-oidium variety, Albarello. However *Wine Grapes* suggests that this is in fact the rare Portuguese Alvarelhão, which is known as Brancellao in Galicia.

The plots Mateo tends may be as much as 40 kilometres apart, which makes day-to-day management hard. The altitude ranges from 300 to 900 metres, with steep slopes. Given the warm climate, he says his biggest challenge is preserving acidity, which is where the higher altitude vineyards come in. He works the vineyards organically with minimum intervention, focusing on restoring the abandoned bush vines. In the winery, he says, 'I try to make the whites like reds, and the reds like whites.' He works with whole bunches and wild yeasts and is experimenting with different sizes of oak. His consultant is Raúl Pérez who gave him guidance in the early years (he launched the Quinta in 1991 and released his first 'commercial' bottle in 2000). Together they make a wine, A Trabe, named after the vineyard of the same name which has some of Galicia's oldest vines, from a range of varieties. The wines range from the very approachable Alanda red and white, through red and white from the Gorvia vineyard, and Muradella to Sábrego and Berrande, plus several different experimental wines. All are made by a man who clearly loves his vineyards.

RIBEIRA SACRA

Ribeira Sacra means 'sacred riverbanks', and originally referred to the many monasteries and churches that once populated this area. However there is a magical aspect to these steep riverbanks and winding rivers that preserves a feeling of sacredness. They also produce some terrific wines. In particular, Mencía and other local varieties produce remarkably pure, crisp reds. Richard Ford is enthusiastic about the rivers: 'The country is rich and pastoral, the bacon delicious, and the Biscochos [cakes] de Monforte renowned. From Monforte the angler may proceed to the Vierzo [Bierzo] … Take a local guide … and look to your tackle, for hereabouts are some of the finest salmon and trout fishing quarters in Spain; here are virgin unwhipped streams, which would make old Izaak Walton's mouth water.'

The DO covers the province of Lugo and Ourense, running along the Sil river, which is a tributary of the Miño. As a Y-shaped DO it's very diverse, with variations in orientation, altitude and gradient. There are five distinct sub-zones: Amandi, with its vertiginous vineyards on the right bank of the River Sil; Chantada, with a riper, fruitier style to its wines; Quiroga-Bibei, Ribeiras do Miño, on the left bank of the Miño; and Ribeiras do Sil, with its hectic, steep slopes on the left bank of the River Sil. The countryside is spectacular, with vineyards teetering on the steepest of slopes down to the river. They call this 'heroic viticulture' and are right to do so. It's hard to overemphasize the beauty of this region. In the wine world the Mosel is talked about, but these vineyards in canyons are remarkable. In 1956 there were 14,000 hectares. However, as the emigration of the 1950s finished what phylloxera had started, the terraces were abandoned. Furthermore, the creation of the reservoirs by damming the rivers drowned many vineyards. It has been a long journey back. The results are very promising, particularly with the crisp, well-structured reds. When unoaked or carefully oaked the fruit shines through.

Ribeira Sacra was first developed as a VdlT Ribeira Sacra in 1993; in 1995 the DO Ribeira Sacra was provisionally established, finally being recognized in 1996. It still remains something of a secret to many; only 3 per cent of the production is exported. The vineyard area is registered as 1,241 hectares, but the actual vineyard area is much closer to 2,500. The extra is accounted for by growers who make wine for home and local consumption and do not wish to be involved in the usual bureaucratic complications of a DO.

The climate is mainly continental, with Atlantic influences, long hot summers and mild autumns. The Miño valley runs north–south with a relatively open aspect, and is wetter (900 millimetres annually) and warmer (average temperature 14°C) than the Sil valley. This runs east–west and is more closed; with rain at 700 millimetres per year and an average temperature of 13°C.

The soils in Chantada and western parts of Ribeiras do Miño and do Sil are mainly granitic, while Armandi and the eastern parts of the Ribeiras have clay with higher levels of slate. Both of these contribute to a clearly stony, fresh character to the wines.

Ribeira Sacra at a glance

Grape varieties

White: Albariño, Loureira, Treixadura, Godello, Doña Blanca, Torrontés
Red: Mencía, Brancellao, Merenzao, Garnacha Tintorera, Tempranillo, Sausón, Caíño Tinto, Mouratón. Ninety-three per cent of production is red wine.

Size

Vineyard: 1,241 hectares
Growers: 2,438
Wineries: 89

The small print

Ribera Sacra Summum Whites: 100 per cent from the preferred varieties. Barrica: aged in maximum 600-litre casks for a minimum of three months.
Ribera Sacra Summum Reds: 85 per cent of preferred varieties, of which a minimum of 60 per cent must be Mencía. Barrica: aged in maximum 500-litre casks for a minimum of six months.

Producers

Abadía da Cova/Moure

Avda Buenos Aires 12, 27540 Escairón
Tel.: +34 982 452 031
www.adegasmoure.com

The address above is the winery office. For a sense of the drama of the site, type the bodega name Abadía da Cova into Google maps and look at the satellite view. The winery is on a terrific site overlooking the steep slope over the bend in the river and is a must-visit in terms of tourism. Just remember to ask someone else to do the driving on the hairpin bends.

Moure has been making wine since the 1950s; the wines are sold under the brand name Abadía da Cova. The winemakers were pioneers in Ribeira Sacra, the first to make a Barrica, a barrel-aged red, and first to make an Albariño (though today the Albariño also has Godello in the blend). The Mencía Barrica is fermented in tronco-conical deposits and then aged in French oak for 18 months. The winery also makes a range of *orujos* and flavoured liqueurs.

Algueira

Doade s/n, 27460 Doade
Tel.: +34 982 152 238
www.adegaalgueira.com

Fernando González Riveiro and his wife Ana Pérez have managed their 11 hectares of vineyards for years, but it wasn't until 1998 that they created the winery. The knowledge of their vines shows in the wines, which are exceptional. A visit to Algueira is practically as breathtaking as their vineyards. I exaggerate, just a little, but one after another the tasting reveals wines that are individual, original, sensitively made and ringingly pure. While they do make Godellos, this is a place to come to discover the originality and diversity of Galicia's reds: Brancellao, Mencía, Merenzao (a personal favourite from Algueira) and more. There's a Burgundian delicacy to these wines which enchants.

Dominio do Bibei

Langullo s/n, 32781 Manzaneda
Tel.: +34 986 657 856
www.dominiodobibei.com

Dominio do Bibei put Ribeira Sacra on the international map. There are a number of factors in its success. It could so easily have been dismissed as a modern project, but owner Javier Domínguez and his team have developed wines with authenticity. Undoubtedly he benefited from the insights of Sara Pérez (Mas Martinet) and her husband René Barbier Jr (Clos Mogador, Espectacle) from Priorat, both of them skilled *terroiristes*. The resident winemaker is Laura Lorenzo.

The estate is 123 hectares, though nothing is easy to manage in this complex countryside; just 45 hectares are planted, and they are farmed organically. The wines are developing in character as new plantings with cuttings from old varieties continue to come on stream. The growers look for old cuttings: their Albariño came from Do Ferreiro in Rías Baixas. The winery is all about concrete, including concrete eggs, with wooden vats and barrels. Lalama is the lively, spicy red of Mencía, which over time has grown to include Brancellao, Mouratón (Garnacha Tintorera), Sousón and Garnacha; Lacima takes the best Mencía and is matured in barrel and tronco-conic cement vats before spending one to two years in bottle (Dominio do Bibei's wines are released with bottle age). Lapola is Lalama's partner, a blend of Godello, Albariño and Doña Blanca, a lively white with apricot fruits and mineral notes. Lapena is 100 per cent Godello, grown at high altitude on schist. The Dominio do Bibei is a vivid Brancellao and Mouratón blend, a fine expression of the vineyards.

Envínate

Tel.: +34 682 207 160
asesoria@envinate.es

Envínate is a leader in the new generation making and selling wines from different regions across Spain. Its four founders have particularly made their names in Tenerife, and more recently in Montilla-Moriles. One of the quartet is Alfonso Torrente from Ribeira Sacra. His wines are called Lousas, after the Galician name for the slate soils found in the Amandi sub-zone where the wines are made.

Lousas Viñas de Aldea is the village wine, a Mencía blend drawn from south-facing vineyards, averaging 60 years. Foot-trodden, like all the Lousas wines, it is partially whole-cluster fermented. The resulting wine is pure, cherry-fresh and persistent. Parcela Seoane is a Mencía blend from a slate vineyard at 400 metres, aged for 11 months in 500-litre neutral oak barrels. It is intense, lively and, like its cellarmate, pure. Camino Novo is a little different. Made from 70-year-old Mencía with 15 per cent Alicante Bouschet, on slate and schist, it is altogether vivid, an expressive full-flavoured Ribeira Sacra.

Fedellos do Couto

O Couto 19, 32760 Castro Caldelas
Tel.: +34 666 568 159

This is surely the trendiest winemaker on the Ribeira Sacra block. The project started in 2013 and is named after the 'brats' (*fedellos*) of the twelfth-century manor house (Pazo do Couto) amid the vineyards. The manor house has been in Luis Taboada's family for generations. Of his three colleagues, two have worked in Gredos with Dani Landi, and together they work 4 hectares overall, a mix of varieties and soils on the banks of the rivers Sil and Bibei. Their work is all about organic farming, co-fermentation, wild yeasts, whole bunches and ageing in large oak containers. Cortezada is their aromatic, dark and spicy Mencía field blend, grown at 750 metres. Bastarda is their very typical varietal Merenzao (also known as Bastardo). They have a white wine: Conasbrancas, a field blend macerated on skins for 28 days, followed by 12 months on lees without batonnage, to deliver a waxy, spicy wine.

Guímaro
Sanmil 43, Santa Cruz de Brosmos, 27425 Sober
Tel.: +34 982 152 508
adegasguimaro@gmail.com

Guímaro, meaning 'rebel', was the nickname of owner Pedro Rodríguez's grandfather. However, through hard work in Guímaro, Rodríguez will soon be turning his family winery into a modern classic, rather than a rebellious outsider. The family has long grown vines in Amandi and Pedro's parents still work in the vineyards and maintain a typical market garden with animals and vegetables. The commercial winery was set up in 1991 – before that the wine was drunk at home and sold locally. The person who made the difference was Raúl Pérez. He initiated Rodríguez in the importance of the old vines and single vineyards and taught him how to to reduce yields and manage the vines. In the winery they went back to the traditional techniques which have now become so fashionable: wild yeasts, foot treading, using stems in the fermentation and ageing in used barrels to avoid oak influence. Rodríguez is now managing the vineyards organically and continuing to develop the traditional local varieties. The family currently owns 9 hectares and manages another 14.

Guímaro is Pedro's straightforward Godello, planted on slate and granite, while Cepas Viejas is a Godello from his oldest vines, a tense, structured white. Tinto is a very likeable, unoaked, juicy cherry red. Finca Meixemán comes from 70-year-old Mencía which has a month long maceration on skins and stems, for a classically aromatic wine with bramble fruits. Finca Capeliños comes from a small plot of vines that are almost 100 years old. Finally Finca Pombeiras comes from 70-year-old Mencía at 450 metres. Rodríguez also makes Ladredo with Dirk Niepoort.

Last but not least it's important to mention El Pecado, which Raúl Pérez makes from Finca Capeliños and its centenarian vines. It is laden with damsons and dark stone fruits, and has exceptionally fine tannins.

Ponte da Boga

Lugar do Couto-Sampaio, 32764 Castro Caldelas
Tel.: +34 988 203 306
www.pontedaboga.com

The winery was built in 1898, and wine was produced until the 1960s, when it closed. In 1999 local growers decided to relaunch the enterprise, receiving the necessary financial step up in 2005, when it was taken on by the drinks group Hijos de Rivera, whose original product was – and remains – Estrella Galicia beer. Ponte da Boga owns 20 hectares of vineyards, as well as purchasing grapes from different soils and climates. Winemaker Dominique Roujou de Boubée and his wife Laura Montero consult here, working with rather than against the steep landscape, avoiding the carving up of the hillsides with wide terraces.

The wines reflect the local varieties, and make a very clearly structured range. There is a bright, crunchy Mencía, Expresión Histórica (a Mencía blend), Capricho de Merenzao (another lovely, elegant Merenzao from Ribeira Sacra), Bancales Olvidados (a Mencía from 'forgotten' sites, from growers), Porto de Lobos (100 per cent Brancellao), as well as a Godello and an Albariño.

Epicure Wines (www.epicure-wines.com) make Licis, a single vineyard Mencía here.

Rectoral de Amandi

Amandi, 27423 Sober
Tel.: +34 988 384 200
www.rectoraldeamandi.com

The winery gets its name from the seventeenth-century church that used to be here. Rectoral de Amandi has its own part in Ribeira Sacra's history as a DO, as it was founded in 1990 and was a pioneer in the making of the DO. It's the largest producer today, focusing on Mencía.

Regina Viarum

Doade s/n, 27424 Sober
Tel.: +34 986 288 212
www.reginaviarum.es

This modern winery, on an impressive site over the valley, was established in 2002 and is now a member of the HGA bodegas group, which owns properties across north-west Spain. It produces fresh, crisp Mencías. If there must be one criticism it is of their bottle shape and packaging, which were not destined for international appeal. (The Regina Expresión is a lively red, but the bottle, reminiscent of those used for olive oil, does not sell the wine.) However the link with HGA is undoubtedly improving communication and marketing.

On the radar

One to watch is **D. Ventura**, from Ramón Losada. Gerardo Méndez of Do Ferreira in Rías Baixas has been advising here.

OCTOPUS AHOY

You haven't visited Galicia if you haven't eaten *pulpo* (octopus). In fact if you make a habit of visiting wineries then it's probably the first thing you will eat. The best octopus I've eaten wasn't on the coast at all, but inland in Ribeiro and Valdeorras. The experts come from O'Carballiño, a town in the Ribeiro DO. When cooking for an event they will come in a van and set up their stoves and vast pots. (Smart city people would call this a pop-up.) The octopus is cooked in the pan, using a technique that ensures that it's tender and not in the least rubbery. It is then cut up into small pieces with scissors and served on wooden plates, seasoned with paprika, salt and good olive oil, to be eaten by skewering the pieces with cocktail sticks. Despite the delicate way of eating, piece by piece, sixteen of us managed to get through 25 kilogrammes of octopus at a lunch in Ribeiro by the River Sil. This was only the start: after the octopus came the fish, then the meat and potato stew, and the pudding to follow.

RIBEIRO

Ribeiro, in the western part of Ourense province, was the first DO created in Galicia, in 1976. This early beginning is not in the least surprising given Ribeiro's long history in wine and wine export. After the Romans the religious orders fostered the development of wines around the end of the first millennium and in medieval times Ribeiro became a noted exporter of wines, which were well received by the English. The distinctive wine of the time was Tostado, made from grapes hung up to raisin before fermenting. Politics and war turned the English against Spain, so they substituted Port for Ribeiro. Ribeiro went into a slow decline, not helped by oidium, phylloxera and civil war. In the twentieth century it became a machine for home production and bulk sales.

Ribeiro, named after the river bank of the River Avia, is a land of *colleiteiros* (small harvesters/growers). The presence of almost 6,000 of them in the DO complicates decision-making and innovation. Only very recently has Ribeiro started to come out of its shell and show us some exciting wines. To a market that has come to see Albariño as the only variety of Galicia, Ribeiro's textured and complex whites are something original.

It's important to mention here Arsenio Paz, from the gloriously situated Finca Vilerma (www.vilerma.com), with its views over the vineyards down to the Avia. Paz purchased A Vilerma in 1977 and in due course developed an exceptional home, garden and winery in the old Pazo. He intended to make 'a little good Ribeiro wine for friends' but was bemused by the Palomino and Garnacha Tintorera that confronted him, as well as the generally poor quality of the resulting wine. He set out to research the traditional varieties, with the Experimental Cellar of Ribeiro carrying out trials, and in 1987, a decade after his arrival, he launched his own wines: a red blend of Sousón, Brancellao, Caíño, Ferrón and Tempranillo, and a white blend of Treixadura and all the local varieties. Paz was not alone. The other pioneer was Ricardo Carreiro. His son Ricardo runs the influential Coto de Gomariz (below).

Richard Ford has a helpful tip, or 'Mem.' as he calls it, if you are in the area: 'The province of Orense is the most fertile of this corner of Spain, especially near the banks of the Sil, Avia, and Miño. Linen is the chief manufacture. The hams made at Caldelas [between Orense and A Rúa] are excellent. Mem.: always have one in the commissariat, and a bota full of Tostado wine.'

Ribeira is carved up by three rivers, the Miño, the Arnoia and the Avia, with the charming old city of Ribadavia at its centre. The soils along the river banks are alluvial. Much more interesting are the slopes, many of them steep, which have soils of decomposed granite, known as *sabrego*.

The climate is humid, with moderate temperatures in general and hot summers. The rainfall is between 800 and 1,000 millimetres per year, and there is a definite risk of frost. Ribeiro was strongly affected by the April 2017 frosts, with 30 per cent of vineyards in the Miño and Arnoia river valleys affected, and 77 per cent of those in the Avia valley – overall 50–55 per cent of Ribeiro production. The microclimates are varied here given the influence of the rivers and the variety of slopes and aspects.

Ribeiro at a glance

Grape varieties

White: Treixadura, Torrontés, Palomino, Godello, Macabeo, Loureira, Albariño, Albillo, Macabeo, Lado, Caíño Blanco

Red: Caíño, Alicante, Sousón, Ferrón, Mencía, Tempranillo, Brancellao

Only 10 per cent of Ribeiro production is currently red wine, but the future is promising, and that percentage should grow.

Size

Vineyard: 2,646 hectares
Growers: 5,812
Wineries: 107

Tostado: a tradition revived

Tostado is a naturally sweet wine achieved by unforced drying of clusters of grapes in roofed and well-ventilated places for a maximum of three months. The maximum yield is 40 litres of wine from 100 kilogrammes of raisined grapes. The must yielded from the grapes should contain a minimum of 300 grammes of sugar per litre. The finished wine will be between 13 and 15% abv, with residual sugar between 100 and 150 grams per litre. It spends a minimum of 180 days in oak or cherry-wood barrels, and 90 days in bottle. It may be made from: (white) Albariño, Godello, Loureira, Torrontés and Treixadura; (red) Brancellao, Caíño Bravo, Caíño Longo, Caíño Tinto, Ferrón, Mencía and Sousón.

Producers

Campante/Bodegas GRM

Finca Reboreda s/n, 32941 Puga
Tel.: +34 988 261 212
www.bodegasgrm.com

Otherwise known as Grupo Reboreda Morgadío, this unites the Morgadío winery in Rías Baixas with the Reboreda bodega in Ribeiro. In Ribeiro they produce mainly whites including the A Telleira Godello. The real treat here is their Alma de Reboreda Tostado Naturalmente Dulce. The Tostado style may be traditional, but it is not always loveable. Alma, though, is worth seeking out. It is made from Treixadura which is picked and hung up to raisin very slowly for about three months. After pressing, the must is fermented in French Allier oak; given the sugar levels it takes at least ten months. The wine has vital statistics of 14% abv with 175 g/l of residual sugar. This is balanced by 6.5 g/l of acidity. Altogether it is bursting with dried fruits, honey and spice, with a clean, silky finish.

Casal de Armán

O Cotiño, 32400 San Andrés de Camporredondo
Tel.: +34 699 060 464
www.bodegascasadelarman.com

This is an impressive project with a winery, a seven-room hotel and a restaurant, in a property that dates back to 1727 – providing a fine chance to sleep among the vineyards. The winery was started by the González Vázquez family in the 1990s, and they own 20 hectares of vineyards as well as buying in grapes from different soils and sites in the area. Casal de Armán is their polished, well-made Treixadura blend; there is a red version too which is perhaps less evenly balanced. The two top wines are white, the Treixadura blend Finca Misenhora and the barrel-fermented 100 per cent Treixadura Finca Os Loureiros.

Coto de Gomariz

Barro de Gomariz, 32429 Leiro
Tel.: +34 610 602 672
www.losvinosdemiguel.com

If for nothing else Coto de Gomariz would be famous for its claim to be the first walled vineyard or *clos* in Iberia, dating back to the tenth century.

Along with San Clodio and Vilerma it shares the site of what were once the San Clodio monastery lands. Their wines are also amongst the best in the DO. Gomariz has 28 hectares, with lovely stone terraces; the oldest vines were planted in 1979. The whole project was at one time farmed organically; now it's just the top wines. The range of parcels enables them to blend and add real complexity to the wines drawing on schist as well as clay and granitic soils. The Coto de Gomariz white is a blend of Treixadura with Godello, Loureira and Albariño. It may be the winery's 'standard' wine but it has a long, refreshing finish, with notes of jasmine and dried peaches. Gomariz X is a single vineyard wine grown on schist – the X being from the Galician *xisto* – and fermented in stainless steel. Owner Ricardo Carreiro works with winemaker Xosé Lois Sebio (see p. 79), and together they are continuing to develop an exciting range of young and oak-aged whites and reds. The Flower and the Bee is the label for a popular pair of wines produced from young vines in the Avia valley. There's a Treixadura and a Sousón, approachable and fresh.

Eduardo Peña

Lugar de Barral s/n, 32430 Castrelo de Miño
Tel.: +34 629 872 130
www.bodegaeduardopenha.es

A relatively young business with a winery that is beautifully sited amid 7 hectares of vineyards overlooking the river. The vineyards were planted in 2005 and the winery built in 2008, and today two wines are made. The top wine is the eponymous Eduardo Peña, fermented in 300-litre oak barrels, a blend of Treixadura, Albariño, Godello, Lado and Loureiro, giving a creamy, spice and pink grapefruit character. The second wine, María Andrea, is a blend of Treixadura, Loureira and Albariño.

Emilio Rojo

Rei de Viana 5, 32420 Leiro
Tel.: +34 988 488 050

If you only try one wine from Ribeiro, then it has to be this. There *is* only one wine here, of course, because that's all that Emilio Rojo makes. I first discovered it at a blind tasting of 100 Galician non-Albariño whites, and it stood out head and shoulders above the rest. Perhaps that doesn't sound like stiff competition, but it certainly was. This is one of Spain's great white wines, made by a former Siemens engineer who returned to his homeland to work in wine, transforming his family vineyards. From his low-yielding 1.2 hectare terraced vineyard of sandy decomposed granite he produces just 5,000 bottles. The wine is two-thirds Treixadura, with Loureira, Albariño, Lado, Torrontés and Godello. Rojo is his own man; not a person to be drawn into the world of marketing and sales. There is no need, since his wine speaks for itself: pure, vivid, with a passion fruit acidity, wonderfully complex, thrilling.

Finca Viñoa/Pazo de Casanova

Finca Viñoa, Banga, 32821 O Carballiño
Tel.: +34 988 488 741
www.fincavinoa.com

Another young brand, this is making impressive progress. Finca Viñoa was founded in 2003 and in 2010 became part of Grandes Pagos Gallegos de Viticultura Tradicional, which owns Quinta de Couselo in Rías Baixas. Latterly (2015) nearby Pazo de Casanova joined the group. As a matter of wine trivia, one of the joint owners of Grandes Pagos Gallegos is Carlos Mouriño, entrepreneur and President of Celta football club in Vigo.

Viñoa is in a lovely position, tucked away in the Avia valley, with its 10 hectares spread across 23 *socalcos*, or terraces, on granite and schist at 150–325 metres altitude. The vines were planted in 2003 and the first wines launched in 2010, following further investment and enlargement of the estate. The estate wine is Finca Viñoa, a Treixadura–Albariño–Godello–Loureiro blend which spends eight months on lees. It's a very polished wine, with fine aromatics and a refreshing finish.

Pazo de Casanova also has 10 hectares of vineyards overall, planted with native varieties. Its estate wine is mainly Treixadura, with a little Godello, Albariño and Loureiro. Finca Viñoa and Pazo de Casanova are really promising wines, also nicely packaged. With the backing of the Grandes Pagos Gallegos group and winemaker José Manuel Martínez these have strong potential to build Ribeiro's international profile.

Luis Anxo Rodríguez Vázquez/Viña de Martín

Laixa 7, 32417 Arnoia

Luis Rodríguez owns 5 hectares of vineyards spread over 100 tiny plots around Arnoia, with its precipitous slopes of decomposed granite. From these few hectares this quiet man has developed wines that have become something of a cult. He has been converting the vineyards gradually from the existing Palomino and Garnacha Tintorera, which were so commonly used after phylloxera, to Treixadura and Lado, as well as Ferrol. His winery, and his wines, are named after his uncle. He works with both white varieties and red (some 40 per cent of his production). Os Pasas he makes in both a white and a red version. The white is light and fresh; but a year on lees has developed fine complexity. Escolma, his special selection white, only made in the best years, is Treixadura fermented in French oak and aged for 12 months, plus a further 36 months in bottle. These are wines that blossom with some bottle age. A Torna Dos Pasos Escolma is the top red, made from a selection of the best varieties in the best plots in the best year – again with a year in barrel and three in bottle. This medium-bodied wine is cherry-fruited, fresh, savoury and long, with finely balanced acid and tannin.

Manuel Formigo
Cabo de Vila 49, 32431 Beade
Tel.: +34 627 569 889
www.fincateira.com

Formigo is the Spanish word for ant, and Manuel Formigo has been sure to make good use of the image in his packaging. Formigo's family have been winegrowers in Beade for generations. The family owns some 5 hectares of vineyard in different parcels the area. Formigo launched the winery in 2006 under the 200-year-old family home, bringing at the same time a fresh and appealing style to their wines. The vineyard is nearly all white, and includes a little of the almost defunct Alvilla variety, as well as some Palomino, the variety which dominated the region after phylloxera. Formigo is recuperating red varieties as well as white. A winemaker to watch, he is loyal to his locality and to the purity of its wines. He produces Finca Teira Blanco and Tinto, while Teira X is an electric blend of 60 per cent Treixadura, with 15 per cent of Alvilla, 15 per cent Albariño and 10 per cent Loureira. There is also Formigo Blanco, a young, lively white blend.

Ramón do Casar
Paraxe de San Sebastián s/n, 32430 Castrelo do Miño
Tel.: +34 638 433 611
www.ramondocasar.es

Take a boat trip on the Miño and you will see this very modern winery from the water. It's a new project but well embedded in the history of the region. Ramón do Casar was one of the many Galicians who left Spain, many to earn money to send back to their impoverished families, others to escape the Civil War. Do Casar went to Venezuela. On his return he purchased some 7 hectares of vineyards on the slopes above the river. His children now make the wines, using these grapes and also some purchased fruit. The labels of the wines are a particularly touching memorial to those early years, using black and white photographs from the 1950s. The winery currently produces Ramón do Casar, a blend of white varieties, lush and aromatic; Treixadura, a limpid refreshing wine; and Nobre, a lightly oaked Treixadura.

San Clodio

Cubilledo, Gomariz, 32429 Leiro
Tel.: +34 686 961 681
www.vinosanclodio.com

San Clodio is the project of the film-maker José Luis Cuerda. Wine has been grown here since the monks cultivated vines seriously in the Middle Ages; Cuerda's first harvest was in 2005. Over the years Cuerda has been reviving the vineyards, rebuilding the *socalcos* or terraces, with a specific commitment: '*Nunca voy a comprar uva ajena*' ('Never will I buy someone else's grapes'). His San Clodio is a blend of the typical white varieties from the DO.

It's important to separate the winery San Clodio from the former monastery of the same name which is next door. The former Cistercian monastery dates back to the twelfth century, and San Clodio is a historic name in Ribeiro as it is across Spain. Its picturesque cloisters are a popular site for public events such as the Ribeiro tastings I've attended; it's also where I received an award from the DO. Most famously, in the later twentieth century it belonged to Manuel Fraga Iribarne, a pro-Franco politician whose career covered both the dictatorship and the transition to democracy (he was president of the Galician government 1990–2005). Today it's a hotel, with large, comfortable bedrooms.

Viña Mein

Lugar de Mein, San Clodio, 32420 Leiro
Tel.: +34 988 488 400
www.vinamein.com

Viña Mein is a lovely property, a charming house comfortably settled amid its vines, grown on 18 hectares of 'pure granite'. As they point out, this means they are in a frost pocket, and hence they have created a lake to take the edge off the frost. Viña Mein is a significant name in the modern history of Ribeiro, given that it demonstrated the potential of the region's wines with its local varieties. The Galician lawyer, Javier Alén, and a group of friends and family, started work on the project in 1988. The first vines were planted then, and the first wines were released in 1994. Viña Mein, mainly Treixadura and unoaked, rapidly became a classic, representing the potential of the revived Ribeiro.

Since 2015 Comando G, which made its name with Garnacha in the Gredos area, has been consulting here. As different approaches are introduced – using foudres instead of barrels for fermentation, defining single vineyards, developing the red wine portfolio, working with whole bunches – Viña Mein should once more be making headlines in Ribeiro.

Xosé Lois Sebio

www.xlsebio.es

Sebio is the winemaker at Coto de Gomariz. An irrepressible figure, he is involved in many projects. He works across north-west Spain, including with growers in Rías Baixas, Valdeorras and Bierzo. Some of the projects are farmed organically or following the theories of the late Masanobu Fukuoka, the Japanese farmer interested in no-intervention, natural farming. He is interested in low-sulphur wines, minimum intervention, leaving the wine on skins. His 'Vinos de Encostas' range is in his words 'authentic', determinedly expressing terroir. Salvaxe ('wild') is a field blend of old vine white varieties, with minimum intervention, partly fermented in and aged in 500-litre oak, fleshy and textured. Hush, made only in the best years, is a red field blend, fermented and aged in 500-litre barrels. Super Héroe is a delightfully named red blend: 'mulberry on steroids' was my tasting note. It was so named because as a superhero it is fighting against 'cloned wines ... and also represents the fight of good against bad, the individual against the globalized. The personal against the impersonal, the distinctive against the common and the vulgar.'

On the radar

Terra do Castelo (www.terradocastelo.com) was founded in 2004 by 104 families farming 100 hectares. **Pazo Tizón's** (www.pazotizon.com)

first wines were launched in 2005. Oscar Aragón from Ribera del Duero's Cillar de Silos is consulting here.

VALDEORRAS

Valdeorras was founded as a DO just one year after Ribeiro, in 1977, and is next door to Ribeira Sacra, just across the River Sil. Indeed, critical growers can look down or across from one side or the other and criticize the 'opposition'. It is the most easterly of the Galician DOs, in the valley formed by the rivers Sil and Jares. Despite their influence, the climate is less humid than in most of Galicia and the region has distinctly hot, dry summers. Rainfall is between 700 and 1,000 millimetres annually. The risk of frost is severe, as growers found in the destructive April frost of 2017. The best vineyards here are south-facing, and rise up to 500 metres. There are valley-floor vineyards too, but these are generally less impressive. While the historical, post-phylloxera varieties persist – Palomino, Garnacha Tintorera – the distinctive feature is Godello. The very best Godello here makes one of Spain's greatest white wines.

The name, literally 'valley of gold', recalls the gold that was mined here in Roman times. My colleague Pedro Ballesteros MW points out the link between mining and wine. When the climate allowed, wine was a source of nourishment for miners: 'California's top Zinfandel owes its existence to the nineteenth century Gold Rush; Rutherglen's finest wines in Victoria, Australia, are direct descendants of the gold.' In the same way, local wines were welcomed by the Roman miners and armies who famously mined for gold in Las Médulas mines in Bierzo, as well as Valdeorras.

The other mineral resource of Valdeorras is slate: 90 per cent of Europe's slate is produced here. Our home in London was recently re-roofed with Valdeorras slate (when the builder gave me a choice of Valdeorras, Wales or Canada, I naturally chose Valdeorras). Even the humblest shed in Valdeorras is finished off with a smart blue-black slate roof.

Critics have commented on the role of outsiders here, and the apparent lack of local skill. Initially Rafael Palacios, Telmo Rodríguez and Guillermo Prada Gayoso all brought investment and expertise from Rioja, while the consultants Ana Martín and Pepe Hidalgo have made Guitián great, but are not locals. In one way or another, all the wineries I have listed below are owned by non-Galician businesses, or are benefiting from non-Galician expertise. This will surely change.

Valdeorras at a glance

Grape varieties

White: Godello, Doña Blanca, Palomino, Loureira, Treixadura, Doña Branca, Albarín, Torrontés, Lado, Palomino

Red: Mencía, Merenzao, Grao Negreo, Garnacha, Tempranillo (also known as Araúxa), Brancellao, Sousón, Caíño Tinto, Espadeiro, Ferrón, Gran Negro, Garnacha Tintorera (Alicante Bouschet), Mouratón

Size

Vineyard: 1,171 hectares
Growers: 1,460
Wineries: 44

Producers

A Tapada/Guitián

A Tapada s/n, 32310 Rubiá de Valdeorras
Tel.: +34 988 324 197
www.guitianvinos.com

The winery is formally called A Tapada, but it was founded by the Guitián family in 1985, and it is the family name, used as the brand, that has stuck. Their 10 hectares of vineyard dedicated to Godello sit on slate at one of the highest parts of Valdeorras, at 500 metres. They used a very old, pre-phylloxera clone for planting, back in 1985. Ramón Guitián launched and initially led the project but he was killed in a car accident in 1996, and so today it is run by Mari Carmen and Senén Guitián. Significant in the partnership have been consultants Pepe Hidalgo and Ana Martín.

Hidalgo designed the winery with Ramon Guitián, specifically only for estate wines. Given the altitude, the grapes here ripen more slowly and as a result gain greater aromatic appeal. The majority of the wines are fermented in stainless steel, in fact Guitián was a pioneer in ageing wines with lees in stainless steel, something that has subsequently become much more common. Some of the wine is fermented in oak, American and French, and a small amount in acacia. They also make a 50-month aged Godello, to show the ageing capacity of the wines; and a late harvest version. Try them all.

Avancia

Parque Empresarial a Raña, 32300 O Barco de Valdeorras
Tel.: +34 952 504 706
www.jorgeordonezselections.com

Wine merchant Jorge Ordóñez has built an impressive portfolio of wineries across Spain. Avancia was the result of his mission to have a Godello to introduce to the US market. He has 23 hectares of vineyards on slate and quartz. From the dry-farmed bush vines, planted between 1904 and 1970, there are two Godellos, two Mencías and a Mencía *rosado*.

Godeval

Avda de Galicia 20, 32300 O Barco de Valdeorras
Tel.: +34 988 108 282
www.godeval.com

Godeval is notable in the history of the DO for being the first winery to make a single varietal wine based on Godello. That was in 1986, when they had just 2 hectares of vineyard. In 1988 the winery was launched inside the refurbished monastery of Xagoaza. Today there are 21 hectares producing 150,000 bottles across three wines: a monovarietal Godello; Cepas Vellas ('old vines'), which spends five months on lees; and Revival, named after the research project to revive Godello.

Rafael Palacios

Somoza 22, 32350 A Rúa
Tel.: +34 988 310 162
www.rafaelpalacios.com

All credit is due to Rafael Palacios for a single-minded focus on a single variety in a single DO. And with what results – the wines just go on getting better! Palacios' family wine business in Rioja, Palacios Remondo, was predominantly in red wines. He created a new style of white Rioja, Plácet, at the winery before moving to Valdeorras in 2004. Little by little, he purchased tiny parcels of neglected vineyards, slowly putting them together to make his wines, always with a very clear vision. The parcels are in the most westerly part of the DO, at between 580 and 720 metres. Palacios currently has 32 plots totalling 19.5 hectares. Most are farmed with organic-based treatments and the oldest vineyards are farmed biodynamically. The creation of the ladder of quality has been sure and steady, with wines increasing in loveliness, produced in ever smaller quantities, the higher you go.

Louro is Godello with a dash of Treixadura, grown at 600–720 metres on sandy decomposed granite terraces. Fermented in French oak casks of between 300 and 500 litres, it then spends four months on lees in the casks. As Sortes is named after the drawing of lots or *sortes*, by which inheritances were settled. The vines range in age from 9 to some 90 years old and are a mix of bush and espalier. To avoid evaporation, the soil is covered with straw in the summer – another laborious piece of work. As Sortes is fermented in 500-litre French oak, and spends seven months on lees in cask. Both these wines have 20 per cent new oak each year.

Sorte O Soro, by contrast, is fermented in 500-litre new French oak and spends eight months on lees. The fact is that this is an exceptional selection from exceptional grapes. I had no trouble recently voting it my best white wine in Spain, for *Decanter*. Palacios' latest project is Antiga Godello Tradicional – as the name suggests, a wine that commemorates the old ways, from ungrafted bush vines of Godello planted in 1920, north facing at 680 metres. The wine is fermented in the traditional way, on skins and in open vats. It is then aged for ten months in used barrels, resulting in a wine that is concentrated and mineral with a lively acidity and a long finish.

Compañía de Vinos Telmo Rodríguez

El Monte, 01308 Lanciego
Tel.: +34 945 628 315
www.telmorodriguez.com

Telmo Rodríguez is best known today for his work developing single vineyard Garnachas in Rioja. However he long had his eye on Valdeorras, from whence his latest wines are full of interest. His 'entry level' wines are Gaba do Xil, red and white, made both with estate grapes and from contracted suppliers. Both the Mencía and the Godello are unoaked, and speak vividly of their variety. The new range of wines from the Santa Cruz zone has delightful period labels. Branco de Santa Cruz comes from an organically farmed vineyard and is a blend of Godello with a field blend of Loureiro, Doña Branca and Palomino, aged for 12 months in neutral vats. As Caborcas, its pair, from vineyards on the slopes of the River Bibei, is a blend of Mencía with Merenzao, Sousón, Garnacha and Brancellao. The wine is fermented in stainless steel and in wooden vats, and then aged for 12 months in large oak casks.

Valdesil

Ctra a San Vicente OU-807 Km 3, 32348 Vilamartín de Valdeorras
Tel.: +34 988 337 900
www.valdesil.com

Valdesil is a must-visit winery, to see what are some of the oldest Godello vines in the DO, planted in 1885, just after phylloxera. The remarkable, sprawling, gnarled trunks are propped up by stones and poles. The winery is using these very old vines to provide the plant material for their new vineyards. The revival of Valdesil began in 1990, when Francisco Prado Gayoso, one-time chairman of the Olarra winery in Rioja, began to recover the plots, or *pezas*, which had been distributed across the family over time or been sold off. The business, managed by his three sons, now has 20 hectares.

Valdesil is of course taken from the name of the River Sil. The vineyards are mainly slate with some granite. The entry-level wine is the lively Montenovo Godello; Valdesil Godello Sobre Lías is the step up. Pezas da Portela is barrel-fermented Godello, and exceptionally well-balanced, while Pedrouzos is from the very oldest vines, and O Chao is a single vineyard wine from granite. There are also reds in the portfolio – the youthful Valderroa Mencía, the barrel-aged Carballo, and Valteiro, which presents a rare opportunity to sample the variety María Ardoña. (*Wine Grapes* says that as María Ordoña it is otherwise known in the region as Merenzao or Bastardo.) It is well worth the detour to visit this property.

On the radar

Alberto Orte of **Compañía de Vinos del Atlántico** (www.vinosatlanticos. com) has created Escalada do Sil, a Merenzao, Mencía, Garnacha Tintorera blend.

ON THE RADAR: GALICIA'S IGPS

- **Barbanza e Iria** is an IGP in the region of Ribera de la Ría de Arosa. White wines come from Albariño, Caíño Blanco, Godello, Loureiro Blanco, Treixadura and Torrontés. Reds are made with Brancellao, Caíño Tinto, Espadeiro, Loureiro Tinto, Mencía and Sousón.

- **Betanzos** is an IGP in La Coruña. The white varieties are Blanco Legítimo, Agudelo (Godello) and Jerez; the reds are Garnacha, Mencía and Tempranillo.

- **Valle del Miño-Ourense** lies, as the name suggests, along the River Miño. The whites are made from Albariño, Godello, Loureira, Palomino, Torrontés and Treixadura. The reds are Brancellao, Caíño, Garnacha, Mencía, Mouratón and Sousón.

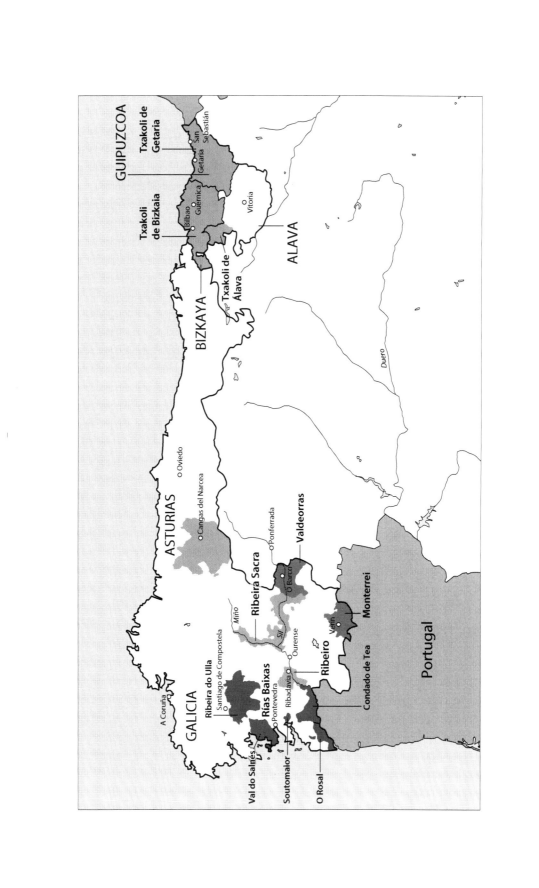

4

ASTURIAS AND THE CANTABRIAN COAST: HEROIC VITICULTURE AND GASTRONOMIC DELIGHTS

Referred to by Richard Ford as 'the Wales of the peninsula', Asturias is tucked in between Galicia and the Basque Country. It seems there was little mutual friendship. In one of his many delightfully sweeping observations, Ford comments: 'The Asturians hate their neighbours, and the Gallicians especially'.

Wine in Asturias dates back to the ninth century, when the Benedictine monks fostered wine culture on the banks of the River Narcea. But in time the style of these wines fell out of favour. In many other parts of Spain it was oidium and phylloxera that killed the wine industry but in Asturias taste played its part. The hard-working miners and fishermen of the chilly coast preferred warm, ripe wines from the south. But the region's isolation, both physical and stylisitic, has its benefits for today's wine lovers. What is so exciting about this almost forgotten region is that it lays claim to some extremely rare grape varieties.

CANGAS

Cangas is surely the most impressive wine region in Spain. Not the prettiest, but certainly dramatic. It is also remarkable for its lovely isolation. In this most southerly part of Asturias, bordering León and Galicia, the vineyards are sheltered from the north winds and there is good sun exposure. It can feel like stepping back into the Middle Ages, to a place where life was slower and access to wi-fi did not rule our lives. Cangas' isolation has come at real cost to its people, but has meant that the region has its own grape varieties. This is one area that has not been overrun by Tempranillo – or Cabernet Sauvignon, or Merlot. Wine lovers should come here to walk in the countryside, and to enjoy old, unique varieties. Gradually the wines are being exported, but the process is slow, and with only six wineries in the DO there are not the resources to export widely.

Initially vines flourished in Cangas. By 1858 there were 5,493 hectares. But just 20 years later, after oidium and phylloxera took hold, there were just 1,903. Winemaking very slowly recovered. Yet it faltered in the face of the Franco government's push for Asturian coal – and of the miners' demand for bigger, bolder beverages. The vineyards were further weakened by the famously destructive hailstorms of 19 June 1959, which stripped the vines. In due course, coal mines proved no more reliable in terms of employment and in the end closed in the face of cheaper, cleaner energy. In the 1990s a movement was started to preserve the vineyard heritage. In 2009, Cangas became a Vino de Calidad and subsequently a DO.

Cangas rightly classifies itself as high mountain viticulture and heroic viticulture (alongside Priorat and Ribeira Sacra), with vines above 500 metres, on steep slopes and terraces, and held in small plots. The vines here experience lower rainfall (although still more than 1,000 millimetres a year) and more sunshine than the rest of the province. The soils are slate and sand, which give the necessary drainage.

Cangas at a glance

Grape varieties

White: Albarín Blanco, Albillo, Moscatel de Grano Menudo
Red: Albarín Negro, Carrasquín, Verdejo Negro, Mencía

Size

Vineyard: 70 hectares
Wineries: 6

For newcomers to the region the fascination is tasting the varieties in as pure as possible a state, without the layers of polish that barrel ageing gives. Understandably producers want to add that glamour; in due course, there may be less new oak, or larger casks used. In the meantime there are wineries in Cangas that are inside the DO and wineries that are not. To build a united profile for the world, it is to be hoped they can forget their differences.

Producers

Dominio de Urogallo

Las Barzaniellas, 33817 Cangas del Narcea
Tel.: +34 985 810 384
www.dominiodelurogallo.com

Nicolás Marcos Vicente is getting a lot of attention for his biodynamically farmed wines, and his no- and low-sulphur, wild yeast ferment, whole bunch, foot-trodden approach. He comes from a winemaking family in Toro and is well known, as his brother was a leading bullfighter. He studied under Alain Graillot in Crozes-Hermitage and has found in Cangas a freshness that eluded him further south. He farms 14 hectares, making reds and whites from the local varieties, and is not a member of the DO. Francisco Asensio of the new project in Sanlúcar de Barrameda, Bodegas Alonso, is his co-owner.

Monasterio de Corias

Monasterio de Corias s/n, 33800 Cangas del Narcea
Tel.: +34 670 659 579
www.monasteriodecorias.es

The Benedictine monastery of St John the Baptist of Corias dates back to the eleventh century. The monks are gone, but it is still possible to enjoy its magnificence, and sleep in more comfort, as it has been turned into a Parador. The vineyard work once so familiar to the monks has been resumed. The Monasterio winery, owned by Juan Redondo, Chairman of the Cangas del Narcea DO, has been recuperating the local varieties: Albarín Tinto and Blanco, Verdejo Tinto and Carrasquín. The most interesting wines in the range are Corias Guilfa, a blend of Carrasquín and Verdejo Negro which is matured in French oak. There is also a selection of single varieties: Albarín Tinto, Carrasquín and Verdejo Negro.

VidAs

El Carrascal 7, 33800 Cangas del Narcea
Tel.: +34 626 754 225
www.bodegavidas.com

A small family project run by Beatriz Pérez and Pepe Flores, VidAs (Vides y Vinos de Asturias) makes wines from Carrasquín, Verdejo Negro, Albarín Negro and Mencía, and Albarín Blanco for white wine. They have two lines. Siete Vidas are their young wines, none of them aged longer than three years. Cien Montañas (100 mountains) is their monovarietal range, expressing all the character of the mountain vineyards, in the best years. This is an opportunity to taste single varietal Carrasquín with its purity and dark fruit.

On the radar

Also on the radar in Cangas del Narcea are **Chacón Buelta** (Tel.: +34 985 818 498) and (not in the DO) **Obanca** (Tel.: +34 985 811 539).

ON THE RADAR: IGPS IN CANTABRIA

• **Costa de Cantabria** is a small IGP. It runs inland from the coast up to an altitude of 600 metres. There are a number of white varieties – Godello, Albillo, Chardonnay, Malvasía, Hondarribi Zuri, Picapoll Blanco and Verdejo Blanco. The reds are Hondarribi Beltza and Verdejo Negro.

Producers

Casona Micaela

Los Henales s/n, 39880 Valle de Villaverde
Tel.: +34 634 934 429
www.casonamicaela.com

This new (2004) project is building a profile in Costa de Cantabria. The 7-hectare vineyards, at 400 metres on calcareous soils, have been planted with Albariño and Riesling. The first wines were produced in 2008. The winery architecture is glossy and stylish.

Palacio de Nevares

Arriondas-Ribadesella, Asturias

This new project has 4.5 hectares of vineyards, planted in 2016. The Palacio de Nevares is a joint hotel-spa-winery initiative. The owners have various luxury hotels in the region including Pueblo Astur (www.puebloastur.com). There have been no vineyards here before but soil and climate studies indicate that the Asturian variety Albarín will flourish. There are apple orchards on the estate, so cider is also planned. The buildings are still to be restored, before the winemaking can be established.

• **Liébana** is the IGP bordering Asturias, León and Palencia. The white varieties are Albillo, Albarín Blanco, Chardonnay, Godello, Palomino and Verdejo. The reds are Albarín Negro, Cabernet Sauvignon, Garnacha, Graciano, Mencía, Merlot, Pinot Noir and Syrah.

TXAKOLI AND THE BASQUE COUNTRY

The history of the Basque people is remarkable. Their courageous sailors went out whaling in open boats and it is possible that the Basque people were the first Europeans to reach the United States of America. The language, Euskera, seems unrelated to any other European language, and the people themselves are in general in the Rhesus negative blood group, when the rest of the world is mainly Rhesus positive. There is a rich culinary culture, including a tradition of men's dining clubs. The Basque people suffered greatly during the Civil War, which included the terrible bombing of the city of Guernika, and retain a strong political and cultural identity. And then there's the remarkable success of Athletic Club Bilbao, created with the help of the football-playing English miners who worked there, hence its English name. The club is rare in its commitment to its locality, with only Basque players permitted. Make time for a match if you can; the newly rebuilt stadium with its multiple bars and restaurants is worth a visit. East of Bilbao, on the coast, San Sebastián is the top Spanish destination for fans of fine dining with Michelin-starred restaurants and street upon street of tapas bars of which the region is rightfully proud.

Within a matter of kilometres of each other there are three denominations making wines so distinctive that you can spot them in a blind tasting. These have nothing to do with the rest of Spain; in fact they have more to do with the south of France. From west to east the DOs are Txakoli (or Chacoli) de Vizkaya, Txakoli de Álava and, close to the French border and the Pyrenees, Txakoli de Getaria.

Local wines were first controlled in the fourteenth and fifteenth centuries. San Sebastián has had a guild of grapevine pruners since 1509, with 400 members today. The first extant document citing *vino chacolin* was in 1616. By the end of the nineteenth century Txakoli was in decline. Phylloxera and the repealing of protectionist laws, enabling the import of foreign wines, put paid to the local industry until late in the twentieth century.

The term Txakoli comes from *etxakoa* (home-made) or *etxeko ain* (enough for home). The popular image of Txakoli is of a light, greenish white wine poured from a height into tumblers, offering a spritz and a mouth-puckering punch of acid. Yet it's so much more. For a start the three DOs are noticeably different. Furthermore, there are 'traditional method' sparklings and *rosado* Txakolis, with even a few reds, an orange wine and the occasional exceptional sweet wine. The uniting feature is that they are all Atlantic wines – or at least, Cantabrian wines. With their toes in the ocean they offer what so many people are looking for nowadays in their wines: moderate alcohol and freshness.

In terms of winemaking, fruit has usually been harvested around the time of the festival of Our Lady of Pilar (12 October) and is fermented and finished by the winter. Typically the bottles are kept for some further weeks to allow them to settle and develop. Increasingly producers are working the lees, some are using concrete eggs and oak barrels, while others are focusing on parcel selection, and on longer bottle ageing.

Txakoli is in transition. It is building international appeal, driven by a few wineries. However, as one might expect from wines with strong local sales, the packaging does not give a clear message. Some of the bottles are green glass, some brown, most are German Riesling shapes, though the more ambitious and pioneering ones are Burgundy bottles. These are just growing pains, but they are awkward while they last.

TXAKOLI DE GETARIA/GETARIAKO TXAKOLINA

This is the DO clustered around the gastronomic capital of Spain, if not Europe, San Sebastián. By the 1980s there were only 21 hectares of vineyards. However the DO, created in 1989, is today the largest of the three, making the wines with spritzy freshness that have defined Txakoli. It also has the most diverse range of varieties permitted, though the traditional varieties are the most widely found.

The soils in the DO are rich in organic matter. The climate is humid, given the closeness to the Bay of Biscay, with rainfall as high as 1,600 millimetres annually.

Txakoli de Getaria at a glance

Grape varieties

White: Hondarribi Zuri (95 per cent of vineyard), Gros Manseng, Riesling, Chardonnay, Petit Courbu
Red: Hondarribi Beltza

Size

Vineyard: 402 hectares
Growers: 211
Wineries: 45

Producers

Ameztoi

Eitzaga 10, 20808 Getaria
Tel.: +34 943 140 918
www.txakoliameztoi.com

The logo on the Ameztoi bottles celebrates the great Juan Sebastián Elcano, a sailor from Getaria who was the first to circumnavigate the world, though his profile has never been as high as it should be. He sailed with Magellan, and after Magellan's death brought the *Victoria*, the surviving ship from the initial five that set out, back to Sanlúcar de Barrameda in 1522.

Today the fourth and fifth generations are in charge of the winery and its 20 hectares, in a glorious position overlooking the sea. They make a zesty, typically spritzy white from Hondarribi Zuri; a *rosado* – Rubentis – from a 50–50 blend of Hondarribi Zuri and Hondarribi Beltza, again with a light sparkle; and Primus, a white that has had some skin contact before fermentation to build a creamier palate. They also make a red wine and 'traditional method' sparkling white and *rosado*.

K5

Andatza Diseminado Barreiatua 16, 20809 Aia
Tel.: +34 943 240 005
www.txakolina-k5.com

The modern K5 winery sits at 300 metres in the midst of its 15 hectares of vines. Hondarribi Zuri is grown here on soils which are a mix of chalk, limestone and shale. There are two wines in the portfolio, K5 Argiñano and K Pilota. Pilota spends five months on its lees in stainless steel, to deliver fruity aromas, and very brisk acidity, while Argiñano with eleven months on lees has a clean, savoury note.

Txomin Etxaniz

Barrio Eitzaiga 21, 20808 Getaria
Tel.: +34 943 140 702
www.txominetxaniz.com

One of the established names of the DO, this winery has plenty of history: in 1649 the Guipúzcoa archives mention Domingo de Etxaniz as being linked to vine growing. Today the Txueka Etxaniz family owns 35 hectares of vineyards on strikingly sited slopes overlooking the sea. All but 10 per cent is Hondarribi Zuri; the remainder Hondarribi Beltza. They make three categories of wine: Txakoli, of which their regular version is a classic; 'traditional method' sparkling; and late harvest.

On the radar

Adur (www.adurtxakolina.com), founded 2010, produces vivid, fresh Txakoli. **Hiruzta** (www.hiruzta.com) occupies a beautiful hilltop site. **Rezabal** (www.txakolirezabal.com) makes a crisp, fresh Hondarribi Zuri, grown in the sight of the sea.

TXAKOLI DE BIZKAIA/BIZKAIKO TXAKOLINA

Despite the growing urban sprawl Txakoli has held on in Bizkaia. After the decline in the first half of the twentieth century, producers finally came together in the 1980s and in 1994 the DO was created.

The vineyards are mostly on slopes at 50–200 metres above sea level. The soils are shallow, mainly clay-loam over limestone and marls. The climate is mild and humid from the influence of the Bay of Biscay, while yearly rainfall is as high as 1,300 millimetres. To counteract the climate, says José Ramón Calvo of Gorka Izagirre, with vineyards so close to the sea, he needs south-facing, well-ventilated slopes for the vines. He green harvests and leaf plucks to expose the bunches to the sun for ripening.

Txakoli de Bizkaia at a glance

Grape varieties

White: Hondarribi Zuri, Folle Blanche
Red: Hondarribi Beltza

Size

Vineyard: 391 hectares
Growers: 211
Wineries: 45

Producers

Doniene Gorrondona

Gibelorratzagako San Pelaio 1, 48130 Bakio
Tel.: +34 946 194 795
www.donienegorrondona.com

Tucked away above the bay at Bakio, a town with a long history in Txakoli, in a small house that is both home and bodega, is Doniene Gorrondona. The house was built in 1852 and the current owners have the documents to show that Txakoli was produced there then. Wine production resumed in the 1960s, so it is one of the oldest wineries in the DO. The lovely wines are not showy, but rather a very pure expression of the place. The team has pioneered barrel-fermented Txakoli, and sparkling wine (from Hondarribi Zuri and Mune Mahatsa), and this is the only winery within the Bizkaia DO to have its own distillery. There is also a red from Hondarribi Beltza.

It's an enjoyable visit since the team is constantly experimenting – with cryomaceration, with oak, with new techniques. Gorrondona is the 'basic' Txakoli, crunchy and bursting with energy, while Doniene is a step up with lees ageing and creamy complexity. The barrel-fermented Doniene spends four months on lees in new French oak – the result is subtle and polished.

Gorka Izagirre
Barrio Legina s/n, 48195 Larraabetzu
Tel.: +34 946 742 706
www.gorkaizagirre.com

A number of wineries have restaurants attached, but how many of them have a Michelin three star upstairs? What is more, the chef is a member of the family, rather than a name hired to add glamour to the wine brand. The restaurant is Azurmendi and the chef Eneko Atxa; for details see page 309.

The bodega started life as Aretxondo in 1994, and is run by the current technical director José Ramón Calvo. In 2005 Gorka Izagirre launched the joint winery/restaurant project with his nephew. The result is a winery that is as shiny and stainless steel as the chef's kitchen above, although perhaps just a bit more spacious – it has a capacity of 400,000 bottles. They manage 40 hectares of their own or other growers' vineyards. From these they produce a wide range of wines, including their regular Hondarribi Zuri–Hondarribi Zerratia blend, one of the rare Txakolis to be closed with a sensible, non-contaminating screw cap. Particularly interesting is 42 by Eneko Atxa, made in conjunction with the chef, which is fermented and aged in 500-litre vats. The smoky notes of oak, sweet spices and creamy texture all add individuality.

Itsasmendi
Barrio Arane 3, Apdo 241, 48300 Gernika
Tel.: +34 946 270 316
www.bodegasitsasmendi.com

Itsasmendi was launched in 1989 by a group of friends. Today they have 35 hectares of vineyards around the Urdaibai Biosphere Reserve, across a range of soils and aspects. Itsasmendi no 7, a blend of Hondarribi Zuri Zerratia, Hondarribi Zuri and Riesling, is made from selected parcels for ageing on lees, the Txakoli version of an aged Albariño. A fascinating project, revealing how the stone fruit of the young wine is replaced by mineral notes. Artizar is a vineyard selection that is aged for eight months in oak vats. It varies with the vintages, but in good years is outstanding. Latest in the portfolio is Bat Berri, my first experience of an orange wine from Txakoli. It is made from whole bunch Hondarribi Zuri fermented on skins. The wine is lightly opaque, orange with notes of coral pink. The aromas are smoky with red fruits; it remains fresh on the palate and is followed by a grip of tannin. Although not Txakoli as we know it, this has a long, satisfying finish.

TXAKOLI DE ÁLAVA/ARABAKO TXAKOLINA

The earliest records of wine in the valley of Ayala date back to the ninth century. By the thirteenth to fifteenth centuries the vineyards were well established; writers in the eighteenth century were commenting favourably on the wines of the region. From 550 hectares of vineyard in 1877 the production of wine collapsed in the twentieth century: phylloxera arrived in 1919 and was followed by heavy industry, farming and changes in consumer taste. In 1988 Álava was dying, with fewer than 5 hectares left. Today it is back on its feet, with 95 hectares and some exciting projects. This is the smallest DO, but in my latest tasting it produced the highest scoring wines.

The soils are mixed, from clay to stones. The climate shows less influence from the Bay of Biscay, so it is less humid and drier.

Txakoli de Álava at a glance

Grape varieties

White: Hondarribi Zuri; Petit Manseng, Petit Courbu, Gros Manseng

Size

Vineyard: 95 hectares

Growers: 50

Wineries: 8

Producers

Astobiza

Jandiola 16, 01409 Okondo
Tel.: +34 945 898 516
www.astobiza.es

Astobiza spells out its philosophy loud and clear: 'single vineyard, dry farmed, hand harvested, estate bottled, indigenous grapes, low production Atlantic wine'. They are not the only ones who can lay claim to this approach, but they are undoubtedly the most articulate, and it is most apparent in their wines. This may well be because of the clear thinking of their consultant, Ana Martín, herself Basque, who works on a number of projects with her business partner Pepe Hidalgo.

The winery is housed in the eighteenth-century Señorío de Astobiza. The property has 10 hectares at 300 metres, an elevation which protects it from humidity and frost. In the vineyard they have Hondarribi Zuri and Gros Manseng. They emphasize the use of double selection of grapes and cold maceration, and temperature controlled ferments. As a result the regular Astobiza is aromatic and fresh, with a lively stone fruit palate. Malkoa is a selection of the oldest parcels of Hondarribi Zuri, and is made in concrete eggs which develop the texture of the wine by the regular movement of the liquid with the lees. The wine has a very fine, elegant interplay of citrus and wild herbs.

On the radar

Bat Gara (www.txakoliuno.com) is an impressive project, launched by three friends: a farmer, a priest and a restaurateur. Wines are made at the Goianea Cooperative in Amurrio. The regular Uno has a firm, lean style with a very long, punchy finish.

5

CASTILLA Y LEÓN: THE TRANSFORMATION OF OLD CASTILE

Castile is often thought of as the heartland of Spain, not only because of its central and dominating position, but also because its early counts and kings were the first to make an organized stand against the Moors. Furthermore the people and landscapes of this region have been seen by many as representing the 'quintessential Spain'. The hackneyed image of the Spaniards as a proud, melancholy and mystical race, obsessed by death and visions of past grandeur, has its roots in Castile, and is based to a large extent on an interpretation of the extraordinary Castillian landscape, which is quite unlike any other in Europe … it is a land of endless plateaux, scorched by the sun, blown by the wind, framed by distant glimpses of gaunt mountains.

Michael Jacobs

Old Castile, what we now call Castilla y León, is indeed a vast landscape, home to some of the more exciting wines in this book. In addition to the well-known denominations – Bierzo, Cigales, Rueda and Toro (Ribera del Duero has its own chapter) – there are people making fine wines all over the region. Many producers I highlight below are working in vineyards that pre-date the creation of nearby DOs. Producers like the Compañia de Vinos Telmo Rodríguez, for instance, have remarkable pre-phylloxeric

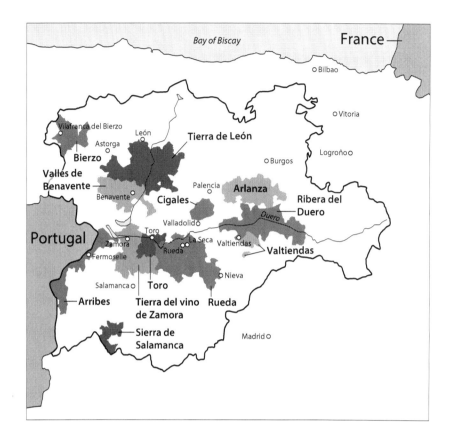

vines. Others, such as Vega Sicilia's neighbour Abadía Retuerta, were left outside the map when the lines were drawn. Still others make wines which for one reason or another do not obey the current DO regulations. The great bonus is that Vino de la Tierra de Castilla y León has restrictions on varieties, yields and ageing, but it is much less narrow than the DOs. This gives producers the freedom to use the varieties they wish, and vinify them and age them as seems best for the wine. Prieto Pariente, for instance, has Viognier, and Abadía Retuerta has certainly taken advantage of the relative freedom to good effect with Syrah and Petit Verdot. Here you will also find Touriga Nacional which has tiptoed across the border from Port country.

BIERZO

There is a strong case for not including Bierzo here at all. It would do better in Galicia, in green Spain, where climatologically and spiritually it belongs. However, in the end, political map-making puts it here.

Bierzo is the showcase for Mencía – other varieties may appear, but Mencía, at its most glorious, stands out. It is popularly referred to as the Pinot Noir of Spain, the most Burgundian of wines. However there is no reason to justify Spanish wines in terms of their red neighbours. Enough to say that it can have a floral fragrance, with a bright and refreshing line of acidity. Delicacy can be its second nature. On the slate soils frequently found in Bierzo it is often exceptional.

It may be hard to believe that red wine in Spain goes beyond Tempranillo, or its synonyms. But in the distant north-west corner Mencía has broken through, and from Bierzo its influence has spread up north through Atlantic Spain. It's surprising to discover that despite its growing reputation Bierzo still exports less than 28 per cent of its production.

The DO was only created in 1989, and the winery members are mainly small family businesses, a number of whom created their own brands after years of making their wines for sale locally or to the local co-ops. It's taken time for growers and winemakers to learn how best to work with the variety. Historically it was rustic, with that underlying charge of acidity which can seem refreshing or simply harsh, depending on the way it is handled.

Wine has a long history in Bierzo. The Romans came here to mine for gold – Las Medulas can still be visited today – and they needed wine. Pilgrims on the Camino de Santiago needed wine, as did the monasteries and churches that succoured them. It may be the pilgrims who brought Mencía, known in Portugal as Jaen, over the border with them. Mining continued through the centuries. Ponferrada is the capital of mining and iron ore.

Bierzo at a glance

Grape varieties

White: Godello, Palomino, Doña Blanca, Malvasía

Red: Mencía, Garnacha Tintorera (Alicante Bouschet)

Size

Vineyard: 2,982 hectares

Growers: 2,400

Wineries: 77

Relish the beauty of the Bierzo countryside – chronicler Ford certainly did, and puts it better than I could: 'El Vierzo [is] the Switzerland of León. This is a district of alpine passes, trout-streams, pleasant meadows, and groves of chestnuts and walnuts … The Vierzo is one of the most interesting nooks in the whole Peninsula, and is all but unknown to the English antiquary, artist, angler and sportsman.'

Bierzo is a natural amphitheatre inside mountains rising to 2,000 metres. The vineyards lie at between 500 and 850 metres. Bierzo falls into two zones: upper and lower, and the best vines are in general on the poor soils of the higher ground. The soils have a mixture of mineral elements including quartzite and slate. (It was the latter that drew Álvaro Palacios and his nephew to Bierzo, after their experience on the slate soils of Priorat.) At the lower level the soils are alluvial. This diversity of altitude and soil means that the start of harvest can vary by as much as five weeks across the DO. The climate varies between the mild character of Galicia, and the heat of the Duero and Castilla y León DOs.

Producers

Casar de Burbia
Travesía de Constitución s/n, 24549 Carracedelo
Tel.: +34 987 562 910
www.casardeburbia.com

This family business, launched in 1998, is based on an investment in old vineyards of Mencía in the late 1980s, in the area of Valtuille de Arriba. The business now owns 27 hectares, divided into 52 plots. In blind tastings the wines have performed well, especially the straightforwardly juicy, young and unoaked Casar de Burbia, and its partner, the unoaked Godello.

There are two top wines. Tebaida 5 draws on the old vineyards, notably one from 1903, with a very high iron content. Tebaida Nemesio is grown on clay, giving a richer, fleshier palate of dark plums, but maintaining an underlying freshness.

Cuatro Pasos
www.cuatropasos.es

The Bierzo winery of successful Rías Baixas cooperative, Martín Códax.

Descendientes de J Palacios
Chao do Pando 1, 24514 Corullón
Tel.: +34 987 540 821
info@alvaropalacios.com

Where should one begin? Perhaps with the latest news, which is the opening for the 2017 harvest of the splendid new winery, up amid the vines. It was designed by Rafael Moneo, and part of his brief is said to have been to build a winery that was big enough to grow. It's certainly that. Already Ricardo notes that wines are benefiting from the underground cellaring, by ageing more slowly.

This new building is a great contrast for Ricardo Pérez, Álvaro Palacios' (see p. 247) nephew, who was used to working in a confined space in the middle of town. Now he has all the space he wants and is close to his biodynamically farmed vines. The project has developed step by step since they arrived in 1999, as he and his uncle have identified vineyards and purchased a variety of plots in different places, or as they put it, 'a constellation of minute plots of old vines on steep, rocky slate soils'. Over the years, the vision has become clear. The village wine, Villa de Corullón, is made up from no less than 200 plots. Its make-up reflects the field blend: 89 per cent Mencía with a mix of red varieties, plus 9 per cent white: Valenciana, Jerez (Palomino) and Godello. The grapes that do not make it into Corullón go into the more commercial brand Pétalos.

Las Lamas is a wine from a vineyard of just 1.73 hectares at 800 metres. Wonderfully floral, silky and very fresh, it has a firm powerful grip on the finish. The single vineyard (1.39 hectares) Moncerbal has an overwhelmingly pretty beginning, elegant with notes of redcurrant, cranberry and very fine tannin. This is followed up by a punch of freshness and a very long finish.

The top wine is La Faraona, from a vineyard of just 0.55 hectares. Pérez manages it all himself, the work, the harvest, the winery. The steep slope of the vineyard lies over a tectonic fault, so there are volcanic minerals in the soil which add to the character and complexity. The aromatics are subtly mineral; in the mouth the wine almost explodes with flavour. Bright freshness lifts the richness, and it finishes with a very long, almost savoury sign-off.

Dominio de Tares

Los Barredos 4, 24318 San Román de Bembibre
Tel.: +34 987 514 550
www.dominiodetares.com

Dominio de Tares was founded in 2000 with a focus on Mencía and Godello, and since then has really impressed. It works with small plots, owning and managing 30 hectares in all, aged between 40 and 90 years. Some are in lower Bierzo, others higher up on the slopes of Bierzo Alto. Out of the blends of that selection, there are some fine expressions of terroir. Baltos is the young, generous, lightly oaked red. Their key brand is the eponymous Dominio de Tares Cepas Viejas, which spends twelve months in oak. Finally the very oldest, ungrafted vines, growing on schist on steep slopes, go to Bembibre. There are two Godellos, the young La Sonrisa de Tares and the barrel aged Dominio de Tares Godello. They also own Dominio dos Tares in León.

Estefanía

La Lechería 3, 24390 Dehesas
Tel.: +34 987 420 015
www.mgwinesgroup.com

Estefanía is owned by the MGWines Group, which now has wineries in Alicante, Bullas, Bierzo and Vinos del Tierra de Castilla. The company also recently established a bodega producing Fondillón, Alicante's historic wine. Estefanía's winemaker is none other than Raúl Pérez, which ensures quality and reputation. The typical style is polished, modern wine. Estefanía is sometimes better known by its brand name Tilenus. There is one white, a Godello; the rest are Mencías, the more mature wines aged in French oak.

Losada Vinos de Finca

Ctra A Villafranca LE-713 Km 12, 24540 Cacabelos
www.losadavinosdefinca.com

Losada sits on one of the pilgrim routes of the Camino de Santiago. Pilgrims who have made it this far can begin to feel they are closer to their destination, with the countryside and climate becoming more green and less extreme. The winery was founded in 2005 and now draws on 8 hectares of vineyard. In contrast to other producers who focus on vines grown on slate, the Losada wines are typically grown on clay, which gives them a less angular character.

In recent blind tastings the wines have been performing well. They are less oaky, less powerful than they were, and express much more of the potential elegance of Mencía in Bierzo. The juicy El Pájaro Rojo is the fruitiest of the range, with a short time in oak. Losada is a successful new style of Bierzo, much more finely balanced, with fruit and a note of oak. Altos de Losada is a flagship wine, with deep, savoury flavours, wrapped in fine oak. At the top end, Losada's winemakers are developing their understanding of its vines. La Bienquerida 1906 ('the loved one') from a centenarian vineyard, has a splendid dark intensity from concentrated fruit. Diablo, meanwhile, is a small production of Alicante Bouschet, often known as Garnacha Tintorera, not often found in a single varietal like this. It reveals the energy and potential of this inky grape. It has been aged in amphorae and barrels for 12 months which has soothed its rough edges and tamed its tannins just a little. Pobladura is altogether more genteel, and another tiny production. Half the Garnacha is aged in amphorae, an innovation which is helping to soften the wines. Losada has turned a corner, and the future developments will be worth watching and tasting.

Luna Beberide

Antigua Ctra Madrid-Coruña Km 402, 24540 Cacabelos
Tel.: +34 987 549 002
www.lunabeberide.es

The Luna family founded their winery in 1987, and have 80 hectares of vineyards including some unexpected varieties – Sylvaner, for instance. Within their plots there are some 50- and 60-year-old vines. However overall they have replanted the vineyards, restoring to dominance the historic local varieties of Mencía and Godello. The young unoaked Godello and Mencía are very approachable, juicy wines, modern and well made. Nevertheless they do still make a Gewürztraminer, a rare find in Bierzo, and an unexpected, but good, white blend of Gewürztraminer, Chardonnay and Sauvignon Blanc.

Paixar is their top wine. This originated as a project of Alejandro Luna, with Eduardo and Alberto García, to create a wine from parcels of old vines grown on slate. It has been highly rated, and reflects perhaps the expertise of the García brothers in making big wines in Ribera del Duero and its surrounding areas. Originally made and sold independently it is now in the Luna Beberide portfolio.

For a surprise, don't miss La Renacuaja – she's a sweet blend of Petit Manseng and Moscatel with 80–100g/l of residual sugar and 12 months in French oak barrels.

Mengoba

Avda del Parque 7, 4544 San Juan de Carracedo
www.mengoba.com

Grégory Pérez is another of the new generation of French producers to settle in Spain. His choice was Bierzo, and the village of Arganza, with its slate soils. It is mountainous round here with his vineyards going up to 600 metres. In this highland fastness he works with different sizes and types of vats. He farms with the least intervention in the soils. One of the factors that sets him apart is his use of Garnacha Tintorera in Mencía reds.

Despite the fact that he chose Bierzo, the Bierzo DO has not always chosen to accept his wines into the DO. So you will find a number under the useful Vino de la Tierra Castilla y León umbrella, or with no appellation at all. What's important is the liquid, and Pérez makes a growing range of exciting and individual wines. Most accessible – in style and availability – is Brezo, for which he makes a white, a *rosado* and a red. His most elegant wine is La Vigne de Sanchomartín, a co-fermented blend of Mencía, Garnacha Tintorera and Godello, a field blend of varieties found together in the vineyard. For lovers of rare varieties Estaladiña wins the prize, because it is a grape variety not yet recognized by the DO. This red grape, possibly related to Merenzao, possibly not, is foot-trodden and amphora-aged. Las Tinajas is his amphora-aged Godello, which has four months of skin contact to produce a complex and fascinating orange wine. One should not overlook Las Botas, which is aged in Manzanilla butts from Delgado Zuleta for ten months. Sherry is a fascination for producers all across Spain, and Las Botas shows the complexity that a Sherry butt can give.

BIERZO OR BURGUNDY?

Bierzo is currently at a moment of great promise. A new generation is making its own rules, exploring the distinctive characteristics of the soils. Ricardo Pérez Palacios is active in the DO and in the community. He has helped to construct a quality classification for the wines of Bierzo which is the closest to Burgundian of any of the classifications so far proposed. That's to say, generic wine, village wine, *cru*, *grand cru*, or words to that effect. This puts a single vineyard at the summit of the pyramid, which works for Bierzo, but is much less popular in Rioja, where many producers blend across vineyards and sub-zones. Hence the continuing debates in Rioja.

In Bierzo the proposal was agreed by the CRDO in 2017, although a key concern is whether all the producers will sign up to it.

Pittacum

La Iglesia 11, 24546 Arganza
Tel.: +34 987 548 054
 www.terrasgauda.com

Founded in 1999 by three partners who were fans of Mencía, the business is named after a Roman-era clay pot which they found while excavating the cellar. The winery was purchased by Terras Gauda of Rías Baixas in 2002. They own 5 hectares, and buy in from local contractors. The entry level is the juicy young Petit Pittacum. One of the top wines, La Prohibición, is 100 per cent Garnacha Tintorera. Aurea is the top wine, from 110-year-old Mencía, with 14 months in new French oak.

Raúl Pérez

Finca El Barredo s/n, 24530 Valtuille de Abajo
Tel.: +34 987 562 148
www.castroventosa.com

Castro Ventosa or Castro Bergidum is the name of the Roman settlement on the hill by the family winery. The family can date back their vinegrowing in Valtuille at least to 1752, and the founding of the current winery to their grandmother's generation. A step change was made when Raúl Pérez returned to the winery to work.

Pérez' influence across north-west Spain has been electrifying. He has regenerated the wines at his family winery and through that work attracted international attention for his work elsewhere. He has also been fundamental in offering winery space to up-and-coming projects and in welcoming like-minded winemakers, such as the Michelini brothers from Argentina, to work on special projects with him. He studied at the wine school in Requena and I watched him recently speaking to an audience of growers at a conference in Utiel-Requena. Although he has become a celebrity in the wine world he talked with the utmost humility about how he works with grape varieties. He is not a producer of *vinos de autor* – his style is a much more sensitive expression of the grape varieties. That was clear in the way he talked to the growers about not imposing your rules or recipe book on the variety and not treating it in exactly the same way each year.

This sensitive approach is just what Mencía needs. Pérez makes a range of Castro de Valtuille wines of which Cepas Centenarias is a bottling of rare old vines. He also makes the Ultreia series of Mencía blended with local varieties. Cova de la Raposa is one of the rarities: made from pre-phylloxeric Mencía blended with Bastardo and Garnacha Tintorera among others. The grapes go through a natural ferment in whole clusters and are left to macerate for no less than 90 days. After that the wine is aged for 20 months in French oak barrels. Like so many of his wines, it is in short supply; just 500 bottles are made.

It is worth tracking down his other wines. Outstanding are the wines he makes in the Amandi district of Ribeira Sacra at Guímaro: El Pecado ('the sin') and La Penitencia ('the penance'). Then there's Sketch, a Rías Baixas Albariño and Le Batard, made using grapes from Sierra de Gredos. There's more besides – with wines from Tierra de León (Margón), and the wines he makes for Estefanía. There really is never a dull moment at a wine tasting with Pérez, with one remarkable wine after another coming out of the box(es) from this generous, creative, thoughtful man.

Vinos Valtuille

Promadelo s/n, 24530 Valtuille de Abajo
Tel.: +34 987 562 165
www.vinosvaltuille.com

Dimas García's predecessors had been growers in the region since 1910. That is when they acquired the vineyard in Valdoneje, which now gives its name to their top wine, Pago de Valdoneje. García launched the winery in 1999, though it is now in the hands of his son Marcos. They have 12 hectares of vineyards, averaging 90 years old, right in the heart of the Camino de Santiago. They underline the fact that they are a small, artisanal winery making wine in the traditional way.

The results are very promising as they handle the fruit of their old vines with sensitivity. Pago de Valdoneje is a straightforward, honest reflection of the quality of their vines, very finely balanced. The Valdoneje Viñas Viejas has the added intensity of the older vines.

El Valao is fermented in large stainless steel vats, and aged in used oak barrels. There is not enough oak to dominate the fruit, just enough to give it complexity and allow the old vines to express themselves. Cabanelas is a single vineyard wine, with a more thoroughgoing oak treatment. Last but very much not least is the complex, characterful Godello.

On the radar

Mencías de Dos

Tel.: +34 616 920 648

This is the winery of Ada, José Luis Prada's daughter, who paired up in 2004 with Ricardo Sanz, winemaker in Rueda, when they studied winemaking together. They work on organically farmed plots from Prada's family vineyards, with slate and quartz soils.

Michelini I Mufatto

This is the brand of the husband and wife winemaking team of Gerardo Michelini and Andrea Muffatto, and their son Manuel. Their home is in Gualtallary, Mendoza, Argentina, where they are making fascinating wines. They are clearly having fun discovering the terroir here and making fine wine, facilitated by Raúl Pérez. They use wild yeasts, grapes are foot trodden and left on skins in amphorae, and the wine is matured in French oak. Mundo Zepelling is another typically quirkily named and fascinating project from the Michelinis. Look out for more interest – and more quality – where this comes from.

Verónica Ortega

www.veronicaortega.es

Ortega has a perfect pedigree, having worked for Daphne Glorian, Álvaro Palacios, Dirk Niepoort and at Domaine de la Romanée-Conti as well as in New Zealand and the Rhône. Returning to Spain she worked with Raúl Pérez before launching her own cellar in 2014. She makes two wines, Quite and Roc.

CIGALES

When you are planning a trip to Ribera del Duero, add in an extra day for a detour from Valladolid to Cigales. It's just a half hour drive along the road to Burgos, following the River Pisuerga, to the quiet town of Cigales. Make the pilgrimage to a place that became famous for its *claretes*, its pale reds/deep-coloured *rosados* in a land where big, rich reds are king. In Castilla y León white wines were scarce, until Rueda appeared on the scene. The only alternative to red was the *rosados*. However three-quarters of Cigales wine is sold in Spain, the majority within the region. The *rosados* in particular find it hard to fight in the international marketplace with the demand for Provençal-style rosés. Still, as the profiles below show, some producers, like some of the Riojanos, have decided to take on the French at their own game and make pale pink drinks.

Cigales at a glance

Grape varieties

White: Verdejo, Albillo, Sauvignon Blanc, Viura
Red: Tinta del País (Tempranillo), Garnacha Tinta, Garnacha Gris, Merlot, Syrah, Cabernet Sauvignon.

The small print

Rosado contains a minimum of 60 per cent Tinta del País, and a minimum 20 per cent from white varieties. Wines may be sold from 31 December of the year following the harvest.

Red contains a minimum of 85 per cent Tinta del País and Garnacha Tinta. In September 2011 the regulations were changed to permit the production of white, sparkling and sweet wines.

Size

Vineyard: 2,000 hectares
Growers: 430
Wineries: 34

The DO was only created in 1991, but the area's wine history dates as far back as the Romans, as in Ribera del Duero. The first documented evidence comes in the tenth century, with a written record of vineyards in municipalities. The arrival of the monasteries ensured the production of wine. By 1888, before the arrival of phylloxera, the region was producing 15 million kilogrammes of grapes a year. As elsewhere in Spain, there was a successful business shipping wine to France in those days. Today instead you will see vast expanses of cereal stretching to the horizon, replacing the former viticulture.

The vineyards are at 700–800 metres, and the soils are sand and loam over clay, with limestone varying between 1 and 35 per cent. The gravels and large rounded rocks that lie across the surface of the vineyards are distinctive, and valuable, as in Châteauneuf-du-Pape, for reflecting heat back up to the vines. Generalizing wildly, Cigales is higher, stonier and drier than its neighbour Toro. The climate is continental, although the DO says that it also has Atlantic influences. At Finca Museum they say that Cigales never suffers the late autumn frosts that Ribera del Duero has experienced, and the spring is typically less extreme too. Average rainfall is 407 millimetres.

The DO is made up of eleven municipalities, many of them with their own castles, reminders of the region's centuries of warfare. One of them, at Mucientes, was the castle of Juana 'la loca' (the mad), the unfortunate daughter of Ferdinand and Isabella, inheritor of the united crowns of Aragón and Castile, who was declared insane.

As across the whole of the region, there are underground cellars scattered throughout the landscape, each marked by the mounds which are the staircase entrances. These are accompanied by apparently random air vents, rising up out of the ground for light and ventilation to the cellars.

For many years, Cigales was synonymous with *rosado*, a deeply coloured pink wine made by blending red and white, and often oak aged. Reds became established more recently. Undoubtedly many of the reds are still a little rustic, but there are some very enjoyable, characterful wines too. Since it lies almost ignored in the shadow of Ribera del Duero, the wines are certainly much more affordable. A small DO then, but worth exploring as it develops.

Producers

César Príncipe
Ronda 22, 47194 Fuensaldaña
Tel.: +34 983 663 123
www.cesarprincipe.es

Three wise men are behind this winery. The original, grandfather Eutiquio, the eponymous father César, and the third generation, grandson Ignacio, who describes himself as 'father, *viticultor* and communicator'. Eutiquio passed down his vinegrowing wisdom through the family. The current project was founded in 1982, and the bodega was opened in 1990. The significant year for the business was 2000, when the first vintage of César

Príncipe was released, winning high scores with the critics. Cigales – and the bodega – hit the international headlines.

The vineyards are mainly in Fuensaldaña and range from 25 to 100 years old. As was typical a century ago across Spain, the vineyards would have been interplanted with a mix of different varieties. Today Ignacio Príncipe has up to 50 per cent white grapes – Jerez (as Palomino is known here), Albillo and Moscatel – amid the Tempranillo, which means pickers need to be sent through the vineyard twice to harvest grapes at their optimum ripeness.

César Príncipe is the flagship wine, from very low yielding vines of between 70 and 100 years old. It has 14 months ageing and is a well-structured, finely balanced wine as the world discovered in 2000, when it revealed the potential of the 'unknown' DO of Cigales. As its label shows, 13 Cántaros Nicolás is a memorial to Eutiquio who would do his accounts in chalks on the rock walls of the underground cellar where he made his wine. It's a younger, fruitier style with eight months in oak. Ignacio Príncipe also makes a Verdejo from Rueda, a classic *clarete*, and a new wave *saignée*, very pale and Provençal. Eutiquio would be proud.

Finca Herrera

Pintor Ribera 35, 28016 Madrid
Tel.: +34 914 158 259
www.fincaherrera.es

As the address here suggests, Finca Herrera is not a grand business with a showy bodega fit for oenotourism. Nevertheless it is firmly rooted in the wines of Castilla y León. The first Herrera, Pascal, was winemaker for the cooperative in Manzanares, Ciudad Real. His son, also Pascal, was a generous and expansive character with enormous experience, who died suddenly in January 2017. As an agricultural engineer he had been involved in the drawing up the initial definitive map of Spain's DOs. Latterly he was president of the CRDO Ribera del Duero, before doing the same job for Cigales. He had also run the Wine Museum in Valladolid, and been closely involved with wine competitions across Spain (which is where I first got to know him, across the judging table). His restaurateur son Manuel, who already makes wines in the Madrid area, started his own project in Cigales, and gratefully acknowledges the guidance of his late father.

The Tempranillo (with 9 per cent Garnacha) is made from 60- to 80-year-old bush vines, and spends eleven months in a blend of French, Hungarian and American oak. But Cigales is not all Tempranillo/Tinta del País. Manuel's wine Garnachas proves that point: it's an on-trend pale-coloured, aromatic, textured blend of Garnacha Tinta, with 5 per cent Garnacha Tintorera (strictly speaking, it's Alicante Bouschet) and 3 per cent Garnacha Gris. The wine uses very old bush vine Garnachas from 90 years up to more than 110 years old. Still, Manuel remains true to Cigales with his Musculoso Clarete, a *rosado*. His chosen blend is 85 per cent Tempranillo, 10 per cent Garnacha, and just 5 per cent Albillo. Like many of Cigales' *rosados*, it spends some time in oak. However, the usage is subtle – six months in 500-litre used French barriques. These wines are a fine memorial to the Herreras, with a promising future.

Finca Museum

Ctra Cigales-Corcos Km 3, 47270 Cigales
Tel.: +34 983 581 029
www.bodegasmuseum.com

Surely Cigales' most glamorous winery, this is set at the end of a long drive through the 72-hectare vineyard, with manicured gardens, a statue to Vinea, and as much space as a winemaker could want for fermentation and barrel storage. The clue to the level of investment is that it is owned by Baron de Ley from Rioja. The vineyard is the result of careful research. After much enquiry the owners found the site, including remarkably stony vineyards, a former lake in the Tertiary period. They own 185 hectares, and manage another 60. Four wines are made here. The eponymous Museum is a Reserva with 22 months in new French oak and is bold and forthright but with polish. Vinea, like Museum, is 100 per cent Tinta del País, a Crianza with 14 months in a blend of American and French oak. There's also a Vinea Rosé, with its French name, and the French method of *saignée*, by 'bleeding' the juice off the skins of red wine grapes, and not blending it with white grapes. It's still a full-coloured rosé, despite the different method of winemaking, and full of strawberry fruit. The top wine in the line-up is Numerus Clausus, made from the craggy old vines from the gravelly vineyards. This has 30 months in new French oak, plus another three years in bottle and has the density and richness expected of this category, as well as aromatic charm.

Among the Cigales wineries, this is one of the more active in wine tourism, and has several options for visits, including traditional lunches in local restaurants after the visit.

Sinforiano Vaquero

Ctra Villalba Km 1 dcha, 47194 Mucientes
Tel.: +34 983 663 008

The business goes back as far as 1966, when Sinforiano Vaquero and Daniela Gómez decided to take on the family underground cellar, and the old vines. They have turned it into a modern winery with 70 hectares of vineyard, and put their children in charge.

The popular Sinfo range has Roble, with just four months in oak; a classic *clarete*; and Rosado which has been fermented in American oak (500 litres) and aged in French oak for five months. It is both well made and well balanced. Raimun is a popular range, with a late harvest Verdejo–Sauvignon Blanc in the line-up. Most interesting is the innovation of Quelías, a new-wave pale *rosado* that is a multi-varietal blend. It may not yet be perfect, but it demonstrates a recognition of market demands. Top of the range is 50 Vendimias 2009 made to celebrate Sinforiano's fiftieth anniversary in the business. Careful selection in the vineyard combined with American oak have led to a sumptuous and spicy wine.

Traslanzas

Barrio de la Bodegas s/n, 47194 Mucientes
Tel.: +34 639 641 123
www.traslanzas.com

When you discover the people behind this project, you know that it is going to be good. The vineyard belongs to the Pinacho family, and María Pinacho makes the wine with Ana Martín. Ana and her business partner Pepe Hidalgo pop up in a number of wineries in this book, as they consult widely, always developing projects of interest. Traslanzas reckon they made the first serious red in Cigales. They used a vineyard planted in 1945 by María's grandfather, south-east facing at 800 metres, yielding less than a kilogramme per vine. The fermentation is with native yeast, and the wine is aged in French and American barriques for 12–15 months in the family's underground cellar. They stress the fact that this is freestyle ageing, so the wine follows the vintage expression and not the fixed timetables of the classic categories of ageing. Their first vintage was back in 1998, and since then they have developed a polished, intense expression of the vineyard.

Valdelosfrailes

Ctra Cubillas de Santa Marta s/n, 47290 Cubillas de Santa Marta
Tel.: +34 983 485 028
www.valdelosfrailes.es

The winery is an offshoot of Ribera del Duero's Matarromero group. Carlos Moro's family had been making *claretes* for many years, in an area which was first put to vine by the Cistercians at the monastery of Palazuelos. With the launch and growth of Cigales, investing in a major winery here must have seemed natural. The winery draws on 90 hectares of vineyards, mainly Tempranillo, with some Verdejo and some Cabernet Sauvignon. The average age of the vines is 35 years, although some parcels are centenarian. Their first vintage here was 1999.

RUEDA

There is no need to get out the altimeter app on your phone in Rueda, it may be flat but there's something about the light that tells you that you are far from the sea and fairly high up – around 600–700 metres, in fact. The ground is covered with small pebbles stretching to the horizon, which is only broken by pine trees. The soil is poor, and well drained, with limestone, some of which is sandy. The climate is continental.

The area we know as Rueda was devastated with the retreat of the Moors during the Reconquista, in a policy of burning everything in sight. The region was abandoned for many decades. However King Alfonso VI stepped in, in the eleventh century, and encouraged a return to the land, and farmers and the Church returned to settle. In the meantime the abandoned *meseta* had become fertile again. Wine was one of the necessary products for the Church, and they were easily able to make oxidative Sherry-style wines. Thus they continued until phylloxera came. The sandy soils resisted the pest, although many areas were wiped out. Replanting encouraged the selection of Palomino: with its high yields and ease of growing it provided a good source of income for farmers who were paid for volume not quality. The only problem was that there was little market for these mildly Sherry-ish wines outside Rueda, let alone in the export market.

Rueda at a glance

Grape varieties

White: Verdejo, Viura, Sauvignon Blanc, Palomino Fino

Red: Tempranillo, Cabernet Sauvignon, Merlot, Garnacha (reds were introduced from vintage 2001)

The small print

Rueda: A blend of minimum 50 per cent Verdejo and other varieties listed above

Rueda Verdejo: Minimum 85 per cent (but usually 100 per cent) Verdejo

Rueda Sauvignon: Minimum 85 per cent Sauvignon Blanc

Rueda Espumoso: 'Traditional method' sparkling wine, minimum nine months ageing.

Rueda Dorado: Dry liqueur wine, minimum 15% abv, aged in oak barrels for a minimum of two years

Size

Vineyard: 13,517 hectares
Growers: 1,479
Wineries: 69

With great foresight, the Marqués de Riscal identified this apparently unlikely area in the early 1970s as a good place for clean, fresh white wines from Verdejo. How right he was! With the founding of the DO in 1980 the producers involved took the decision to relaunch Rueda as a producer of similar fresh, young white wines. So the traditional Dorados, the oxidized wines aged by the solera method or in demijohns, were set aside. Now a few producers are returning to make these wines as a tribute to their predecessors. Hijos de Alberto Gutiérrez is one example, and Félix Lorenzo Cachazo another.

This is what Richard Ford encountered on his favourable visit to Rueda: 'Rueda, population 2500, has a fine parish church, and a handsome long street. It is one of the best towns in this district as the quantity of good wine grown here is a source of profit to the inhabitants. The vineyards lie on a stony broken soil; the wine is kept in deep cellars in large oaken barrels, and is considered to be a specific against the gout.'

BOOM OR BUST?

Verdejo has been the star of the last two decades. Between 1996 and 2006 production almost trebled, and between 2006 and 2012 it doubled again. It is easy to understand the demand: the Verdejo grapes made a Spanish wine with international appeal. Fermented in squeaky-clean stainless steel, released within six months or so, the wines are young and punchy. In commercial terms, it was an ideal variety that could be harvested and sold within the year. In marketing terms what was important was that it was a local grape, and was different, so it did not have to get down and dirty with Chardonnays the world over. In fact the benefit was both its similarity to and its difference from Sauvignon Blanc. It didn't generally have the overpowering methoxypyrazines that give Sauvignon Blanc its classic green pea character, fine in small doses, but sometime too green. Instead it has a characteristic balancing note of bitterness in the finish.

The Rueda vineyard hasn't just grown, it has also changed. In 1996 Palomino accounted for 20 per cent of the vineyard. Now it is less than 0.5 per cent. A good thing, probably, although the Verdejo and Sauvignon have not always been of the best. The issue is the demand for the wine. In addition there has been competition from cheaper production areas in Spain who can undercut growers here. In terms of winemaking the use of straightforward yeasts delivering a quick and reliable ferment, with no lees ageing, plus firm filtration makes for much anonymous wine. Rueda is at a turning point. There are some outstanding producers below, but they are working in a market where Verdejo is sold too cheaply, unsustainably.

Producers

Agrícola Castellana

Ctra Rodilana s/n, 47491 La Seca
Tel.: +34 983 816 320
www.agricolacastellana.com

Cooperatives are important in Rueda, and Agrícola Castellana is one of the oldest (1935) and largest (it makes almost 20 per cent of all of Rueda's wine). The statistics go on: they control more than 2,150 hectares of vineyards, producing 40 different labels under DO Rueda and 12 under VdlT Castilla y León. Under the separate, more prestige, brand Cuatro Rayas, there are another dozen or so wines. The Cuatro Rayas Viñedos Centenarios is a speciality, made from the very oldest vineyards; a reliable, likeable Verdejo.

Álvarez y Díez

Juan Antonio Carmona 12, 47500 Nava del Rey
Tel.: +34 983 850 1136
www.alvarezydiez.com

Álvarez y Díez record that their home town was called Nava del Medina at the time of the Reconquista. However in 1560, Felipe II renamed it Villa de la Nava del Rey and established the first of its regal privileges. The region did not recover from the ravages of phylloxera until well into the twentieth century. Thus it was not until 1941, just after the end of the Civil War, that Modesto Álvarez and Eladio Díez created today's winery, specializing in the traditional wines of the region. Modernization came in 1992 when the winemaking and winery were updated, although the business continues to use the underground cellar formerly owned by the Church. They now own more than 100 hectares of vineyards. The Mantel Blanco Verdejo is a popular classic, and the Mantel Blanco Verdejo Fermentado en Barrica, fermented in new French and American oak and aged in barrel for one year and bottle for another, is a successfully rich, spicy style.

Belondrade

Quinta San Diego, Camino de Puerto s/n, 474891 La Seca
Tel.: +34 983 481 001
www.belondrade.com

The winery was founded in 1994, and rapidly became one of the DO's stars, pointing the way to what could be achieved, in particular through subtle use of oak. Initially Brigitte Lurton was involved, along with her brother Jacques; their brother François has other wineries in Rueda and Toro (see pp. 120, 129 and 130). The owner is Frenchman Didier Belondrade, with 30 hectares of vineyard, of an average age of 30 years, managed across 19 parcels, depending on rootstocks, clones and aspect.

Belondrade y Lurton is their top wine, fermented and aged in 300-litre French oak. The wine is blended at 10–12 months, and bottle-aged for about 6 months. Wonderfully complex, it is definitely a wine to enjoy with a few years of age. Quinta Apolonia and Quinta

Clarisa are named after his daughters, and both are VdlT Castilla y León (see p. 139).

Burdigala

Nueva 12, 474912 La Seca
Tel.: +34 983 034 030
www.burdigala.es

This is François Lurton's joint project with Michel Rolland. It produces two whites here in Rueda, both 100 per cent Verdejo, and two reds in Toro.

After cold maceration the juice for Campo Alegre is run off the skins and macerated for another ten days to develop flavour. One third is fermented in concrete eggs, one third in *demi-muids*, new French oak barrels of 600 litres, and the remainder in stainless steel. In this way they build texture and complexity in the wine before ageing on lees for four months and then blending. The top wine is Campo Eliseo, from older vines, fermented in 600-litre new French oak, and then aged in barrel for ten months.

Compañía de Vinos Telmo Rodriguez

www.telmorodriguez.com

The much-travelled wine business makes two wines here. Basa is a reliable young Verdejo with 10 per cent Viura, based on a mix of bush vine and cordon vineyards, grown in gravel and limestone, fermented in stainless steel. El Transistor is the big brother. Entirely Verdejo handpicked from bush vines, it uses native yeasts and is fermented in casks, barrels, concrete and stainless steel. It's altogether more complex, textured and serious.

Félix Lorenzo Cachazo

Ctra Medina del Campo Km 9, 47220 Pozáldez
Tel.: +34 983 822 008
www.cachazo.com

One of Rueda's pioneers is now relaunching the classic wine of Rueda. The Carrasviñas Dorado was known as Amontillado in the old days. Today it is made with Palomino and Verdejo fortified after fermentation and aged for 18 months in 16-litre glass demijohns or *damajuanas*. The glass jars are exposed to the extreme cold of winter and heat of summer in order to develop a complex oxidative character in the wines. The new release is small, just 1,800 bottles. Their regular Verdejos are fine, but this return to tradition is very exciting.

Herederos del Marqués de Riscal

Ctra N VI, 47490 Rueda
Tel.: +34 983 868 029
www.marquesderiscal.com

Rueda owes a great deal to the Marqués de Riscal. It took the vision of this Riojano, and his French adviser Émile Peynaud, to recognize the potential in the soils and varieties, and to bring the wines to international attention through the Riscal brand and sales network. His arrival in 1972 pre-dates the creation of the DO. The Marqués transformed the wines by using stainless steel tanks with temperature controls, technology which is standard now, but was unheard of in those days. Riscal continues to innovate, producing the first barrel-fermented Verdejo, and then developing native yeasts for cool fermentations.

With the latest purchase of land, Riscal owns over 300 hectares of vineyard and controls now between 300 and 350 further hectares. Despite the sheer volume of grapes the brands are very clearly tiered in terms of quality. It's not always the case that a family business can work in different DOs and get it right, but Riscal has managed it beautifully. The production is directed by Luis Hurtado de Amézaga, who oversees the quality of the Herederos de Marqués de Riscal estates.

The regular Riscal Verdejo is a fresh, good value choice. Next up is Finca Montico, a single vineyard wine which has more complexity. Above that is the Limousin, a carefully and sensitively made oaked Verdejo. It used to be much oakier, but in recent years there has been an encouraging move to larger vats and shorter times in oak. The latest release and the most impressive is Baron de Chirel. However, and unfortunately for the DO, this has been released as a VdlT Castilla de León. Castilla de León does not lack for prestige wineries now, a sign of growing confidence in its reputation and the flexibility it allows. Some wineries may have been forced to use the appellation because their grapes do not come from any other DO. But here it was more a case of dissatisfaction with the authorities and the overall poor quality perception of Rueda wines that led Riscal to make a wine outside the

DO. Chirel is the white partner of their modern Rioja Reserva, and it more than lives up to the task.

Hijos de Alberto Gutiérrez
Ctra de Valdestillas 2, 47231 Serrada
Tel.: +34 983 559 107
www.dealberto.com

This historic winery, with its rabbit warren of underground cellars, is based in a farmhouse founded by the Dominicans in the seventeenth century, and purchased by the Gutiérrez family after the Desamortización de Mendizábal. The fourth generation of the family is now in charge. Of particular interest here is the Dorado they make in the style of Rueda's traditional wines. It's solera-aged Verdejo, oxidized, and 17% abv: a classic revived.

Javier Sanz Viticultor
San Judas 2, 47491 La Seca
Tel.: +34 983 816 669
www.bodegajaviersanz.com

It's easy to get confused in Rueda – there are plenty of people called Sanz. Javier Sanz is part of a long line of Rueda *viticultors*, who started his winery in 1990 and now farms 104 hectares of vineyard. Villa Narcisa is his 'regular' Verdejo. Malcorta is his top wine, the result of working with an old clone of Verdejo, which he has named 'Malcorta'. He says that it is more aromatic, and fresher.

José Pariente
Ctra de Rueda Km 2.5, 47491 La Seca, Valladolid
Tel.: +34 983 816 600
www.josepariente.com

In 1998 Victoria Pariente established the winery, naming it after her father, José. Victoria is now one of Rueda's top names. Over the years she has honed her vineyards and her winery, polishing and developing her techniques. Her winery is also remarkable, all of it precise and clean. She installed concrete eggs long ago, and the pipework for those is all just-so – not always the case with egg owners in wineries. Her approach to the winery is reflected in the wines. The 'regular' Verdejo is a clean, refreshing, lively style. She also makes a Sauvignon Blanc. The name of the Fermentado en

Barrica suggests it might taste really oaky, but it's anything but. It comes from old vines and has a honeyed, mineral complexity, needing time to age. The Cuvée Especial really is a special cuvée – fermented in concrete eggs to emphasize the lees character, with lower sulphites, it is wonderfully aromatic and vividly fresh, with a lean finish. Unmistakeably José Pariente. A particular treat is Apasionado, a late harvest sweet wine made with Sauvignon Blanc.

Victoria's daughter Martina works in the winery, but along with her brother also has Prieto Pariente, her own winemaking project in Castilla y León (see p. 142).

Menade
Ctra Rueda - Nava del Rey Km 1, 47490 Rueda
Tel.: +34 983 103 223
www.menade.es

This is a Sanz family winery, set up in 2005 by Richard Sanz with his siblings, producing wines from organically farmed grapes. Over time they have transformed both the packaging and their viticulture. The environment and sustainability are top of their agenda. They make one wine in DO Rueda, their 'regular' Verdejo. All their other wines are VdlT Castilla y León, to give them the freedom to make their own choices. Their top wine is undoubtedly La Misión, which is what used to be called V3. This is a Verdejo, which was grafted over with an old clone of Verdeja [sic]. It is aged partly in vats, partly in 500-litre barrels and partly in amphorae.

Naia
San Martín s/n, 47491 La Seca
Tel.: +34 628 434 933
www.bodegasnaia.com

I find that Naia divides opinion. Some prefer the crunchy, aromatic unoaked K-Naia, a good value Verdejo–Sauvignon Blanc blend, others the lees-aged 100 per cent Verdejo Naia, and still others Naiades, which is sourced from very old vineyards and aged for seven months on lees in French oak. My personal favourite is Naia – a creamy, honeyed, leesy Verdejo. But others may prefer a more overt oak influence, and certainly Naiades has the capacity to age and grow in character.

Launched in 2002, this is another of the Avante Selecta group of wineries. It owns 23.5 hectares of vineyards, and the style of wine is guided by the group's technical manager Eulogio Calleja.

Ordóñez

Julio Romero de Torres 12, 29700 Vélez-Málaga
Tel.: +34 952 504 706
www.jorgeordonezselections.com

Jorge Ordóñez is an importer of Spanish wines into the USA, with a range of wineries across Spain. He produces two wines in Rueda from old vine vineyards. The vines for Nisia were planted in 1942 and 1950; it is fermented in larger sized French oak, and in stainless steel, followed by eight months on lees. The top wine, Nisia Las Suertes, is from a vineyard planted in 1885 that never succumbed to phylloxera because of its sandy soils. This is fermented and aged in larger French oak, and because of the concentration of the fruit stands up well to the oak ageing.

Vinos Sanz

Ctra Madrid – La Coruña Km 170.5, 47490 Rueda
Tel.: +34 983 868 100
www.vinossanz.com

This is the oldest of Rueda's wineries, dating back to the 1870s. Their La Colina estate has the oldest plantation of Sauvignon Blanc in the DO, in addition to Verdejo and Viura. I have a particular affection for their old vine Finca La Colina Cien x Cien, which was one of the wines I tasted way back on my first visit to Rueda. It made and makes a striking impression regarding the potential for this grape variety: aromatic, intense, penetrating and fresh.

Shaya

Ctra Aldeanueva del Codonal s/n, 40642 Aldeanueva del Codonal
Tel.: +34 968 435 022
www.shaya.es

Shaya was launched in 2008, with Australian winemaker Belinda Thomson overseeing production. She makes three wines: Arindo, the young Verdejo; Shaya, the flagship, made from old bush vines, one third fermented in larger barrels to give complexity; and the top wine Shaya Habis. This is fermented in French oak and aged for seven months in barrel. Shaya is part of the Orowines group that belongs to the Juan Gil family of Jumilla, which specializes in smaller, more artisanal projects across Spain.

OUTSIDERS PILING IN

A number of wineries from elsewhere in Spain have set up shop here, following the lead of Paco Hurtado de Amézaga, Marqués de Riscal who, with the advice of French oenologist Émile Peynaud, identified the potential of Rueda for white wine. In those days Rioja needed a fresh option for white wine. The new entrants continued slowly. There were those who settled and stayed – notably Belondrade. Telmo Rodríguez and Pablo Eguzkiza with their Compañía de Vinos are also well-established here. Very recently there has been a new rush to invest, perhaps assisted by the economic crisis, during which much land and property in the wine industry has come up for sale. Some outsiders are neighbours from Ribera del Duero, such as Matarromera. Others, such as François Lurton, have built joint businesses in Toro and Rueda.

Recent arrivals include: Codorníu, Epicure Wines Les 3 Amis, Freixenet, Torres (Catalunya), Beronia (Jerez/Rioja), Bilbaínas, CVNE, Marqués de Cáceres, Martínez Bujanda, Ramón Bilbao, Rolland & Galarreta (Rioja), Gran Feudo (Navarra), Cillar de Silos, Matarromera, Pradorey, Protos (Ribera del Duero), Estancia Piedra (Toro), Vicente Gandía (Valencia). There are plenty more. Some of these are recent projects and have yet to show their full potential; I'd include Epicure Wines, Torres and Ramón Bilbao in this category. It's to be hoped these companies can all invest in serious, top quality wines, and use their marketing power to rebuild Rueda.

Other noteworthy bodegas

Emina Rueda

www.emina.es

The sister winery to Emina in Ribera del Duero, part of the Matarromera group.

Mathilde Chapoutier
www.chapoutier.com
The négociant branch of Chapoutier has added a young, uncomplicated Rueda Verdejo to the portfolio.

Máquina & Tabla
www.maquina-tabla.com
In Rueda they make the partner to their Tinta de Toro Páramos de Nicasia, with the same name. Fermented in concrete, used oak and stainless steel, the winemaking emphasizes the grape rather than the oak. A very interesting project.

Palacio de Bornos
www.palaciodebornos.com
This bodega makes fresh, young Verdejos. The group also owns Señorío de Sarria and Guelbenzu in Ribera del Queiles, and Lagar de Bornos in Rioja.

Veracruz
www.bodegasveracruz.com
Makers of good value, lively Verdejos.

Viñedos de Nieva
www.vinedosdenieva.com
This winery draws on some exceptional old vineyards. It has been under new ownership – the Martúe group – since 2009.

TORO

The peasants about here become as churlish as their country ... all seem poverty-stricken and starving amid corn and wine ... roads, canals and customers are all wanting, yet this Vino de Toro is far superior to what is commonly sold in England as port.

Richard Ford

Since Ford's day, the locals have become much more charming, and the wines have a ready market internationally. Toro has the glamour that Cigales lacks, and kilometre for kilometre even more glamour than Ribera del Duero. Take a look at the smart names below who have invested here. Toro has the edge. At the point where land in Ribera del Duero just became too expensive, Toro was the natural, accessible place to go. Note Ford's comment on the strength of the wine; in 1830 it could be compared to a hearty Port.

Toro at a glance

Grape varieties

White: Malvasía, Verdejo
Red: Tinta de Toro, Garnacha

Size

Vineyard: 5,469 hectares
Growers: 1,352
Wineries: 62

The small print

Red wines in the classic ageing categories are made with 100 per cent Tinta de Toro. *Rosados*, made by the *saignée* method, use a minimum of 75 per cent Tinta de Toro and the rest Garnacha, or Garnacha alone. Whites are made from a minimum of 85 per cent Malvasía with the remainder Verdejo, or with 100 per cent Verdejo.

Up until now, Cigales has always suffered by comparison with its neighbour. Toro's production is twice as large as that of Cigales. At 620–750 metres its vineyards are lower than Cigales', with Tertiary Era soils, a blend of sand, clay and calcareous conglomerates, with brown-grey limestone topsoil and some stony alluvial soils. The rainfall is 350–400 millimetres, and it shares with Cigales the typically extreme cold and heat, and late frosts, that are a feature of Castilla y León. Good viticulture here, in this land of drought, involves balancing the vine, the leaf area and the number of clusters.

Toro takes in twelve municipalities in the province of Zamora as well as three in Valladolid province. At the beginning of the sixteenth century

Toro itself was an important city, and there are plenty of documents recording the importance of viticulture and the wine business. Its bold, well-structured wines were shipped to the New World, as they were powerful enough to withstand the crossing. In time, however, Toro fell into decline for a number of social and economic reasons. There were geographical issues, too: it was just too far from a sea port, or a navigable river, to do business with the outside world. However when, at the end of the nineteenth century, Spain was hit by phylloxera, Toro was one of the rare areas that survived. Its sandy soils ensured that the phylloxera louse could not survive, and this protected the vines on their own rootstocks. Many were subsequently uprooted, but there are some that persist to this day and form the backbone to great wines. The first steps to a DO were made in 1933; however history intervened and it took until 1987 for DO Toro to be created, with just four wineries.

Tinta de Toro, the Tempranillo from Toro, is the DO's grape. Its thicker skins and earlier ripening contribute to a dense, bold wine that easily delivers plenty of alcohol. The issue of high alcohol is one of the early memories of Manuel Fariña whose family have long made wine in Toro. In the late 1960s, he recalls, he had to reduce alcohol levels. The typical Toro easily reached 17% abv, so he worked to bring it down to between 13 and 13.5% abv by harvesting earlier. The same family continued to innovate in the region: they were the first to bring in stainless steel fermentation tanks, and the first to understand the importance of building brands for bottled wines.

Producers

Alonso del Yerro

Finca Santa Marta, Ctra Roa-Anguix Km 1.8, 09300 Roa
Tel.: +34 913 160 121
www.alonsodelyerro.es

This is the second project from Ribera del Duero's Alonso del Yerro bodega. They make one wine, Paydos, 100 per cent Tinta de Toro, firm and four-square. The winemaking style is developing year by year, with partial use of whole bunches, and using only one third new barrels for maturation. Stéphane Derenoncourt, the eminent Bordeaux consultant, is the longstanding consultant to Alonso del Yerro here and in the mother ship in Ribera del Duero. Paydos is named after the initials of the youngest son of the family, Pedro, and his chosen number *dos* (two). They own 9 hectares of vineyards in Morales de Toro.

Bernard Magrez

Pza de la Trinidad 5, 48900 Toro
Tel.: +34 980 698 071
www.bernard-magrez.com

They make just one wine here, Paciencia. What a terrific name for a wine! Magrez has been in Toro since 2003, and it is hard to believe that someone had not chosen the name before that. The name is all of a piece with the winery itself – which is inside an old church in the Plaza de la Trinidad in Toro. From 14 hectares of Tinta de Toro, with vines ranging from 30–100 years they make a polished wine, with baskets of black fruits, and well-managed French oak.

Burdigala

Ctra de Tordesillas 14, 49800 Toro
Tel.: +34 980 082 027
www.burdigala.es

This is one half of a joint project of François Lurton and Michel Rolland (see also p. 120), to make wine in Rueda and in Toro. The wines are complementary, with a couple in each DO. In Toro they work with 100 per cent Tinta de Toro. Campo Alegre is the younger relative, made with bush vines of an average age of 40 years, grown on sand and silt soils with large, rounded stones. The wine is aged in new French oak for 14 months – ripe, supple and likeable. Campo Eliseo is the top wine, with vines that are twice as old as those used for Campo Alegre. The owners undoubtedly bring a Bordeaux insight in their approach to the old vine Tempranillo, which is aged for 16–18 months, giving a silky, powerful wine that needs time in the cellar.

Dominio del Bendito

Pza Santo Domingo 8, 49800 Toro
Tel.: +34 980 693 306
www.bodegadominiodelbendito.com

Is there something about French winemakers and Toro? Antony Terryn is one such who travelled the wine regions of the world, but finally ended up in Toro. Toro, he says, gave him the ideal climate and soils, vines on their own rootstocks, some very old vines and a culture of the vine and wine: 'I love these vines of mine, I see them as an inheritance, and I pay homage to the brave *viticultors* from whom I bought them, and to their predecessors, who cared for them before that.' He now has 15 hectares of his own and manages a further 15, all dry-farmed organically.

If you want to learn, it's often best to learn from a convert, an outsider like Terryn, who has become an insider through affection and sheer hard work. He makes three wines with Tinta de Toro which he feels reflect his terroirs best. El Primer Paso, from younger vines, which sees six months in French and American oak; Las Sabias, from old vines, a much more structured approach to Toro; and finally El Titán del Bendito, a wine as bold and generous as its name suggests, from the zone of La Jara. This has a fine undertone of minerality, alongside the powerful fruit.

Don't miss his Dulces Locuras, 'sweet indulgences'. These are not permitted within DO Toro rules. Thus Antojo Rubio is a VdlT Castilla y León, a *capricho*, as he calls it, from a blend of Verdejo, Malvasía, Palomino, Moscatel, Viura and more, which he dries on straw in the autumn, presses in December and ferments in French barriques for 18 months: caramel and spicy, it is delicious. Its partner in crime is La Chispa Negra, a *vino de mesa* made from raisined Tinta de Toro, a rare treat, as Spain has only a few sweet reds.

El Albar Lurton

Camino Magarín s/n, 47529 Vilafranca del Duero
Tel.: +34 983 034 030
www.francoislurton.es

Year by year François Lurton polishes and perfects the wines from the estate, named after the distinctive pine trees in the region. The Albar wines are made in the classic ageing categories of Crianza and so on, and are fresh, with good fruit. The young ones are closed with a screw cap, which is good to see.

Elias Mora

Juan Mora s/n, 47530 San Román de Hornija
Tel.:+34 983 784 029
www.bodegaseliasmora.com

Victoria Benavides' winery is named after the previous owner of her vineyards. She founded the business in 2000 and, between the vineyards she owns and those of the growers she works with, she has 70 hectares at around 800 metres. The distinctive feature of the vineyards is the large pebbles on the surface, which lie over a layer of limestone. 'These young wines in Toro need plenty of tannic oak,' she says, and certainly her young wine with six months in American oak has a bold structure, but it is counteracted by plenty of fruit and the power behind it. Her personal favourite is the Gran Elias Mora, which spends 17 months in French oak. It has a chalky freshness from the soil, and is as elegant as Toro can be. Top wine 2V Premium is a more classical, typical Toro, four-square and structured. Her sweet treat is the Dulce Benavides, made from raisined Tinta de Toro, with three months in French oak; it's wonderfully fresh, despite the richness.

Fariña

Camino del Palo s/n, 49800 Toro
Tel.: +34 980 577 673
www.bodegasfarina.com

Fariña is one of the great names of the early days of Toro, as it was founded in 1942, well before the DO. Bernardo, Manuel's son, and Salvador's grandson, is the third generation in charge. The family took the lead in many areas of viticulture and winemaking, bringing Toro into the twentieth century. If they have been overtaken somewhat by a new generation, then that does not lessen the charm or appeal of their traditional wines. The Colegiata and Gran Colegiata wines are particularly good. Their *maceración carbonica* – a juicy Beaujolais-style youngster – is a welcome spin on the usual Toro styles. Above all, you can be sure of a warm, traditional welcome at Fariña. This is important as a number of wineries, offshoots of projects elsewhere, do not make a priority of wine tourism here.

Liberalia Enológica

Camino del Palo s/n, 49800 Toro
Tel.: +34 980 692 571
www.liberalia.es

Founded in 1996, Liberalia launched its first wines in 2000. They produce a wide portfolio, but they are fairly easy to track as the different wines are numbered Cero, Uno, Dos, Tres, Cuatro, and so on. Juan Antonio Fernández releases the top range with a good number of years' ageing. This ensures that while they are undoubtedly firmly oaked, they are well integrated.

Numanthia

Real s/n, 49882 Valdefinjas
Tel.: +34 980 699 147
www.numanthia.com

The property of the luxury goods giant LVMH, Numanthia produces three powerful, concentrated reds, in particular Numanthia itself and the top wine Termanthia, from pre-phylloxeric vines, all of them 100 per cent Tinta de Toro. The godfather of these exceptional wines is Rioja's Marcos Eguren, for Numanthia was an Eguren property from its first vintage in 1998 until 2008. The foundation of the wines which built the reputation of Toro is of course the vineyard. The business manages 83 hectares of old vineyards, 200 parcels in all. The estate has many pre-phylloxeric vines, and the vineyard age is from 30 to 140 years. The low yields guarantee concentration and power.

The winery is named after the city near here that famously withstood the Roman legions. It is also the name of the estate wine, which is made from vines aged between 60 and 100 years and has 18 months of ageing in French oak. It is silky, powerful, generously black-fruited, with exceptionally refined oak, and very elegant – Toro tamed. Termes is the wine from younger vineyards (30–50 years old); while fresh, it is also boldly oaky. The top wine, Termanthia, comes from 140-year-old vines of the 4.8 hectare Teso Los Carriles vineyard. Hand destemmed and foot trodden, the wine is aged in 200 per cent new French oak (that is to say, new barrels for each of two years). This is an intensely powerful wine that needs bottle age and cellaring.

In 2017, in a partnership of the utmost luxuriousness, consumers were offered the chance to purchase a barrel wrapped in leather from the equally luxurious Spanish leather fashion house Loewe. For €95,000 (US$120,000) the buyer could have the wine equivalent of the capacity of the barrel – 300 bottles – in any size from 75 centilitres through to 12-litre Balthazars. They could also choose the tint colour of the leather, which would be inlaid with the purchaser's initials.

Pintia

Ctra de Morales s/n, 47530 San Román de Hornija
Tel.: +34 983 680 147
www.vega-sicilia.com

Vega Sicilia acquired the property, formerly known as Alquiriz, in 1997, and with it 45 hectares of vineyard. They now have 96 hectares at 700 metres, mainly ungrafted bush vines, with an average vine age of 35 years. They launched their first vintage from the estate in 2001. The wine undergoes malolactic in 70 per cent French oak barrels, with 25 per cent American and 5 per cent Hungarian. The style is altogether Vega Sicilia, but it's also Toro: bold, a little rustic. Give it time to calm down in the bottle.

Rodríguez Sanzo

Tel.: +34 983 150 150
www.rodriguezsanzo.com

A name to follow. The enthusiastic Javier Rodríguez makes wines almost everywhere. That's to say: Bierzo, Jumilla, Navarra, Priorat, Rías Baixas, Ribera del Duero, Rioja, Rueda, Toro, VdlT Castilla y León, and the list may have grown by the time you read this. His wines in Toro can be oaky, but there is always something new and interesting to look out for, recently including a Garnacha project. My latest favourite is Las Tierras de Javier Rodríguez Original; great value, and from vines planted in 1945. A surprise was Tras la Yesca, that's to say a wine made from vines rescued from the trunk disease Esca, known as Yesca in Spanish.

San Román

Ctra N122 Km 411, 47112 Villaester
Tel.: +34 983 784 118
www.bodegasanroman.com

The García family's footprint spreads wide across Castilla y León. Father Mariano spent three decades in Vega Sicilia before moving over to Aalto. He set up Mauro, just outside the Ribera del Duero border, where his sons joined him, and Garmón is the latest family launch, also in Ribera del Duero.

The Toro project, founded in 1997, enabled Mariano García to explore a new zone, and to approach Toro winemaking in a more modern way, expressing fruit and minerality. He began in 1995 by researching the old vineyard plots in the north-east of the DO. The family now has 100 hectares, mainly Tinta de Toro with some Garnacha. The soils range from a fine, sandy loam to a more structured clay soil covered with pebbles. Three wines are made in the technically pristine and carefully planned winery. It may not be a glamorous structure but García has a fine selection of vats in different materials to charm the wine geek.

San Román draws on a selection from the different parcels which are each vinified separately, with 22–25 months in barrel, while the younger Primo has 85 per cent Tempranillo with Garnacha and 'others' (which is to say, varieties not yet recognized by the DO). French and American oak is used for ageing in both wines with only 20 per cent new each year. The style is to control the oak, and to aim for elegance. However García has never been afraid of a bold wine, and there's plenty of character here.

The latest wine in the line-up – the launch vintage, 2012, was released in 2017 – bears a historic name, Cartago (Carthage), and comes from a single vineyard, Paraje del Pozo. Here, beside the Duero river, there's a vineyard of 45-year-old ungrafted vines at 700 metres. The grapes for Cartago are selected from the vines at the freshest and highest parts of the 5-hectare vineyard. They are destemmed, which enhances the richness, and the wine is rounded and finished with 36 months in new and used French oak. This Gran Reserva style looks to be a very promising, almost classical, addition to the range.

Teso La Monja

Ctra Toro-Valdefinjas Km 6.3, Paraje Valdebuey, 49882 Valdefinjas
Tel.: +34 980 568 143
www.sierracantabria.com

The Eguren family of Rioja's Sierra Cantabria sold Numanthia to LVMH in 2007. As testament to the attraction of Toro and its vineyards, they are back with Teso la Monja, working across a patchwork of parcels of vines. Based on their long experience here, they have now prioritized cooler soils, with north-facing aspects giving longer growing cycles, to emphasize freshness. The youngest vines go into the energetic, full-flavoured Romanic and Admires, those aged over 45 go into Victorian and those ungrafted vines that are 100 or more years old, into Alabaster and Teso la Monja. With these they have been able to provide a wider and more accessible range of wines than with Numanthia. With 100 hectares they also have more vineyards to draw upon.

The winery is a geek's delight with a choice of vats for fermentation, enabling foot-treading. Everything is designed for careful extraction and greater elegance. The young wines spend six months in barrel, Victorino and Alabaster 18 months. Alabaster has all the power of Toro, but wrapped in very fine oak, and exceptionally polished. It will continue to blossom in the bottle.

Teso la Monja, the newest arrival, is the ambitiously priced top of the range wine. The attention to detail is exacting: the grapes are hand destemmed; after fermentation in an open-topped vat, the malolactic takes place in one of the treasures of the wine world, an egg-shaped vat made from oak. While concrete eggs have become popular for the way the liquid moves inside, keeping the wine in contact with the lees, French barrel specialists Taransaud are up for everything, and their oak eggs are beautifully made. However because of their cost, these oak eggs are rare in wineries, except the best ones. Here at Teso la Monja, the investment is all the greater as the egg is only used for the malolactic. After that the wine spends two years in French oak barrels.

Anyone who loves the precision of the Eguren Rioja wines will be fascinated by the elegance they find in their Toro wines, despite the muscularity of the region and its terroir.

On the radar

Compañía de Vinos Telmo Rodríguez
www.telmorodriguez.com
The Compañía de Vinos Telmo Rodríguez makes three wines in Toro. The youngest, Dehesa Gago, sees no oak; Gago has 14 months in oak of different sizes; and the top wine, Pago La Jara, is a special selection, fermented in vat, and aged in French oak, of different sizes and ages.

Estancia Piedra
www.estanciapiedra.com
This extensive estate outside Toro was founded in the late 1990s.

Finca Sobreño
www.sobreno.com
This lively family winery with a strong export-oriented commercial outlook produces reliable, well-priced wines.

Matsu Wines

www.bodegamatsu.com

The Riojano group Vintae is behind these wines, which have become very popular because of their labels. Each one has a warts and all portrait of a man, as bold and demanding as the wines themselves, and the climate that helped form them.

Máquina & Tabla

www.maquina-tabla.com

Husband and wife, oenologist and designer/marketeer, Oriol & Susana make wines in Gredos, Bierzo and Castilla y León. Páramos de Nicasia is named after the old lady, Nicasia, who owns the vineyard. As befits a Toro, it is rich, bold and structured.

Ordóñez

www.jorgeordonezselections.com

The established importer of Spanish wines into the US, Jorge Ordóñez, has wineries across Spain. The Toro wines are particularly good: Tritón and Vatan are both exceptionally well made, polished, contemporary Toros, with a good gulp of alcohol and plenty of oak, and the Tritón is great value.

Rejadorada

www.rejadorada.com

Producers of good value classics. Bravo and Sango are the two top reds.

Vetus

www.bodegasvetus.com

There is a bold, structured Toro; Flor de Vetus and Celsus are the top wines.

VINO DE LA TIERRA CASTILLA Y LEÓN

VdlT Castilla y León is the largest wine region of Spain, and the third largest in Europe. It covers the northern half of the central Iberian plateau; Castilla-La Mancha covers the south part, and is known as VdlT Castilla. Castilla y León became a VdlT in 2000 but it has a long history in winemaking. In medieval times, the Cistercian monks were particularly important in building the quality of the winemaking in the region. However the boom came to a sudden halt when Felipe II moved the court from Valladolid to Madrid, and built El Escorial. The demand for wine dried up. The river Duero is fundamental to the region, running across the border to become the Douro not far away in Portugal. Vines are planted on the fertile river banks and up on the windy *páramos* or plateaus. In general the weather is extreme, cold in winter, scorching in summer, with low rainfall.

Despite this, Richard Ford was enthusiastic, noting: 'The very important kingdom of León, because lying out of the hacknied track of travellers, is not visited as it deserves. It abounds with sites of unrivalled military interest; the painted sculpture is of the first class; the scenery in the Vierzo [Bierzo] and Sierras is magnificent, and the fishing excellent. The chief cities, Salamanca, Valladolid and León, are full of architectural and artistical interest.'

Producers

Abadía Retuerta

Ctra Nacional 122 Km 332.5, 47340 Sardón de Duero
Tel.: +34 983 680 314
www.abadia-retuerta.com

Luxury, your name is Abadía Retuerta! The twelfth-century abbey beside the Duero and next door to Vega Sicilia has been turned into a hotel and spa of the utmost luxury. Once you have stayed there and been given your own personal butler, nothing else quite measures up (though, to be strictly honest, I never called him as I was far too embarrassed and British to do so. And when everything you could possibly want is already in your bedroom, who needs to ask for anything from a butler?). The hotel – Le Domaine – is a destination in itself. The added bonus is a Michelin starred restaurant, and the wines.

The great abbey, one of several convent–fortresses constructed in Castile, was founded in 1143. It is now owned by the Swiss pharmaceutical company Novartis, who have the deep pockets to make the exceptional investment. The estate is huge, 700 hectares rising from the Duero to 850 metres, with woodland and wildlife areas, and tucked inside is 180 hectares of vineyard land at 725–850 metres. Terroir expert

Professor Vicente Sotés did the original soil study in 1992–3, identifying the diversity of soils. The vines were planted in the early 1990s and are now managed in 54 plots, which produce blends as well as single vineyard wines. Tempranillo makes up 70 per cent of the vineyard area. The great benefit of being outside the Ribera del Duero DO is that they can work with Syrah (10 per cent) as well as Petit Verdot, Sauvignon Blanc and experimental varieties such as Touriga Nacional, Tinta de Toro, Sangiovese, Nebbiolo, Riesling, Gewürztraminer, which could prove promising. The winemaking consultant was and remains Pascal Delbeck, a long-time adviser in Bordeaux. He works with Ángel Anocíbar, the winemaker, who has been at the winery since the first vintage in 1996.

The range has changed over the years. Today the most interesting wines are certainly the single vineyard ones, particularly Pago Garduña Syrah, Pago Valdebellón Cabernet Sauvignon, and the much-improved Pago Negralada Tempranillo. The Petit Verdot is a rarity in Spain and well made. They have had great success with Le Domaine, a blend of Sauvignon Blanc (80 per cent) with Verdejo and Godello, and five months in French oak. Individual, thoughtfully blended, enjoyable. It's particularly appealing when the next-door DO still does not recognize white wines.

Barco del Corneta

Impresores 5, Medina del Campo
Tel.: +34 655 890 949
www.barcodelcorneta.com

Beatriz Herranz Sanz founded her winery in 2008. She had been working to seek out old Garnachas for La Fábula, a 4 Monos project in Cebreros. She subsequently returned to her grandfather's old vines in La Seca, a town at the heart of Rueda wines. In 2013 she found some very old vines at 770 metres which she believes are around 150 years old; the Palomino she found there she uses for Bruto (below). She remarks that the old clones of Verdejo she discovered have nothing to do with the new commercial clone selections in Rueda. She makes her Verdejo in 300-litre barrels, keeping it on the lees for nine months. Cucú is her entry-level wine, made with some of her own and some bought-in grapes, fermented in stainless steel.

Her latest project is a revival of Juan García, the local variety of Arribes del Duero in Zamora. These are 80-year-old vines grown on a granite and quartz soil at 670 metres. This is a Vino de Mesa. She also makes a trio of delightfully named and fascinating whites from Rueda's traditional varieties, Bruto (from Palomino), Judas (Viura) and Casio (Verdejo). Bruto is made under a veil of *flor* yeast, like a fino Sherry, though the effect is lighter and more delicate (and unfortified). Her Judas, as unpopular with many wine drinkers as the biblical figure himself, is surprisingly appealing. Not warm, but linear and fresh. Casio is a taste of the old Verdejo, a different style to today's, helped by fermentation and ageing in larger oak barrels. Altogether a very promising enterprise.

Belondrade

Quinta San Diego, Camino de Puerto s/n, 474891 La Seca
Tel.: +34 983 481 001
www.belondrade.com

Didier Belondrade of Rueda makes two wines in his winery that appear under the Castilla y León DO. Both are named after his daughters. Quinta Apolonia is a blend of two Verdejos, one of which is fermented in stainless steel, while the other spends three months on lees. Quinta Clarisa is the bodega's *rosado*, made from Tempranillo.

Comando G Viticultores

Avda de la Constitución 23, 228640 Cadalso de los Vidrios
Tel.: +34 918 640 602
info@comandog.es

The trendiest of the new-wave Garnachistas is Comando G. It was launched in 2008 by Daniel Gómez Jiménez-Landi, Fernando García Alonso and Marc Isart who had all studied winemaking together. They focused on Garnacha from Gredos, so choosing the name of a favourite television programme from their childhood for the brand was obvious. In due course Isart left to focus on Bernabeleva, his winery in Vinos de Madrid.

Sierra de Gredos is a treasure trove of old vine Garnachas, and there is a tapestry of villages to locate and to interpret, exploring the soils and styles. Telmo Rodríguez showed many the way, including García, who worked for him at one time. They are influenced by Burgundian winemaking, and by the Burgundian classification structure from *village* to *premier cru* wines. The portfolio includes a wide range of vineyard expressions in Méntrida as well as VdlT Castilla y León. In the latter VdlT, Rumbo al Norte is grown at 1,150 metres amid rocks and boulders, on granitic soils, with a round expression of fruit. Tumba del Rey Moro, which is very pure in style, is a single vineyard wine made from pre-phylloxeric vines scattered amid the trees.

Compañia de Vinos Telmo Rodríguez

El Monte s/n, 01308 Lanciego
Tel.: +34 945 628 315
www.telmorodriguez.com

Cebreros is Telmo Rodríguez' stamping ground in the south part of Castilla y León. What attracted him were the slate and granite soils of this traditional viticultural area, where farmers still use horses to work the vineyards. In particular, the lures were the slate-strewn slope of the Arrebatacapas mountain which dominates Cebreros, with vineyards that rise to 1,200 metres, and the quality of the Garnacha bush vines.

Rodríguez was one of the early arrivals, back in 1999, though the region has been discovered by others since. They produce two wines here, a fascinating pair. Pegaso Barrancos de Pizarra is from the slate soils; Barrancos de Granito is from granite. Pizarra has a pure, limpid, saline character; Granito is bold, lively, spicy and, yes, perhaps a little stony.

Dehesa La Granja

Real 2, 47315 Pesquera de Duero
Tel.: +34 983 870 037
www.grupopesquera.com

Whichever of Alejandro Fernández' properties you visit, be sure to call in at the shop. They will naturally be selling wine, but you also need to shop for the excellent products from Dehesa La Granja: the chickpeas are very good, and the olive oil. The place is a farm with an on-site restaurant where you can enjoy the home-grown produce.

Fernández acquired the estate in 1998. It is just outside the Toro DO, and almost 850 hectares in size, including 150 hectares of Tempranillo. One of its striking features is the maze of underground cellars used for the winery, which were excavated by hand between 1750 and 1767. These are testament to the long history of winemaking in this region. Over time Fernández has introduced old-vine clones of Tempranillo from his Ribera del Duero vineyards. Here his daughter Eva makes two wines, both 100 per cent Tempranillo. Dehesa La Granja is aged in American oak and released with at least five years of ageing. The Selección is the top wine, with no less than thirty months in French oak and 6–10 years in the cellar. These are bold, traditional wines, which develop well with the bottle age of their choice, since they don't need to follow classic Reserva categories.

Daniel Landi Viticultor

Avda de la Constitución 23, 28640 Cadalso de los Vidrios
Tel.: +34 918 640 602
info@danilandi.com

Dani Landi has been a leader in the Garnacha transformation in Spain in recent years, alongside a handful others. Spain has claimed back its rightful reputation as a producer of top class Garnacha, though in a number of styles depending on the terroir and climate. Landi started on the Garnacha path in his family's winery in Méntrida and then branched out in 2012. He has consolidated his reputation with his wines from the Sierra de Gredos, grown on quartz and clay, schist and slate, and with Comando G (see p. 139). Las Iruelas is from a plot at 1,000 metres, a complex blend of granite, slate, schist and quartz soils. The style is, as always with his wines, elegant with a long, dense finish. El Reventón is slate through and through, from a tiny vineyard at 900 metres. Fermented in open vats, and aged in a foudre and barrels it is superbly aromatic and structured. Biodynamic.

Mauro

Cervantes 12, 47320 Tudela de Duero
Tel.: +34 983 521 972
www.bodegasmauro.com

Founded in 1978, when the lines were drawn for the new Ribera del Duero DO, Mauro fell just outside what was to become the DO Ribera de Duero. This was in spite of the fact that the quality of the vineyards from Tudela del Duero was recognized as far back as Felipe II in 1562. Mariano García, formerly of Vega Sicilia now of Aalto, Garmón and San Román, named the winery after his father. The winery reflects the history of the vineyards – a seventeenth-century house, naturally enough in Calle Cervantes.

García now works with his sons, and they have begun to introduce biodynamic farming. They make four wines from their 80 hectares, three of them red: Mauro, Mauro Vendimia Seleccionada (VS), and Terreus. They benefit from being just outside the DO, with the flexibility that gives. Thus, for instance, Mauro is Tempranillo with a dash of Syrah.

The VS is 100 per cent Tempranillo. The top wine, Terreus, comes from a small (3 hectare) parcel of Tempranillo. García's wines are full of power and energy, a signature wherever he works.

The Godello, the newest wine, is from Bierzo fruit, and sold as Castilla y León. It is rich, textured and spicy, from eight months on lees in used French oak.

Ossian

Cordel de las Merinas s/n, 40447 Nieva
Tel.: +34 983 878 020

Ossian, the winery's eponymous wine, has been in its time one of Spain's great white wines, confounding those who believe Verdejo can only be a commercial beverage. The winery was launched by local viticulturist Ismael Gozalo, and Javier Zaccagnini, now of Aalto and formerly managing director of the CRDO Ribera del Duero. They made outstanding wines from the historic pre-phylloxeric Verdejo vines which had outlived phylloxera because of the sandy soils. The wines had a striking freshness. It was the first winery to receive organic certification in Rueda. Both men felt that the rules of the DO prevented them from making the best wine, which is why they chose to make their wines VdlT Castilla y León.

The business is now owned by the Pago de Carraovejas winery, which bought out Zaccagnini and latterly Gozalo, who still continues to sell grapes to his former business. Ossian remains a wine of absolutely singing purity. Amongst the other wines in the line-up they have Verdling, which is Verdejo, but made like a Riesling, in *trocken* and *dulce* styles. The classics are Ossian itself and Capitel, both barrel-fermented giving a subtle complexity.

Prieto Pariente

Ctra de Rueda Km 2.5, 47491 La Seca
Tel.: +34 983 816 484
www.prietopariente.com

Not to be confused with Prieto Picudo – the grape variety – or indeed with José Pariente, the highly rated Rueda Verdejo producer run by Victoria Pariente. This particular business is run by Victoria's children Martina and Ignacio, and they make a great team. Ignacio is in charge of the business, while Martina is the winemaker. Family businesses are never easy, especially when the parent is as well known as Victoria is. But Martina has a clear vision of their brand. The wines are intended to be a reflection of Castilla y León. She also specializes in red wines, while Victoria is known for whites.

The wines from Valladolid grapes are sourced from the *páramos* well known for their quality: Mucientes, Pedrosa del Rey and Valbuena de Duero. El Origen is Tempranillo with 20 per cent Garnacha and 5 per cent Cabernet Sauvignon. La Provincia, as the name suggests, is all about the character of the province of Valladolid; it is 55 per cent Tempranillo with the rest Garnacha from vineyards planted between 1941 and 1955. Particularly exciting is Los Confines, which comes from two old vineyards in the Sierra de Gredos, one in Cebreros and the other in San Bartolomé de Pinares. It reflects the slate and granite soils of the two sites. A very different expression from the wines of Valladolid, it is taut and elegant. Finally in the line-up is a Viognier, discovered in a small vineyard in the *páramos*. A bit of a rarity in these parts, it could so easily be fat and overly ripe. Quite the opposite turns out to be the case: this is no more than 13% abv, only partly oaked and very refreshing, with a zesty, pink grapefruit character. Overall an enterprising project and one to follow.

Quinta Sardonia

47329 Sardón de Duero
Tel.: +34 983 032 883
www.terrasgauda.com

Quinta Sardonia is another of the Ribera del Duero anomalies, as it is just 2 kilometres outside the DO boundary. It has a number of features of a great site, most importantly, the 22 hectares of biodynamically farmed vineyards are on steep slopes with different aspects, unlike so many of the vineyards on the flat within Ribera del Duero. The Tinto Fino planted in 1998 came from the Pingus vineyards (for Peter Sisseck of Pingus was behind this project). Sardón is the latest wine. In addition there is 22 per cent of Cabernet Sauvignon in the vineyard, and smaller amounts of Merlot, Syrah, Petit Verdot, Cabernet Franc and Malbec. The land is divided up into 18 different soils, which forms the basis for winemaking, each of the soils receiving different handling and compost. The winemaker is Jerome Bougnaud. He makes three wines: Sardón, which is the entry level; QS2 which has the distinctive character of the Cabernet Sauvignon used; and Quinta Sardonia, which is a blend of all the varieties, and very elegant in style.

In 2010 it was acquired by the Terras Gauda group from Rías Baixas, which also owns Pittacum in Bierzo.

ARLANZA

Arlanza at a glance

Grape varieties

White: Albillo, Viura
Red: Tempranillo, Garnacha, Mencía

Size

Vineyard: 400 hectares
Growers: 300
Wineries: 16

One of Spain's newest DOs, this was created, like Arribes (see p. 145), in 2007, though winegrowing dates back many centuries. It lies between Palencia and Burgos, and the Arlanza river flows through it. The phylloxera outbreak with its consequent destruction of employment prompted mass emigration. More recently the wine business has revived. Some wines are still rustic and oaky, with tough tannins, but the best show a promising freshness.

On the radar

Bodegas Lerma
www.tintolerma.com

Monte Amán
www.monteaman.com

Olivier Rivière

www.olivier-riviere.com

Working in Rioja and Navarra as well as Arlanza, Rivière is making exceptional wines. He has four wines here at present. El Cadastro is a village wine, his single vineyard wine is El Quemado and La Vallada is made with bought-in grapes. In addition he has one white wine not produced every year from Albillo Real scattered among the other vines.

Sabinares

sabinares@sabinares.com

This is a joint project by four friends, two of whom – David González and Juan Antonio Leza – are otherwise to be found at Gómez Cruzado in Rioja. They are exploring the specific characteristics of the Covarrubias sub-zone, with limestone soils at 900–1,000 metres.

ARRIBES

Arribes at a glance

Grape varieties

White: Malvasía, Verdejo, Albillo

Red: Bruñal, Juan García, Rufete, Tempranillo; also permitted Mencía, Garnacha

Size

Vineyard: 360 hectares

Growers: 280

Wineries: 15

The dramatic Arribes is a small, but up-and-coming name, a land of rugged gorges in the Arribes national park. The vineyards lie between 550 and 820 metres along the banks of the Duero between Zamora and Salamanca, on the Spanish side of the border with Portugal around the town of Fermoselle. It became a DO in 2007. The soils are sandy, with quartz, some granite and also slate. When Arribes was hit by phylloxera, as in so many regions it resulted in major emigration to

South America. Slowly the people and the wine culture are returning. Vines were replanted on rootstocks in due course, and this ensured the continuation of local varieties, particularly Juan García, Malvasía and Bruñal.

Producers

Almaroja

Las Fontanicas 35, 49220 Fermoselle
Tel.: +34 691 916 260
www.almaroja.es

Englishwoman Charlotte Allen, by a circuitous route of winemaking in the Loire with Noël Pinguet at Domaine Huet, and Martin Meinert in South Africa, arrived here on the strong recommendation of a friend working in Rueda. She has 12 hectares and an underground cellar, like so many in the district, and works with a range of local varieties. The wines are fresh and lively, like the woman herself.

Arribes del Duero

Ctra Masueco s/n, 37251 Corporario
Tel.: +34 923 169 195
www.bodegasarribesdelduero.com

Here, they make bright, juicy, young wines for drinking now. Some are named Vettonia after the Vettones who were the original residents.

Hacienda Zorita Natural Reserve

Ctra Zamora-Fermoselle Km 56, 49220 Fermoselle
Tel.: +34 980 613 163
www.haciendas-espana.com

This is part of the Marqués de la Concordia group (including Lagunilla and Federico Paternina in Rioja and Hacienda Zorita in Ribera del Duero, as well as a hotel and restaurant, and an organic farm). New Zealand viticultural expert Richard Smart was the vineyard consultant here. He advised planting Syrah, among others, in the vineyard, which sits at 800 metres. The Natural Reserve Syrah is a bold, well-oaked wine, with a polished, ripe finish.

La Setera

Portugal 7, 49232 Fornillos de Fermoselle
Tel.: +34 980 612 925
www.lasetera.com

A family business in the village, this is named after the river that flows down into the Duero. Run by Sara Groves-Raines, Francisco José Martínez and their children, La Setera was founded as a dairy in 1993, with the winery added a decade later. Their intention, as one-time city-dwellers, was to work within the landscape and support the local economy and culture. Their production of wines and goats' cheeses is artisan, small scale. Seek out their 100 per cent Touriga Nacional, and the Tinaja Varietales – made from Juan García, Mencía, Rufete, Tinta Madrid, Bruñal and Bastardillo.

VINO DE CALIDAD SIERRA DE SALAMANCA

VC Sierra de Salamanca at a glance

Grape varieties

White: Viura, Moscatel de Grano Menudo, Palomino
Red: Rufete, Garnacha (known as Calabrés), Tempranillo (known as Aragonés)

Size

Wineries: 5

Sierra de Salamanca is in the southern part of the province of Salamanca and takes in no less than 26 villages. Part of Sierra de Salamanca is inside the Natural Park of Las Batuecas, and the whole zone is a UNESCO biosphere. Wine has been here for two millennia – there are remains of pre-Romanic *lagares* in the region.

The vineyards range in altitude from 400 metres to almost 1,000. The climate is humid with Mediterranean influences, much less extreme than other parts of Castilla y León, with hot summers, but wet springs and autumns. The soils are very diverse, ranging from sandy and granitic soil to clay shales and some slate. The Rufete grape, a speciality, makes very drinkable reds.

On the radar

Cámbrico
www.cambrico.com

Compañía de Vinos la Zorra
www.vinoslazorra.es
An energetic team with a lively range of wines from vineyards dating back to 1925.

TIERRA DE LEÓN

Tierra de León at a glance

Grape varieties
White: Verdejo, Albarín, Godello
Red: Prieto Picudo, Mencía
Rosado: *Rosados* must be made of at least 60 per cent Prieto Picudo or Mencía

Size
Vineyard: 1,413 hectares
Growers: 500
Wineries: 34

This is one of the most southerly DOs in Castilla y León, and one of the more recent, created in 2007. Prieto Picudo is what really sets it apart, as it does VC Valles de Benavente. Raúl Pérez, the *viticultor* and winemaker from Bierzo who campaigns for local varieties and traditional winemaking methods, and works with Margón (see below), expressed his frustration to me at the rapid loss of vineyards in Tierra de León. The frustration verged on outrage as he spelled out the radical shrinkage of the vine heritage: 'They have reduced from 20,000 hectares to less than 2,000 today.' The changes in the region are remarkable: in 1984 León had 14,000 hectares of vineyards, while Ribera del Duero only had 3,000.

Wine has long been important here. Not only did the thirsty pilgrims on the Camino de Santiago pass this way, it also lies on the much-travelled path of the Ruta de la Plata, the silver route, which ran from the silver mines in the north down to the port of Cádiz.

The vineyards are on alluvial terraces with limestone and brown rocks, at around 800–900 metres. The climate is continental, with frosts and fog in winter, and hot summers, though the temperature never falls below -15°C or exceeds 20°C.

Producers

Leyenda del Páramo

Ctra de León s/n, Paraje el Cueto, 24230 Valdevimbre
Tel.: +34 987 050 039
www.leyendadelparamo

Launched in 2010 by a group of seven people led by Pedro González Mittelbrunn, to revive Prieto Picudo. The focus has been on buying vineyards of centenarian Prieto Picudo. The name comes from the high, windy plateau, or *páramo*, where the vines grow. At Leyenda they also work with the white variety Albarín Blanco, of which only 100 hectares of old vines are extant. Underlying the work of the winery is a strong commitment to sustainability. Visitors can take a tour which will explain their organic treatments in the vineyards, and their policy of using geothermal energy and solar panels. Wines are well made and fresh; the lightly oaked styles are my personal preference.

Margón

Avda de Valencia de Don Juan s/n, 24209 Pajares de los Oteros
Tel.: +34 987 750 800
www.bodegasmargon.com

The bodega specializes in Prieto Picudo, working with centenarian vineyards. The brand is Pricum. The Bierzo winemaker Raúl Pérez works with them, and his influence can be seen in the winery: gravity fed, fermentation in French oak vats not stainless steel and a range of cooperages for the barrels. They also make a white with Albarín.

Pardevalles

Ramón y Cajal 22, 24230 Valdevimbre
Tel.: +34 987 304 222
www.pardevalles.es

Pardevalles' heritage is one of the historic underground caves, excavated some 300 years ago, where the wines are now aged in French and American oak. The business was founded in 1949, and today the second and third generations run the estate, specializing in Prieto Picudo and Albarín Blanco. The most interesting are the red and white single varietal pair, Carroleón. The red has two years in oak; the white five months on its lees in French oak.

TIERRA DEL VINO DE ZAMORA

Tierra del Vino de Zamora at a glance

Grape varieties

White: Malvasía, Moscatel de Grano Menudo, Verdejo; also permitted Albillo, Palomino, Godello

Red: Tempranillo (often known as Tinta Madrid), with Cabernet Sauvignon, Garnacha

Size

Vineyard: 647 hectares
Growers: 190
Wineries: 10

Tierra del Vino de Zamora is one of the last staging posts before Portugal for the River Duero. In medieval times it too had an important role as a producer and exporter of wine. As the Duero travels west, the climate across the vineyards has become a little warmer, and a little less extreme. In Tierra del Vino de Zamora the vineyards are at about 750 metres and the oldest vines are about 60 years. The soils are alluvial, sandy and pebbly.

Producer

Viñas del Cénit

Ctra de Circunvalación s/n, 49708 Villanueva de Campeán
Tel.: +34 980 569 346
www.vinasdelcenit.com

My abiding memory of Cénit is of my boots sinking into the exceptionally fine, deep sand, as I walked to look at the bush vines. Bush vines plus sand is a strong combination, generally ensuring old vines, ones which phylloxera was unable to reach. That's the case with Cénit, where they are able to draw on plenty of old vines. The sand is explained by the fact that three small rivers used to run through the area; what remains is fine sediment, as well as rounded cobblestones on the surface. The younger vines are around 35 years old; the oldest date back 150–180 years. The clone of Tempranillo here, Tinta Madrid, is, they say, a bold one like those of Toro, but with the elegance of Ribera del Duero. The style is savoury, with coffee, liquorice and spice, while Toro has a bolder, black fruit character.

The winery, founded in 2006, is part of the Avanteselecta group (Óbalo, Rioja; Viña Nora, Rías Baixas; Pazos del Rey, Monterrei; Naia, Rueda; Atalayas de Golbán and Dominio de Atauta, Ribera del Duero; Álvaro Domecq, Jerez).

VINO DE CALIDAD VALLES DE BENAVENTE

VC Valles de Benavente at a glance

Grape varieties

White: Verdejo, Malvasía

Red: Tempranillo, Prieto Picudo, Mencía, with Garnacha and Cabernet Sauvignon as complementary varieties.

Size

Wineries: 6

Valles de Benavente is rightly proud of its history. Documents mentioning the wine go back as far as 1274. Then in 1338, a document of King Alfonso XI mentions the great quantity of wine produced in the region, and its importance to the townspeople both for drinking and for its export value to Asturias and Galicia. The same document gives the people a royal privilege not to permit other wines from outside to be allowed into Benavente.

The terrain varies – in the north it is fairly flat, typical of the *meseta*. In the south-east it ranges from gentle slopes to clay-based plains. In terms of climate, the region is dry with very cold winters and hot summers, ranging from -15 to 40°C. The region specializes in Prieto Picudo, and in particular *rosados* made from the variety. These are pretty wines, with good, crisp acidity.

The wineries include **Otero** (www.bodegasotero.es), which started life, typically of many parts of Spain, as a producer of bulk wine (not bottled), in 1906. What's particularly interesting about their range today is the Prieto Picudo *rosado*.

VINO DE CALIDAD VALTIENDAS

Lying to the north of Segovia province, this borders Ribera del Duero on its north-east edge.

VC Valtiendas at a glance

Grape varieties
White: Albillo
Red: Tempranillo dominates, with a little Cabernet Sauvignon, Syrah, Merlot, Garnacha

Size
Wineries: 6
The vineyards lie at about 900 metres on sandy clay and pebbly soils.

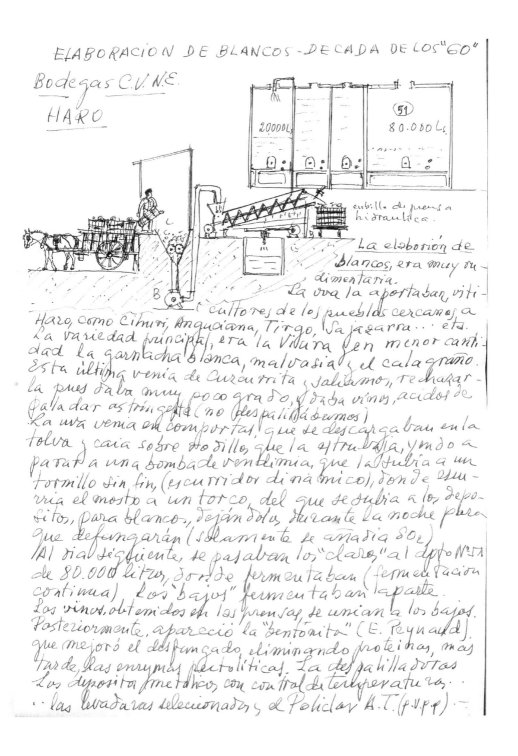

'How we made white wine in Rioja in the 1960s': drawn for CVNE's current winemaker María Larrea by her predecessor Ezequiel García. He says 'it was very rudimentary'. Near the end he lists the later innovations that made life easier, such as bentonite for fining, stainless steel tanks and temperature control.

Left: Rioja has a long history – Javier Hidalgo, far from his home in Sanlúcar de Barrameda, showing the tenth- and eleventh-century necropolis in the beautiful grounds of Remelluri, officially La Granja Nuestra Señora de Remelluri.

Below: Bárbara Palacios makes Barbarot, a Tempranillo with some Merlot. No surprise then, that her regular companion at work in the vineyard, definitely the most famous of Rioja's winery dogs, is called Merlot.

Above: A great combination of traditional amphoras and modern technology makes for fine wines at Sandra Bravo's Sierra de Toloño winery in Villabuena de Álava

Right: Victoria Pariente's wines from Rueda are all about attention to detail, right down to the meticulous pipework for her concrete eggs. (There are more eggs and oak vats out of shot.)

Above: Typically Rías Baixas: the view from Vionta winery over the *minifundia* to the islands and inlets.

Left: Rías Baixas at work: pulling up the ropes on which the mussels grow. In the background, wine consultant Dominique Roujou de Boubée steps across the pontoon.

Above: Garnacha specialist Norrel Robertson MW works in some magical sites. Here in Calatayud's Ribota valley, the Sierra de Armantes looms in the background; foreground are his 80-year-old Garnacha vines, grown on red clay with limestone.

Below: This is the painstaking work of reviving old vine Garnacha: note the rocks propping up the vine to the left. Fernando Mora MW in Valdejalon.

SOIL MAP

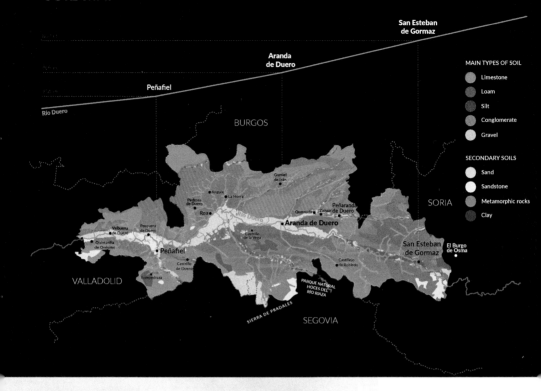

MAIN TYPES OF SOIL
- Limestone
- Loam
- Silt
- Conglomerate
- Gravel

SECONDARY SOILS
- Sand
- Sandstone
- Metamorphic rocks
- Clay

Above: The complexity and potential of Ribera del Duero's soils. Based on data from Bodegas y Viñedos Alnardo, Instituto Geológico y Minero de España and Centro Nacional de Información Geográfica.

Left: Txakoli country: green vineyards and the sea. In the distance to the right, Txomin Etxaniz winery.

Above: Manuel Moldes of Fulcro in Sanxenxo, Rías Baixas: he's recuperating these Espadeiro (red) vines, which are around 200 years old.

Right: A Godello vine in one of Rafael Palacios' vineyards in Valdeorras. Note the amount of hand work required: each vine needs supporting struts, and straw carefully spread out each year.

Above: An impressive *hórreo*, a traditional Galician store for corn.

Left: Lynne Coyle MW learning the art of 'wine tonging' at Marqués de Riscal.

Below: A taste of spring in Navarra.

VINO DE ESPAÑA

Across Spain there are producers choosing to step outside the local DO, for a number of reasons. Some have to, because the grape varieties they use are not currently permitted within the DO; others prefer the freedom of making their own rules. A few also prefer not to be associated with their local DO for marketing reasons, if they feel that its reputation does not add value. Vinos de España is a useful umbrella in that case.

Microbio

Pza de la Iglesia 7, 40447 Nieva
Tel.: +34 626 267 430
www.microbiowines.com

Ismael Gozalo describes himself using the French term, as a 'vigneron indépendant' and is based in Nieva, well-known for its wonderful old heritage Verdejos. His family was connected to Viñedos de Nieva, which had outstanding Verdejos from pre-phylloxeric bush vines that had escaped the phylloxera louse because of the sandy soils. Nieva is now owned by the Martúe group. Gozalo went on to set up Ossian (see p. 142) with Javier Zaccagnini of Aalto – which they did with great success. In due course both moved on, and now Gozalo runs his own winery.

There are two ranges, the Ismael Gozalo wines, and Microbio. The Microbio range features his unsulphured wines, from natural winemaking using old vines, including a pét nat, naturally sparkling. Among the range is Isse, which comes from a vineyard planted in 1868 at 915 metres. It's fermented in *tinajas*, clay pots, and then spends a year settling in stainless steel. It's worth reading his website; he describes the wines and his philosophy in detail. He also makes a wine – Pirata – with Benjamin Romeo of Rioja's Contador. It's a blend of white grapes from San Vicente de la Sonsierra with Verdejo from Nieva. No wonder it's easiest for him to classify his wines as Vino de España.

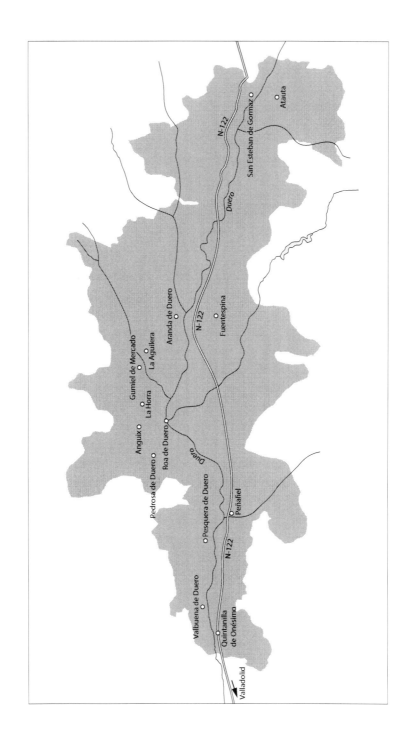

6

RIBERA DEL DUERO: THE GLAMOUR OF TINTO FINO

The DO that has come shooting up the reputation ladder in the last decade or so is Ribera del Duero. Looking back over previous guides to Spain, Ribera del Duero was a small section in the Castilla y León chapter. No longer. For a century the wine of the Duero valley was Vega Sicilia. Today there are some newer exceptional wines populating the region.

The original settlers were the Vaccei – a Celtic people who lived between the rivers Duero and Pisuerga. They were displaced by the Romans, who planted vines. In all probability the Vaccei had also, but the Romans were as in all things systematic. There is a Roman town at Clunia, with a theatre, as well as Roman villas in Baños de Valdearados, Quintanilla de Onésimo, Padilla de Duero and Pesquera de Duero. (Today's Padilla is in all probability at the Vaccei settlement of Pintia – the name which Vega Sicilia took for its Toro winery. A cup with traces of 2,500-year-old wine has been found at the Pintia site.)

Open the map of Ribera del Duero wineries today and you find yourself stepping back into a quasi-medieval world. Names of convents and monasteries abound. If monasteries reflect one part of Ribera del Duero's past, then the castles bear witness to another. Peñafiel is a textbook castle, which has stepped out of a children's fairy tale. Gormaz, in a fine defensive hilltop position over the Duero, just outside the DO's eastern limits, has a terrific castle. It was built in the mid-eighth century by the Emir of Cordoba to form part of the northern defences of the Moors against the Christians. The area is full of watchtowers – *atalayas* – which abound in the DO vineyard zones in Soria.

It's always worth remembering that though the Duero Valley's history in wine goes back millennia – over a century in the case of Vega Sicilia – the second winery was not launched until the 1920s, the cooperative which is now Protos. The DO was only formed in 1982, at which time there were still only nine wineries (or eight, or fourteen, the records conflict). There are some historical reasons for this. When Philip II moved the royal court – and more importantly the wine-drinking courtiers and civil servants – from Valladolid to Madrid, the ready market for the local wines disappeared. Valladolid never developed the transport links as Haro and Logroño did to serve their markets. This may help to explain why Ribera del Duero still has such a strong domestic market, but has only recently begun to focus seriously on export. In the twentieth century government strategy in the post-war period favoured sugar beet over vines. Since 1982, however, growth has been rapid.

Latterly there has been substantial investment from producers in other regions. From Cataluña, Torres established themselves in Fompedraza, Codorníu at Legaris, and Freixenet at Valdubón; La Rioja Alta settled in Anguix with their brand Áster; and Telmo Rodríguez launched Matallana here. From France, Malthilde Chapoutier has a Ribera del Duero wine as part of her family's Chapoutier négociant business; while winemaking consultant Michel Rolland has a joint venture with Javier Galarreta, of the Araex wine group.

Ribera del Duero at a glance

Grape varieties

White: Albillo

Red: Tempranillo/Tinto Fino, Cabernet Sauvignon, Merlot, Garnacha Tinta, Malbec. Red wines must be a minimum of 75 per cent Tempranillo. The rest may be made up of Cabernet Sauvignon or Merlot. If used, Garnacha Tinta, Malbec and Albillo may make up no more than 5 per cent of the blend.

Size

Vineyard: 22,320 hectares (73.34 per cent Burgos, 0.71 per cent Segovia, 5.58 per cent Soria, 20.36 per cent Valladolid)

Growers: 8,255

Wineries: 282 (158 in Burgos, 4 in Segovia, 8 in Soria and 112 in Valladolid)

Land of extremes

Ribera del Duero is scorchingly hot in summer and freezing in winter. One benefit of this climate is a refreshing diurnal temperature variation, essential for keeping freshness in the summer months. It adds up to long ripening, with dense colour and full flavour. To sum up, vinegrowing here is not easy: definitely borderline for growers, with moderate rainfall, extreme heat and cold, potentially damaging frost, all of which risk successful maturation. The rain in Spain may fall mainly on the plain, but not this plain. Vintage variation can be significant here. Nevertheless, for those who understand their soils and vines, rather than following someone else's model, the results can be superb.

Ribera del Duero is part of the northern Iberian plateau. It was formed from a large plinth covered with Tertiary era deposits, mainly sedimentary layers of soils – sandy, silty-sandy or clay-sandy – with distinctive layers of limestone and calcareous outcrops. The Duero running through formed a big basin in the Miocene era. Altitude is important, with vineyards ranged from 700 to 1,000 metres, and an average altitude of 800–850 metres: the lowest of Ribera's are higher than many other Spanish vineyards. In addition, differing aspects are all that one could wish with slopes and hillsides. At the top is the windswept *páramo*, the high plateau.

There are some 35 different soil types. Most are over 60 centimetres deep, but some are less than 40, with outcrops of the mother rock. The contrasts across the DO are remarkable. A CRDO analysis shows for instance that total limestone in the soils varies from 51.5 per cent in the east (with a range from less than 1 per cent to as much as 90 per cent), to 16.8 per cent in the centre, and 32.8 per cent in the west. The chalky whiteness of some vineyards reminds one of the rolling hills of Jerez. Roughly 55 per cent of the vineyard is bush vines, though as the terrain gets flatter to the west trained vines and machine picking are possible. The west is warmer, and the soils are more clay-based. The boom in vineyard growth was 1991 to 2000, with a rush to plant 36 per cent of the overall vineyard in just a decade. As these wines grow in maturity the potential is there for fine wine production.

A STAR STILL TO RISE?

In recent times Ribera del Duero has come second only to Rioja in terms of prestige (with Priorat close behind). Yet personally I wasn't charmed by the wines. For a long time I thought I was alone. However, as I researched this I realized that it was a common reaction for non-Spanish nationals. A Spain enthusiast, a buyer for a top-end independent business in the UK, said despairingly, 'I just can't sell Ribera del Duero; my customers won't buy them, they just don't like them'. He can sell wines from Vega Sicilia, he says, Pérez Pascuas and Emilio Moro, but cannot delve deeper. A common complaint is price: Ribera isn't cheap.

Ribera has a strong domestic market which loves the wines, and some international markets, such as the USA, also demand this style. To get a Spanish perspective I spoke to Amaya Cervera, the perceptive commentator of the award-winning site Spanish Wine Lover (www.spanishwinelover. com). Was this an English malaise? 'You're right,' she said, 'the English critics have never been very keen on Ribera del Duero's wines. The region that produces naturally powerful wines with a very fruity, oaky profile is still the most popular in the Spanish market – above all the mass market "Roble" category which, with rare exceptions, is very marked by oak.'

Riojano Ricardo Arambarri, whose company Vintae makes wine in Ribera del Duero, explains how this has come about: 'It's not necessarily due to the vineyards and the grapes, but the style of elaboration. Ribera del Duero is a very young appellation and has a short history of fine winemaking. Apart from Vega Sicilia, the first successes came at the end of the 1980s through to the early 2000s. Those successes came from a very over-extracted, oaky style that stood apart from the classic Rioja style. During that time, the market, influenced by Robert Parker's preferences, welcomed that style and the appellation had a huge success'.

Ribera del Duero delivers structure, power and intensity as well as freshness, dark fruit and tannin. The clue to the region's limited popularity outside the local market is in that stylistic preference for tannin, and the oak ageing. As one producer, who asked to remain unnamed, observed: 'I often hear bigger winemakers saying, "If it doesn't taste tannic it's wrong". Unfortunately there's this trend among winemakers here in Ribera del Duero – it's an alpha male fight over who can make the biggest.' Given that the high-extract wines were preferred in the region, because they lasted longer in better condition, intense pumping-over was the order of the day. Another producer pointed out that 'if you go into many wineries they have huge machinery and huge tanks. Taking the stalks off is done by big machines. This is going to affect the wine.'

In La Aguilera, one of the towns that is highly rated for its old vines, Germán Blanco of the young project Quinta Milú points out that in Ribera del Duero an additional factor affecting the style of the wines is that, 'Tempranillo makes wines with high polyphenols which deliver colour and tannin, but low acidity.' The longer the grape stays on the vine to ripen, the more the acidity falls, and the freshness disappears: 'The other factor is the boom of a few years back when people planted vines like mad things, and as a result we have lots of young vines ... planted in poor sites.' In that sense, Ribera's future is all ahead of it. For while the region has fine bush vines, and some of them pre-phylloxeric, two-thirds of plantings have been made since 1991. Blanco's comment about sites holds out promise for the future, as producers come to better understand the diversity of their plant material and soils.

One such producer is Maria del Yerro of Alonso del Yerro, who reckons that it has taken almost ten years of effort to bring her wines up to their current level of quality. Her consultant, Stéphane Derenoncourt, is well respected in Bordeaux, but had no prior experience in Spain. 'Our aim has been to make wines with ageing potential, fine wines, with vintage character and which reflect the terroir,' Maria says. 'Stéphane started in that unbearably hot vintage of 2003. Since then we have changed the way we manage the vines, and understand our soils better with the help of [terroir expert] Claude Bourguignon, and of course the vines are older. Since 2012 our soils have begun to produce wines of a really exceptional quality.'

Del Yerro mentions the heat. Ribera del Duero is no easy place to work in terms of its continental climate. With the long winters and short, hot, dry summers there is very little time to wait for ripe tannins. The wines used to be green, as a result. To avoid that involves walking a tightrope in terms of deciding when to pick the fruit. You wait to get phenolic ripeness, but wait too long and you lose the fresh red fruit character, and instead get black fruit without the refreshing finish. The altitude is important here, as is the heterogeneity of the region's soils. There has been work on soil mapping but sub-zones are not yet formally recognized. This will undoubtedly help consumers to understand specific characters of Ribera del Duero and find the sub-zones they prefer. There's an urgent need to preserve the old vineyards and enhance the younger vines. Peter Sisseck has been working in Ribera for a number of years. His PSI project was created to foster Ribera del Duero's vine heritage.

So how might one best enjoy Ribera del Duero, and its changing styles? The simple message is, don't drink it too young (unless it's a Joven, or *roble*). Says Almudena Alberca, Technical Director of Viña Mayor: 'Ribera wines are meant to be aged in the bottle and consumed when they are old, when all the polymerization has been done, and the wine is soft and elegant. But this is not the reality of today's markets. Wine is released when it is still young, when all the tannins are playing rock and roll.' She, like other producers across the region, is adjusting and tweaking in the vineyard and the winery. Even at Vega Sicilia, Technical Director Gonzalo Iturriaga says he is carrying out trials in the wineries across the group, reducing time in oak, using concrete vats, experimenting with coopers.

Oscar Aragón at Cillar de Silos has a new project at Dominio del Pidio, and it's about fermenting in concrete and ageing in the traditional underground cellars in Quintanilla de Pidio. At the east end of the DO, in the vineyards in Soria province, producers like Dominio de Atauta and Dominio de Aguila are releasing wines that have more elegance and less oak. But Cervera warns, 'It's very complicated there in cold years and can produce really tannic wines.'

Ribera del Duero has established success in its national market, and this risks stifling innovation. It's not easy. Alberca says: 'A few of us, and I include myself, want to produce something that is easier to drink – that doesn't mean simple, these are complex wines. However, my clients feel that something is missing. They name another brand and they say, "That wine has more colour than yours, and more oak; yours only has ten months ageing, does that mean yours is lower quality than a Crianza?"' As in Rioja and elsewhere in Spain, the quality of wine is assessed by its time in 225-litre oak. This classification system values time in oak above vineyard quality or age. But things are changing here, as in Rioja: Cervera notes that Pago de Carraovejas, for example, has stopped making its Crianza and Reserva, and produces a 'generic' wine, where they can choose the time in and type of barrel, resulting in less obvious oak.

Ageing categories

Cosecha or Joven: Young wines with no oak ageing.

Crianza: Wines which have spent a minimum of one year in oak, then a minimum of two years in bottle.

Reserva: Wines which have spent a minimum of one year in oak, followed by a minimum of three years in bottle.

Gran Reserva: Wines which have spent a minimum of two years in oak, then at least five years in bottle.

Producers

Alfredo Maestro

Avda Escalona 42, 47300 Peñafiel
Tel.: +34 687 786 742
www.alfredomaestro.com

Maestro started making wine in 1998 and farmed organically from the outset. Although he began conventionally, using every technical trick, in the early 2000s he started to make wines without any additives, including sulphur. At present he makes some 10–15 cuvées, recuperating vineyards in Castilla y León, Ribera del Duero and Cigales, where he has a Garnacha Gris. There is also a pét nat from southern Spanish Pinot Noir with a little Garnacha Tintorera from Ribera del Duero. Sierra de Gredos has been his most recent discovery. Track down and taste these wines for a different, honest expression of terroir.

Aalto

Parajevallejo de Carril s/n, 47360 Quintanilla de Arriba
Tel.: +34 983 036 949
www.aalto.es

How did Aalto make it to the top so quickly? The stated aim in 1999 was, 'to make a wine that in the space of 15 to 20 years should reach the quality of the best wines in the world'. Many would say Aalto has indeed achieved this ambition. There are two factors important in explaining this: insider knowledge and old vines. The insiders are winemaker Mariano García, who was in charge of winemaking at Vega Sicilia for three decades, and Managing Director Javier Zaccagnini. Zaccagnini was director of the

Consejo Regulador of Ribera del Duero for six years, in its early days. They knew where to look for the best old vines and the best soils for their new project.

At first sight they seem an unlikely pair. Zaccagnini has an MBA, speaks four languages, and seems to have boundless ideas and energy, with classical music the soundtrack to his endless journeying. García is tall and long-limbed; with his white hair and silver beard, plus a gold chain round his neck, the adjective 'debonair' could have been invented for him. García was 'born in the vineyards', as his great-grandfather's family had land in Castile. The sites the pair selected for their joint project come from Ribera del Duero's top villages: Roa, La Horra, La Aguilera, Fresnillo and Moradillo. Altogether they own or rent 200 plots, none bigger than 1 hectare, 110 hectares in all. Each plot is harvested and handled separately, with different rackings and oak treatments.

There are two wines: Aalto and Aalto PS (for Pagos Seleccionados – selected plots). Aalto usually spends 20 months in oak, 50 per cent of it new French, the other 50 per cent one- to three-year-old French and American. PS receives 24 months in 100 per cent new French oak. Both PS and Aalto are only blended at the end of the process. These are powerful wines, clearly from a winemaker who knows how to build wines for the long haul. Both are firmly marked by oak, and to my taste need plenty of time in the cellar to calm down and integrate. PS is profound, with liquorice, dark fruits, and spice, and a warm finish of alcohol. The third wine in the bodega is Sei Solo (see p. 186).

Why call the bodega Aalto? Because it is a short, internationally pronounceable word, and one that has the real advantage of appearing top of the list in any guide. Zaccagnini knows about marketing.

Alejandro Fernández Grupo Pesquera

Real 2, 47315 Pesquera de Duero
Tel.: +34 983 870 037
www.grupopesquera.com

Alejandro Fernández has made an outstanding contribution to Ribera del Duero. For many years Vega Sicilia gave the impression that Ribera del Duero was only for the gentry, making wines for the royal family. This founder of the widely used AF tractors proved that you did not need to be an aristocrat to make great wine. A determined figure, a man of few words, a survivor of the harsh Castilian climate, Fernández learnt about vines and wine from his father. In 1972 he founded his own bodega as a second career, in a sixteenth-century stone building in Pesquera as sturdy as the man himself. This was a decade before the creation of the DO, when there were still few wineries. As an engineer, he knew how to manage the technicalities of harvesting and winemaking. His simply named red, Tinto Pesquera, became one of Spain's early cult wines when it won the attention of Robert Parker in 1982. The 'Petrus of Spain' began Ribera's gold rush.

Fernández's secret is the quality of the vineyards. He now has some 220 hectares, at around 800 metres, with glorious views from the top across the region. The soils are sand and gravel over clay and limestone. The Tinto Fino is destemmed, which builds the richness. After fermentation, the wine is racked to French and American oak barrels of varying toasts. The Tinto Pesquera is aged in oak for 18 months and the Reservas and Gran Reservas for a minimum of 24 months. Tasting the wines today perhaps one anticipates too much of these historically high-scoring wines. There's an element of disappointment, but perhaps not unexpected when so many others have subsequently piled in to make wines in Ribera del Duero.

From his initial winery, Alejandro Fernández went on to create three more. Condado de Haza (p. 172) is his other property in Ribera del Duero, Dehesa La Granja in Zamora is a VdlT Castilla y León, and El Vínculo is in La Mancha. Fernández is not just a headline-making producer, he is a canny landowner with a substantial investment in land. Wine tourism plays a part in the business: visitors to the old bodega in Pesquera can see the original press and *lagar*, and can also watch the documentary that shows how the harvest and winemaking were handled in the early days. The other three wineries have restaurants, and in Peñafiel there's the 24-bedroom Hotel AF.

Alión

Ctra N-122 Km 312.4, Padilla de Duero, 47300 Peñafiel
Tel.: +34 983 881 236
www.vega-sicilia.com

This is also part of the Vega Sicilia family, just a few kilometres up the road from its big brother. Launched in the former winery of Liceo, next door, Alión's first vintage was 1991, its first commercial vintage 1992. The vineyards, which average 30 years, are in Padilla, Valbuena de Duero and

Pesquera, and 50 per cent are owned by growers with whom they have long-term relationships.

Vega Sicilia describes the Alión wine as a 'modern, independent … and multicultural' 100 per cent Tinto Fino, though linked to its cousins by the same viticulture. It is younger, with shorter oak ageing (12–14 months in new French oak rather than Vega Sicilia's years in French and American oak) and certainly a little more affordable. By running two separate brands, the mothership is wisely able to keep its traditions separate. In sum, Vega Sicilia has small portions of Bordeaux varietals in the blend, Alión is all Tinto Fino; Vega Sicilia is all about power in a velvet glove; Alión is, as much as a Ribera del Duero can be, about elegance.

Alonso del Yerro

Finca Santa Marta, Ctra Roa-Anguix Km 1.8, 09300 Roa
Tel.: +34 913 160 121
www.alonsodelyerro.es

This is Javier Alonso and his wife María del Yerro's winery. María and her eldest son Miguel are the very obvious faces of the business, hosting tastings and explaining the particular characters of the wines. A number of factors – or, rather, people – served to set Alonso del Yerro apart, right from its foundation in 2002. Javier and María recruited the very highly regarded French consultant Stéphane Derenoncourt to consult, as he still does. For Derenoncourt it was a new step, as it was his first winery outside France. For viticultural advice they also went to the top, employing the French expert Claude Bourguignon to analyse the soils. The soils were carefully mapped, and are managed today with inter-row planting and composts.

Del Yerro recalls that Derenoncourt began in the unbearably hot year of 2003. He saw then the need to focus on freshness. She recognizes now, looking back, just how much time fine wine takes: 'Stéphane always says that it was with the 2012 vintage that our soils began to produce wines of really fine quality, and it's a result of the work we've been doing in the vineyard, the age of the vines, and the understanding Stéphane and Lionel (Gourgue) have of our soils and grapes.'

They have 26 hectares of vineyards in Roa, at 800–840 metres, Tempranillo planted on trellises in 1989. The two wines they make are a pure expression of Tempranillo. Lionel Gourgue joined in 2007 to manage the vineyards and winery in Ribera del Duero, and in their property in Toro. Since then the wines have become ever more elegant and refined.

The Alonso del Yerro is a combination of plots, vinified separately in stainless steel and matured for a year in French oak barrels. Nowadays only 15–20 per cent is new, toning down the power of the oak. This will never be a shy or quiet wine, but it has very fine tannin and pure fruit. The top wine is María. María has also been made since the beginning, but only in the best vintages. It comes from two particular plots, one with chalky clay soil, the other with chalky gravel, combining depth with florality. Since 2007 fermentation has been in oak vats, with malolactic and ageing in French oak barrels. The use of micro-oxygenation and batonnage, which Derenoncourt introduced at the outset, undoubtedly helps the softening of the palate.

The Alonsos have five children and María has discovered the hard way that hosting their joyful wedding parties in the winery can be an expensive business for a fine wine producer!

Antídoto

Ctra de Atauta 63, 42330 San Esteban de Gormaz
Tel.: +34 975 350 493
www.bodegasantidoto.com

Antídoto is one of the few Ribera del Duero wineries in Soria. A special place, it is an almost-forgotten corner of the DO, higher and more continental in climate, with pre-phylloxeric vines. The winery was launched by Bertrand Sourdais, by birth French, the fifth generation of growers in the Loire, in Chinon. He calls himself the 'Vigneron de las Tierras de Soria desde 1999', which emphasizes his vision to discover and recuperate the historic character of Soria. He had previously worked in Bordeaux, and with Álvaro Palacios in Priorat, and then in 1999 became technical director of the Dominio de Atauta project. He remained there for ten years, building an exceptional reputation for the wines and the quality of Soria. After the sale of Atauta, he launched his own business, one that takes in Dominio de Es and Domaine de Pallus in Chinon, as well as Antídoto.

Could the name of this new business – which means exactly what English-speakers would suspect – be a reaction to the change in ownership of Atauta? Perhaps. What is certain is that the character that he developed in Atauta continues. A winery was opened in 2016 in San

Esteban de Gormaz where he works with David Hernando, a former colleague from Atauta days. They currently produce four wines, two *rosados* and two reds. Roselito echoes the traditional *rosados*, a blend of 65 per cent Tinto Fino and 35 per cent Albillo, harvested and crushed together as would have been the case in the old days. Le Rosé is also made from Tinto Fino and Albillo but comes from a single vineyard planted in 1905, an exceptional site at 950 metres, with sand over limestone. As with champagne, only the free-run juice from the press is used. It's then fermented and aged in 600-litre new French oak. While classically made, it's something out of the ordinary for Ribera del Duero.

The mainstay of the reds is Antídoto, the first wine from the new project, launched in 2009 and originally made with fruit from Hernando's vineyards. Today it is a blend of fruit from 350 plots of 80- to 100-year-old vines. The wine spends a year in one-year-old French oak. Energetic and vivid, it is a convincing portrait of the region's potential. Sourdais defines La Hormiga as a great red from Soria. The vineyard was planted in 1922, at 950 metres, on sand over clay. The wine is aged for 18 months in French oak, 50 per cent of which is new. It's more powerful, and the style is bound to develop over the years. Overall, Antídoto and Dominio de Es are worth watching.

Arzuaga Navarro

Ctra N-122 Km 325, 47350 Quintanilla de Onésimo
Tel.: +34 983 681 146
www.arzuaganavarro.com

To be honest, the bodega is not the most attractive building on the highway. However there are fine wines to be enjoyed here for lovers of mature, supple styles. Florentino Navarro bought the extensive estate in the early 1990s in Quintanilla de Onésimo and recognized that it had potential for wine as well as wildlife. As a result the winery has not less than 150 hectares of vineyards: Tinto Fino, as well as Cabernet Sauvignon and Merlot, and in addition Chardonnay, Pinot Noir and Albillo. (They also have vineyards in Ciudad Real, where they make the wine called Pago Florentino.)

The classics are the Crianza, Reserva, Reserva Especial and Gran Reserva series. The Reserva with its dash of Merlot and Albillo to the Tinto Fino is aged in French oak, with a small amount of American oak. The result is supple and traditional. The Gran Reserva has some

Cabernet Sauvignon and Merlot, and is aged for four years in French oak to produce a classic, retro style, with tobacco and spices.

All is not so serious at Arzuaga Navarro; Amaya is from ultra-serious pre-phylloxeric vineyards, but the label is a playful fashion plate; while they too are making a Provence-pale *rosado* from Tinto Fino. There's also a hotel and spa, and a restaurant.

Áster

Ctra Palencia-Aranda Km 54.9, 09313 Anguix
Tel.: +34 947 522 701
www.bodegasaster.com

The record of a Ribera del Duero producer starting a project in Rioja is not altogether promising if one takes Macán, the joint venture of Vega Sicilia and Benjamin de Rothschild as an example. How then, might a Rioja producer fare in the more extreme climate of Ribera del Duero?

La Rioja Alta, one of the great classic Rioja bodegas, did plenty of research – as Vega Sicilia did in Rioja – before purchasing its first land in 1990. It planted the grapes the following year. As with its other properties in Rioja, and in Galicia, they acquired a traditional building, a small manor house, which they converted, with bedrooms for visitors. The grapes from the first six harvests were sold. They made wine in 1999, but it too was sold off. Finally in 2000 they brought their first Áster Reserva to market, and opened a bodega next to the house. By 2005 winemaker Julio Sáenz had been promoted to winemaking director across the estates. They then started to experiment with malolactic fermentation in barrels, and in analysing much more closely the fruit from the different parcels. This resulted in the decision to produce two wines: Áster Crianza and Áster Finca El Otero. The Crianza comes from four of Áster's own vineyards. Like Rioja Alta's own wines it spends longer than the required single year in barrel. In this case it's 22 months in 70 per cent new oak, making it almost a Reserva. The Finca El Otero comes only from the vineyard of the same name. This is aged for 16 months, providing a complement to the fruit. Both wines use only French oak.

Following their company philosophy of owning as much of their own vineyard as possible, La Rioja Alta located good sites in Anguix, planting 80 hectares. The vines are coming into maturity now so the wine can only continue to improve vintage by vintage. The 4-hectare

Finca El Otero has the best soils, dry and infertile with lightly eroded slopes, and the fruit from this goes into the top wine in the best years. The remaining vineyards are divided between supplying the Crianza, and the private wine produced for Áster's club members. So how did this outsider from Rioja do? Very well so far.

Astrales

Ctra Olmedillo Km 7, 093113 Anguix
Tel.: +34 947 554 222
www.astrales.es

The vineyards of Anguix are the key here. The Romera de la Cruz family, the third generation of growers in the village, founded Astrales in 2000, with a view to producing up to a maximum of 100,000 bottles. Eduardo García was signed up to run the winery – his other interests are the family businesses of Mauro, Mauro Dos and Leda, while his father is established at Aalto, and formerly spent more than half a lifetime as winemaker at Vega Sicilia. I first visited the project in the mid-2000s, when the wines coming out of the garage-style winery were really impressive.

The fundamentals are old vines, wild yeasts, short macerations, and ageing in mainly French oak. The result is a fresh expression of Ribera del Duero. Currently they produce three wines. Astrales is made from vines aged over 45 years; while Astrales Christina is from a single vineyard with centenarian vines. It spends 18 months in new French oak. Finally they have a Godello, from Rubiá in Valdeorras, which is aged for more than 50 months in bottle. Since 2014, the consulting team of Pepe Hidalgo and Ana Martín have been in charge of the vineyards and winery. Expect some stylistic changes and innovations.

Bohórquez

Ctra Peñafiel-Pesquera de Duero Km 4, 47315 Pesquera de Duero
Tel.: +34 983 870 123
www.bodegasbohorquez.com

Javier Bohórquez is a Jerezano, now firmly established in the wine business in Ribera del Duero for two decades, in what he calls a kind of marriage between Palomino (Sherry's grape) and Tempranillo (Ribera del Duero's Tinto Fino). While working in Madrid he was searching for the right place to start making wine. He started looking around in Cigales. Then he moved up to Soria, the easternmost of Ribera del Duero's provinces, and finally he stopped off at a petrol station one day in Pesquera and got chatting to the locals. He acquired vineyards in the Pesquera area, some of them at 900 metres, and on the slopes of the Pago de Valderramiro, as well as some vineyards on the right bank of the River Duero. The 17 hectares, planted more densely than is usual, are mainly Tempranillo with some Merlot and Cabernet Sauvignon.

Bohórquez's wines are definitely more elegant than many in Ribera del Duero. That may be partly to do with the altitude, and he emphasizes the role of the limestone soil. But it is just as much to do with the care he takes in the winery.

Carmelo Rodero

Ctra Boada s/n, 09314 Pedrosa de Duero
Tel.: +34 947 530 046
www.bodegasrodero.com

Grower-turns-producer is a regular theme, but Carmelo Rodero is one who has done this with particular success. He comes from a family of growers; his grandparents established the wine cooperative in Pedrosa del Duero. The young Rodero began to establish his own vineyards, 30 hectares in all, and for over a decade he sold fruit to Vega Sicilia. Inevitably this convinced him that he could set out on his own, which he did in 1991. Today his daughters are the fifth generation working in the family business. They manage overall 140 hectares of vineyard, ranging in ages from 30 to 100 years. The majority of it is Tempranillo, with some Cabernet Sauvignon and a little Merlot.

Daughter Beatriz makes all the classic categories. The straightforward young Tempranillo, a regular in local bars, is unoaked with vivid varietal character. The Crianza has 10 per cent Cabernet Sauvignon and 15 months in French oak. Undoubtedly oaky, it retains the youthful expressive style of the house. Above this are the Reserva and two special selections. The Pago de Valterreña, from a single vineyard, is Tempranillo aged for 24 months in French oak, well-polished and nicely integrated. Last in the line-up is the TSM, made from Tempranillo, Cabernet Sauvignon (15 per cent) and Merlot (10 per cent). Although it's an interesting approach to a more modern icon wine, it is less satisfying than the Pago.

Cepa 21

Ctra N-122 Km 297, 47318 Castrillo de Duero
Tel.: +34 983 484 083
www.cepa21.com

Cepa 21, launched in 2007, has a marked air of confidence. That's not surprising since the Emilio Moro family are behind it, in a joint project with other investors. The winery sits in the middle of a vineyard planted with Moro's own Tinto Fino clones selected from centenarian vines in Pesquera. In all, there are 50 hectares of vines, at 750–850 metres, selected with a focus on altitude and cool climate. Cepa 21 sensibly enables Emilio Moro to express a different style without conflicting with the heritage of the parent winery. Stylistically the wines are more modern, bolder and punchier, and eschew the traditional Reserva ageing categories.

Hito is the young label, made from the youngest vines, and aged in French and American oak. Its sister *rosado* is a cherry pink, aromatic Tempranillo. The main label of the winery is the eponymous Cepa 21, from plots in three villages, a mix of chalk and clay with rocky outcrops. It spends 12 months in French oak, and carries a distinctly oaky undertow when new. The top wine is Malabrigo, from an exposed, windy, north-facing plot of loam, sand, clay and pebbles. Eighteen months in French oak give it a fine polish, and this is a very promising style.

Cepa 21 prides itself on its wine tourism. The wine bar is a tasting room for Emilio Moro and Cepa 21, with local vermouths, and the restaurant's chef Alberto Soto has won local awards for his creativity.

Cillar de Silos

Paraje El Soto s/n, 09370 Quintana del Pidio
Tel.: +34 947 545 126
www.cillardesilos.es

The great monastery of Santo Domingo de Silos bought its wine from the vineyards of Quintana del Pidio. When Amalio Aragón set up Cillar de Silos with his children in 1994 in the same village, they named it after the monastery's *cillero*, the monk who looked after Silos' wine and food.

Aragón had started buying plots of vineyards from his neighbours back in the 1970s. Today the family owns 68 hectares between Quintana del Pidio, La Aguilera and Gumiel, at an altitude of 900–940 metres, and spread across small plots, many less than a hectare. The children run the winery between them: Roberto is management and sales, Oscar is technical director and winemaker, while Amelia travels the world running exports. The vine age ranges from 15 to 100 years, with a few pre-phylloxeric vines that survived because of the soils, which are sandy, with a little silt and clay. They grow Tempranillo, with some Albillo. Their white grapes – a blend of Albillo Real and Albillo Mayor over 70 years – are now made into the Blanco de Silos. It's fermented in 500-litre oak, and then aged on the lees. Very promising, especially in a steadfastly red region.

In their line-up, Cillar de Silos include a *rosado*, a reliable young Joven and a Crianza. The Terruños range contains undoubtedly the most interesting wines. Torresilo is a blend of old vines, some of them centenarian. When young it is oaky, but it simply needs time to mature. La Viña de Amalio is the children's tribute to their father. They describe Amalio gloriously: as an expression of a single vineyard, 'it has the grandeur of imperfection', much like the grit in the oyster that makes the pearl. The vineyard was planted in 1964, and its wines are wonderfully aromatic, alongside the expected intensity. The other single vineyard wine is Flor de Silos. It's made from old and pre-phylloxeric vines from a vineyard at 900 metres. Still within the Silos style, it has generous floral aromatics and is fresh and elegant with a fine grain of tannin.

The siblings at Silos don't stand still. Don't miss Golfo, their vermouth, made from Tempranillo, with lavender as well as herbs. Oscar Aragón's recent project is Dominio del Pidio, a natural extension of their history and experience in Ribera del Duero. They have spent some years restoring seven sixteenth-century underground cellars in Quintana del Pidio. What took the time was negotiating with many owners in the village, who each had a small underground cellar, as was the custom, in order to join them up. So far, they make a white, *rosado* and red in the traditional way. Making the white is laborious, as the Albillo grapes have to be picked out from within the Tempranillo vineyards where they are interplanted. The reds are field blends, containing some white grapes. The Dominio wines are fermented in concrete rather than stainless steel, and then aged in 500–1,200 litre French oak casks. The cool, stable environment makes for slow maturation and builds complexity. All of this, they note, brings them back to the ways wine used to be made. The white has a note of oxidative richness; the *rosado* is a real wine, with savoury notes; the red benefits from the winemaking which enables the fruit to sing out, rather than masking it in oak.

Condado de Haza

Real 2, 47315 Pesquera de Duero
Tel.: +34 983 870 037
www.grupopesquera.com

Alejandro Fernández, his fame established with stellar scores for his Tinto Pesquera winery, established this extensive estate in 1987. It has 200 hectares of Tempranillo, and in their midst a chateau or bodega, with an underground barrel cellar. Here he makes three wines, Condado de Haza, Condado de Haza Reserva and Alenza. Alenza is the winery's Gran Reserva, made only in the best years. It takes its name from the first three letters of his first name, and the last three of his wife, Esperanza. Alenza is aged for 30 months in 225- and 300-litre American oak barrels, and aged for a further 30 months in bottle. This is the most interesting wine of the bodega's current production. However even the fine selection of fruit could do with less time in oak.

Dominio del Aguila

Los Lagares 42, 09370 La Aguilera
Tel.: +34 638 899 236
www.dominiodelaguila.com

Jorge Monzón is in charge here, working with old vines, some of them pre-phylloxeric, from exceptional vineyards. He farms organically, using herbal treatments on the bush vines which, given their age, will be mainly Tempranillo, but will also be interplanted with a field blend of others. He has Cariñena, Blanca del Pais, Garnacha and Bobal, amongst others. He works in a restored seventeenth-century bodega, with fifteenth-century cellars. The wines are destemmed, foot-trodden, and fermented in concrete. He makes the wines in underground caves, ensuring a much slower development. His Dominio del Aguila comes from the oldest vines of the much-respected village of La Aguilera, at about 880 metres. The new Peñas Aladas Gran Reserva comes from three small parcels in a windswept valley, one of the coldest parts of the DO, and a tiny production (827 bottles in 2012). A speciality is the Pícaro del Aguila Clarete, made from old vines at 830 metres, a remarkable blend of many of the varieties named above plus

Bruñal, Albillo, Moscatel and Malvasía. This is a new direction for Ribera del Duero, and one to welcome.

Dominio de Atauta

Ctra a Morcuera s/n, 42345 Atauta
Tel.: +34 975 351 349
www.dominiodeatauta.com

When Miguel Sánchez, a wine merchant from Madrid, set up Atauta in 1999 he chose a special place, at the far east end of Ribera del Duero, 50 kilometres from the source of the River Duero, in the province of Soria. Wine has been made here in the valley of Atauta for more than five centuries. Yet this feels a little like the land that time forgot. The vineyards are at around 1,000 metres, with extreme temperature contrasts between day and night and between the seasons. Many of the vines are pre-phylloxeric – this is not an area that gives the impression of vigorous growth and yields. The soils are diverse, but at heart calcareous bedrock.

Bernard Sourdais (see Antídoto) ran the viticulture and winemaking. A decade or so later, the business was acquired by Avanteselecta (a real estate/financial group, with winery holdings in a number of other regions). The team has changed since then. Atauta sources from some 60 hectares, both their own property and from 40 growers, in more than 500 parcels. The vines are 85–140 year old bush vines, 90 per cent of them on their own rootstock. In the winery the approach is straightforward, gravity-fed, natural yeast, open-top fermentation, no filtration or stabilization, with fermentation in stainless steel, concrete, and oak vats. The wines are matured in French oak barriques.

The Dominio de Atauta wine has a remarkable dense and savoury – almost salty – character, which could not be further from any of the baked fruit styles of some Ribera del Duero wines. The three single vineyard wines – La Mala, Valdegatiles and Llanos del Almendro – are all exceptionally fine, offering a more delicate expression of Ribera del Duero than is typical. Parada de Atauta has been introduced more recently to create an entry level, accessible style; it's the largest production of the range.

The Atalayas de Golbán bodega is close to Atauta, and draws on grapes from the Valle de Atauta, as well as from across the zone of San Esteban de Gormaz.

Dominio de Cair

Ctra Aranda a la Aguilera Km 9, 09370 La Aguilera
Tel.: +34 947 545 276
www.dominiodecair.com

Cair, established in 2008, comes from the stable of Luis Cañas in Rioja. It was named after the first two letters of the surnames of the founders, Juan Luis Cañas and his co-investor, the businessman Juan José Irebecampos. In time, the latter greatly reduced his share, selling on to Chinese investors, and giving Cañas the majority. Cair is in La Aguilera, one of Ribera del Duero's great sources of vines, and owns 20 hectares, controlling another 90 from La Aguilera, Quintana del Pidio and Moradillo.

The wines are as modern and polished as the Cañas Riojas. Cair Cuvée, from high altitude vineyards, is the only one of the range to contain a variety other than Tempranillo, with 15 per cent Merlot. It's made from the youngest, 25-year-old, vines. The Tempranillo spends nine months in new and used oak, while the Merlot is put into new French and American oak, before blending. Cair is made from 40–50 year old bush vines. It's fermented in stainless steel, and the malolactic fermentation takes place in new oak, before ageing for 14 months in new French and American oak followed by a year in bottle before release. Next up is Tierras de Cair, which is a blend of different plots from the poor soils in the home village of La Aguilera, with vines aged from 60 to more than 100 years. The fermentation is in oak vats, followed by malolactic fermentation and ageing for 24 months in new French oak. Not produced every year, this is a well-structured, intense Tempranillo. A more recent arrival is Pendón de la Aguilera; its first harvest was 2009. It is named after the banners awarded by medieval monarchs to towns. The vines are more than 80 years old, and like Tierras de Cair fermentation is in French oak vats. Malolactic fermentation is in new French oak barrels and the wine is aged in barrel for 27 months.

Dominio de Es

Ctra de Atauta 63, 42330 San Esteban de Gormaz
Tel.: +34 975 350 493
www.bertrandsourdais.com

The second of Bertrand Sourdais' two projects in Ribera del Duero focuses, like the other, on pre-phylloxeric vines in the part of the province of Soria that is in the DO. He works with a few plots in the *pagos* that he made famous in his time as technical director of Dominio de Atauta: La Mala, Llanos de Almendra and Valdegatiles. As he says, these low yielding bush vines with their delicate fruit deliver '*un líquido divino*' – a divine liquid. He has introduced biodynamic practices to the vineyard. As is typical with such old vines, there is some Albillo interplanted with the Tinto Fino. Thus the Viñas Viejas de Soria has 5 per cent Albillo. Sourdais uses 50 per cent of the stems, and then ages the wine for 20 months in barriques. Famously, these came from Domaine de la Romanée Conti.

La Diva comes from own-rooted north-east facing vines on sandy, limestone terraces, protected by stone walls. As with the Viñas Viejas de Soria, there is Albillo in the blend, but a much higher proportion, as much as 20 per cent depending on the vintage. The grapes are fully destemmed before fermentation in an open-top oak vat, and ageing in just two barriques. Production is tiny – only about 600 bottles a year. Sourdais is on his way; these are wines to follow.

Dominio de Pingus
Millán Alonso 49, 47350 Quintanilla de Onésimo
www.pingus.es

At the end of a quiet road, down by the riverside, there's a faintly nondescript building. As a pilgrimage site it's not especially impressive. Yet it's the home of one of Spain's most famous wines, Pingus. Peter Sisseck, its maker, would undoubtedly say that the important part of the wine is the vineyard. This consists of a matter of three parcels of very old Tinto Fino bush vines, altogether producing fewer than 500 cases of wine. The hardest work has been in the vineyard, coaxing the vines back to life. The grapes are fermented in an oak vat, and then aged in new French oak. Since 2000 the vineyards have been farmed biodynamically.

Sisseck had already made his name at Hacienda Monasterio, not far away, when he decided to launch this terroir wine in 1995. Pingus raised the bar for the price of Spanish wine in the marketplace. An early disaster pushed prices up still further. Robert Parker had praised the wine highly, but a ship sailing with wines to the USA sank off the Azores in November 1997. Prices soared. Pingus' investment potential was established, and it remains one of the rare Spanish wines with a strong presence on the auction market. With vintage 2014, Sisseck believes he has made a wine to match the exceptional 1995. It spent three years in oak, none of it new. This progression into used oak has helped assist the layered texture, without dominating the palate. The wine is exceptionally pure, with rich, supple tannins and an exceptionally long and ringing finish.

Pingus is Sisseck's single vineyard; Flor de Pingus is his village wine, though that is to denigrate its exceptional quality. The village is La Horra, from which he makes this deliciously aromatic, full-bodied and powerful wine, with very fine tannins.

Sisseck's story is well known – the Danish winemaker, with experience in France, who used his childhood nickname as the name of the winery. He lives in the DO amid vineyards – when not winemaking in Bordeaux and travelling the world. His commitment to his adoptive region is deep, and practical. That fact explains PSI. This is a project launched with the mission of preserving the old vineyards, and finding a way of convincing the farmers to preserve their unproductive bush vines and work for quality rather than quantity. The project has made a point of saving the scarce remaining old vine Garnachas. So PSI has some 10 per cent Garnacha along with a tiny amount of the typical interplanting of other varieties such as Albillo. Sisseck explains: 'There are high-potential vineyards, but they need to be managed properly. For this we need people with skills. But there's no prestige to working in the vineyards, so we have to find a way to give that prestige back. That's why we will be doing courses, teaching young people pruning and vineyard work'. The work is crucial: 'The idea of PSI is not just to help the old bush vines. We need to make sure the vines are in the right place. They are our connection to the past. We used to have 9,000 hectares, of which 6,000 hectares were old vines. We now have 22,000 hectares, and 2,000 of them are old. It's not that people aren't replanting. But they are planting in the valley. In ten years' time the kids won't remember where the best places are.'

PSI improves from year to year, and since 2015 the wines have been made in PSI's own winery in Aranda de Duero. There they make the wine in the traditional way, fermenting in concrete vats and then ageing in wooden tanks and oak barrels. The Gran Reserva PSI is a natural extension and launches with the 2013 vintage. Why PSI – apart from the link to your initials, I wonder? 'It's very difficult to find a new name for a wine! The idea was to have the Greek letter psi (Ψ) as the graphic symbol. Then my designer suggested a vine, and then she said you need soil and a house in the background. It was all getting too complicated. So we went back to the image of the roots.'

Emilio Moro

Ctra Peñafiel-Valoria s/n, 47315 Pesquera de Duero
www.emiliomoro.com

The Moros are firmly established in Ribera del Duero. As a family of growers they have the great advantage of owning some vineyards which were planted by their predecessors almost a century ago. The third generation, led by José Moro, has been the driver of the business. The first Moro-labelled wine was launched in 1989, just a few years after the denomination was established. Although the family had long been growers, many of their vineyards had been uprooted in the 1970s. Thus José Moro and his brother Javier started the business with just 5 hectares. By 1998 they decided to abandon the classic categories of Crianza and Reserva, and instead use the straightforward declaration of vintage of a 'generic' wine. Malleolus was their first generic, and within a few years they had also produced two single vineyard wines. Malleolus de Valderramiro comes from a highly rated area, from a 4 hectare vineyard the family planted in 1924. Malleolus de Sanchomartín is from vines planted in 1944; the site is higher up and high in limestone. Both are aged in French oak for 18 months. It's a fascinating contrast. Valderramiro is firmer, more brisk and dense; Sanchomartín is cooler and more elegant. To complete the set Malleolus today is made from the family's younger vines. The largest production of all is the regular Emilio Moro label. It all adds up to a production of over a million bottles a year.

Emilio Moro is a strikingly warm and welcoming business. The website is in six languages, there's a tab asking 'Would you like to work with us?' and the family set up their own charitable foundation in 2008. Theirs are big, forthright wines, no doubt, but they express the character of the people and their terroir. (See also Cepa 21, a new project, on p. 170).

Finca Villacreces

Ctra Soria N-122 Km 322, 47350 Quintanilla de Onésimo
Tel.: +34 983 680 437
www.villacreces.com

Villacreces is in a striking position beside the highway, next door to Vega Sicilia, the house surrounded by 100 hectares of vines and pines. The winery is part of the Artevino group that includes the wineries Izadi and Orben in Rioja, and Vetus in Toro and Rueda. As with so many estates here, it once belonged to the Church, but with the confiscation of the monasteries by Mendizábal it passed into private hands. In recent times it became renowned because Peter Sisseck worked there as a consultant. In all there are 60 hectares of vines, mainly Tempranillo, with some Cabernet Sauvignon and Merlot. There are three wines. Finca Villacreces contains 10 per cent Cabernet Sauvignon and 4 per cent Merlot, and is aged for 14 months in new French oak. It is undoubtedly oaky, but the style is polished and the wine is structured for ageing. Pruno is its well-priced younger cousin, with 10 per cent Cabernet Sauvignon and 12 months ageing in 3-year-old French oak – this undoubtedly eases the sense of oak which is a characteristic of the Villacreces wines. Finally, there is a very small production of the top wine, Nebro, made from centenarian Tempranillo vines from Olmedillo. It spends 14 months in new French oak, and is only made in the best years.

Garmón Continental

Camino de la Ribera s/n, Olivares de Duero
tel.: +34 983 488 708
www.garmoncontinental.com

Strictly speaking the company name is Bodegas Continental, but the project is still so young (first vintage 2014) that it is best known by the name of the wine – Garmón. This is an enterprise from the García family which has a long history in these parts. Mariano García was born at Vega Sicilia, where his father Mauro ran the vineyards. He was the winemaker there for many years, and is now one of the owners of Aalto. At the same time, he runs the well-established family business of Mauro in Castillo y León with his sons, who were formerly at Astrales. He and his sons Eduardo and Alberto García Montaña took the initial letters of their surnames to create Garmón, with an upper limit of 60,000 bottles. None know better than García where to find the best grapes, and his sons had very recent experience from consulting at Astrales. They source their grapes from the villages of La Aguilera, Moradillo and Baños de Valdearados (which became famous in 2011 for the discovery of Roman remains, including, appropriately, a mosaic of Bacchus).

The difference about Garmón for the Garcías is that it is inside the Ribera del Duero DO. As has been their strategy elsewhere, they work with the old vine Tempranillos. They use wild yeast ferments, and age the wine in French oak for 16 months. The result is in the modern style, well made, with polished tannins and a rich, satisfying finish. They also make a Godello from Valdeorras under the same brand.

Hacienda Monasterio

Ctra Pesquera-Valbuena Km 36, 47315 Pesquera de Duero
Tel.: +34 983 484 002
www.haciendamonasterio.com

One of the striking features of Ribera del Duero is just how many wineries are lined up along the flatlands of the highway, with vineyards laid flat out around them. Hacienda Monasterio is entirely different. The drive up from the valley floor runs past south-facing vineyard slopes at around 730 metres to the winery itself at the top, which has the benefit from its position of being gravity fed.

The 160-hectare estate, of which more than half is planted with dry-farmed vines, is rooted in the history of Ribera del Duero wine. It originally belonged to the Lecanda family who were owners of Vega Sicilia. It's in a privileged position, between the great names of the towns of Pesquera and Valbuena de Duero. In the late 1980s it was purchased from the neighbouring Dehesa de los Canónigos. Soon after it was bought by a Seville-based group, before ownership was assumed by partners from Jerez, including Carlos del Río, who is the sales manager for this winery and for the Montecastro project (see p. 182).

Peter Sisseck was recruited as winemaker in 1990, on the recommendation of his uncle Peter Vinding-Diers, on a short-term basis. That was nearly thirty years ago, and since that time his ties with Ribera del Duero have become closer than ever; notably with Pingus (see Dominio de Pingus p. 175), the wine which launched Ribera del Duero on the contemporary international scene. Sisseck planted the Hacienda Monasterio vineyards, which explains just why they look so very convincing. However recognizing that young vines cannot be treated like old bush vines, they used a modified trellis system which has brought the vines successfully through their early years. Today Sisseck continues to consult, advising on yields and blends, though Carlos de la Fuente is in charge.

The vineyards were planted with Tinto Fino, plus some Cabernet Sauvignon, Merlot and Malbec. The vines are farmed organically, according to Sisseck's philosophy. At the winery there is rigorous sorting, fermentation with indigenous yeast, and the malolactic fermentation is in French oak, about half of which is new. Over time the team has developed and refined their handling of the grapes and wine. New vineyards have been bought, and Tempranillo has been regrafted with better clones. In the winery there is experimentation, with some whole clusters and larger barrels. The result is that Hacienda Monasterio becomes ever better.

La Horra

Camino de Anguix s/n, 09311 La Horra
Tel.: +34 947 613 963
www.bodegaslahorra.es

Here's another Rioja winery launching itself in Ribera del Duero, and coming to terms with the differences between Tempranillo and Tinto Fino. As it happens, both Áster (from La Rioja Alta) and La Horra (from RODA) come from the same place, Haro's Barrio de la Estación. And both are demonstrating promise. Behind the La Horra project are Agustín Santolaya, RODA's general manager, and Mario Rotllant, the thoughtful, thorough businessman who founded RODA. After careful research, they homed in on La Horra as the best site. They have agreements with local growers – they manage the vineyards, and the growers will have a 10 per cent stake in the business. Their first vintage of Corimbo was 2008, which was launched in 2010. Following the model of RODA, Corimbo is made from the younger bush vines (around 20 years). There's a native ferment in stainless steel, followed by malolactic in French oak vats, before ageing for 14 months in barrels that are 80 per cent French rounded out by 20 per cent American.

Corimbo 1, launched with the 2009 vintage, comes from bush vines with an average age of 50 years. The fermentation is in French oak vats, followed by malolactic in barrels. The wines are aged a little longer – 16 months – in the same combination of oak as Corimbo. Both wines bring the polish of a successful winery. The team may be new to Tinto Fino, and to the climate, but they handle the fruit respectfully.

At Corimbo, as they have been doing in RODA, they are taking part in a project to build a gene bank of Tinta del País, with the intention not only of preserving biodiversity, but also combating climate change by having more material to draw from.

Legaris

Ctra Peñafiel-Encinas de Esqueva Km 2.5, 47316 Curiel de Duero
Tel.: +34 983 878 088
www.legaris.com

When Codorníu, the Cava company, launched Legaris in 2003, adding it to other major projects including Bilbaínas in Rioja, Raimat in Costers del Segre and part ownership of Scala Dei in Priorat, not counting other wineries outside Spain, it felt like a step too far. I must confess to being less than enthusiastic about the wines. At the beginning they felt safe and predictable. The first vines – Tinto Fino and Cabernet Sauvignon – were planted in 1999, so the vines were relatively young. The vineyards are in San Martín de Rubiales and Curiel de Duero

The viticulture sounds textbook: a mix of bush vines and trellising, with 50 per cent machine harvested. The investment in the winery enables separate handling of different plots. The best grapes are fermented in open casks. Wines are fermented in French and American oak barrels from different coopers. In the end I admit that I have changed my mind. Today the vineyards have more years on them, and Legaris like Ribera del Duero in general is learning about how best to manage its vineyards. The most successful of the wines are currently the reserva and Calmo. The latter is anything but calm, and all the better for that, a bold, impressive blockbuster of a wine, all Tinto Fino and French oak.

Martín Berdugo

Ctra de la Colonia s/n, 09400 Aranda de Duero
Tel.: +34 947 506 331
www.martinberdugo.com

The Martín Berdugo project began in 1990. Joséfina Martín Berdugo planted the vineyards and the grapes were sold to other wineries until the family launched their own wines in 2000. The winery is in the midst of 104 hectares of riverside vineyards, of which 87 hectares are Tinto Fino. The building won an award for its architecture, and the business was progressing well until it came to a momentary halt one evening in September 2013.

The winery was struck by lightning and set alight, and many of the facilities were destroyed. However the family has recovered from the setback and has a portfolio of young and Crianza wines, with its top of the range being 'mb', which is fermented and aged in new French oak.

Matarromera

Ctra Renedo-Pesquera, 47359 Valbuena de Duero
Tel.: +34 983 683 315
www.bodegamatarromera.es

Matarrromera was launched in 1988. The group consists of seven wineries and a distillery; these include Emina and Rento in Ribera del Duero, Carlos Moro in Rioja, Cyan in Toro and Valdelosfrailes in Cigales. Rento, the family's *vino de autor*, was launched in 2000, in a former Jesuit abbey. The vineyard from which it comes is the Moro's only holding on the left bank of the Duero, at Quintanilla de Arriba, planted in 1999. It's fermented in stainless steel and aged in French barriques from a range of coopers for a bold, confident style.

Montecastro

VA-130, 47318 Castrillo de Duero
Tel.: +34 983 484 013
www.bodegasmontecastro.es

Montecastro is one of Ribera del Duero's newer projects, founded in 2000 by a group of partners from Madrid. In 2012 Hacienda Monasterio became a 50 per cent shareholder, in the process bringing in their well-recognized winemaking and sales expertise. It was a smart decision. Montecastro acquired a partner with international recognition for the quality of its Ribera del Duero wines. Hacienda Monasterio in turn acquired a partner that can provide it with a complementary style, a second wine of sorts.

The founders planted 27 hectares of vineyards in separate plots at 860–923 metres, high even for many parts of Ribera del Duero. This altitude guarantees cooling in the extreme summer heat. The soils are poor and rocky, with calcareous bedrock and some black limestone. Organic farming has been introduced, with home-produced compost. Ninety per cent of the vineyard is a clonal selection of Tempranillo, with the remainder Bordeaux clones of Cabernet Sauvignon and Merlot. Fermentation is in temperature controlled concrete vats, with 90 per cent of the malolactic fermentation also in concrete. The wine is then aged in 90 per cent French oak and 10 per cent American oak barrels, new and one year old, for 14–20 months, followed by a few months in concrete after blending. The first vintage with the Hacienda Monasterio team was 2012, released in 2015. The new phase of Montecastro is still in its early days, but the results are promising.

O. Fournier

Finca El Pinar s/n, 09316 Berlangas de Roa
Tel.: +34 947 533 006
www.ofournier.com

O. Fournier could not exist without the dynamism, enthusiasm and vision of its founder, José Manuel Ortega. He started life as a Goldman Sachs banker, and soon found the most pleasurable way to spend his earnings was investing in and enjoying fine Spanish wine. From there it was a short step to entering the wine world himself. Today he has two wineries, one in Chile and one in Ribera del Duero. Far apart though they are, he travels constantly, keeping up with each and developing new ideas.

The O. Fournier group bought the winery of Hermanos San Juan López in 2002 (the original winery had been established in 1979). With the winery came 105 hectares of land, of which 60 hectares were planted with Tinta del País, plus a little Merlot, to which they have added some Malbec, given their Argentina experience. A course of study of the terroir followed to recuperate the vines and improve wine quality, and the winery was rebuilt. The wines are fermented in stainless steel tanks and wooden vats, and aged in French oak, with a small quantity of American or Central European oak (about 20 per cent).

A distinctive feature of the Fournier portfolio is that they have chosen to avoid the typical ageing categories. Thus each wine has a distinctive name, but the ageing in oak depends on the quality of the wine that year. The Urban wines are intended to be young, fruit-driven styles, for drinking young with just three months or so of oak ageing. Spiga, the second wine, sees around 12 months in barrel and up to a year in bottle. The top wine is O. Fournier, only produced in the best vintages. The early wines were bold and had generous oak, but recently the style is becoming more elegant, while still full of flavour.

Pago de Carraovejas

Camino de Carraovejas s/n, 47300 Peñafiel
Tel.: +34 983 878 020
www.pagodecarraovejas.com

Every visitor to Segovia goes for two things, to see the Roman viaduct, and to eat roast suckling pig. One of the restaurants that made its name for its cooking in the 1970s was Restaurant José María, run by an award-winning local sommelier, José María Ruiz. In 1987 he brought together a group of wine lovers from Segovia to create a winery in the new but scarcely developed area of Ribera del Duero. They chose the Carraovejas hillside site just outside Peñafiel as it had an established reputation for its grape ripening so they could build on the foundations of what was already established.

The winery was designed by Basilio Izquierdo, for a long time the winemaker at CVNE, an influential figure. So they enjoyed the benefit of his innovative designs of 'flying saucers' which carried the wine from one tank to another, without pumping. The wines are fermented in stainless steel and oak vats, and aged in French and American oak. From the beginning they always had Cabernet Sauvignon and Merlot in the vineyard. Their first vintage was produced in 1991 and from there they have continued to grow. Their wines are very popular, especially the Crianza, which is a supple, well-oaked choice, and has the kind of appeal that one would expect from someone such as José María Ruiz, with his experience as a sommelier and restaurateur. (Only a sommelier might complain at the hard to pronounce name of the winery – certainly hard for an uncertain customer to request for the first time.) El Anejón is an approachable selection from specific plots, and while the top wine, Cuesta de las Liebres, is perhaps less loveable, it may blossom with bottle age.

The group now also owns Ossian, which produces lovely Verdejos in the village of Nieva in Segovia, choosing to be outside the confines of DO Rueda.

Pago de los Capellanes

Camino de la Ampudia s/n, 09314 Pedrosa de Duero
Tel.: +34 947 530 068
www.pagodeloscapellanes.com

This winery recalls its previous monastic origins – the 'vineyard of the chaplains' belonged to the Church until the forcible handovers by the state in the 1850s. It now belongs to the Rodero family, who established it in

1996. Across their 100 hectares, divided into 35 plots, they have 80 per cent Tempranillo, the remainder being Cabernet Sauvignon and Merlot. They make lively young wines, while El Picón and El Nogal are their two top wines, each aged in a blend of different French oaks. They have also started to make a Godello under their own label.

Pérez Pascuas

Avda Ribera del Duero 30, 09314 Pedrosa de Duero
Tel.: +34 947 530 100
www.perezpascuas.com

A visit to the Pérez Pascuas family feels like a day with the classics. Winemaker José Manuel's father and two uncles founded the business in 1980, building on a family history as growers. That's why they are fortunate enough to have some seriously old vines. They have 110 hectares of vineyard – Tempranillo with 10 per cent Cabernet Sauvignon, which gives extra backbone – so they can manage the wine right from the vine. In the winery they use French and American oak in equal proportions. All in all this is a model of Ribera del Duero winemaking.

The young wine in the line-up, Cepa Gavilán, is made from the younger bush vines, and has a year in oak. It's always a good choice if you see it in a wine bar or the Crianza. While they make the other classical aged categories, my preference is the Gran Selección.

Protos

Bodegas Protos 24-28, 47300 Peñafiel
Tel.: +34 983 878 011
www.bodegasprotos.com

The fact that the bodega has the street named after it is a sign of its longevity and importance. While Protos is known now for its Richard Rogers architecture, its original claim to fame is that in 1927 it was the first winery to be founded in Ribera del Duero since Vega Sicilia.

For any architect, building in the sightlines of one of the classic castles was going to be hard. Peñafiel is a chocolate box castle, a childhood dream which towers over the landscape. But the bodega itself stands up well to the competition, the terracotta tiles of its dramatic roof toning with the surrounding roof tiles, although it is not embarrassed to flaunt its grandeur. It's a suitably grand tribute to the success of the pioneers. For Protos, as its name taken from the Greek suggests, was the first cooperative in the region. Today it has three wineries: Peñafiel; Anguix, for the reserve styles; and La Seca, for Rueda wines.

Protos owns 600 hectares, with another 500 belonging to independent winegrowers. With the capacity of the new winery they can handle 5 million kilos of grapes per harvest. The cooperative has travelled a long way: apart from Vega Sicilia, it was the first to build a brand and to enter wine competitions, making an international name for Ribera del Duero. It was a long time before others came to join it. Today the winery makes the full range of wines, including *blancos* and *rosados*.

Raiz de Guzmán
Ctra Circumvalación R30 s/n, 09300 Roa
Tel.: +34 947 541 191
www.raizdeguzman.es

If you are making a visit to the Consejo Regulador to pick up their very good maps and other printed materials – or simply to admire the architecture of the impressively modern building – then call in at Raiz de Guzmán. There's a hotel and restaurant, where the Páramo de Guzmán sheep's milk cheese goes well with a young Crianza from their range of classic Tempranillos.

Sei Solo
47360 Quintanilla de Arriba
Tel.: +34 619 710 000
www.seisolo.es

This is the child of the ever-inventive Javier Zaccagnini. Once upon a time he ran the CRDO Ribera del Duero; then he moved on to founding Aalto with Mariano García. He set up Ossian with Ismael Gozalo, making lovely Verdejos in Segovia. He eventually sold his share and purchased old vineyards in the much-respected town of La Horra in 2007, followed more recently by further plots in Gumiel and Moradillo. The first commercial vintage was 2011. The wines are made in a corner of the Aalto winery, in small 20-hectolitre vats. They mature for two years in French oak of 225 and 600 litres, and there's no new oak anywhere. Zaccagnini makes two wines – Sei Solo, the first wine, and Preludio the second. The names come from J. S. Bach's violin sonatas, and the labels have Bach's original script. Classical music is the soundtrack to his life as he drives from one appointment to another. As a novice winemaker, he has successfully applied all the lessons he has learned, and should be proud of his successes.

Telmo Rodríguez

El Monte, 01308 Lanciego
Tel.: +34 945 628 315
www.telmorodriguez.com

Telmo Rodríguez and his business partner Pablo Eguzkiza had long experience with Tempranillo in Rioja. Turning to Ribera del Duero they studied the differences with Tinto Fino, monitoring the ripening of Vega Sicilia's fruit, and noting the contrastingly greater thickness of the skins of Tinto Fino grapes. The other distinguishing feature from Rioja was the mix of soil types. In due course they started working with an abandoned bush vine vineyard. From that beginning, have come Matallana, M2 de Matallana and Gazur. Gazur is the youngest in the family, a cross-DO blend of bush vines from other growers, grown on calcareous clay and fermented with native yeasts in oak and stainless steel casks. M2 comes from a selection of vineyards in Sotillo, Roa and Fuentecén, totalling 20 hectares in all, of which just over half is owned by independent growers. The wine spends 14 months in French oak, 50 per cent of which is new. Matallana is the step up, a tiny production selected from a number of vineyards also used for M2. These are wholly owned by the business, and are being farmed organically. Fermented in oak casks, the wine then spends 15–18 months in new French oak, but carries it lightly. At a time when single vineyard wines are hitting the headlines in Rioja and elsewhere, these wines make a strong case for the traditional cross-village, cross-DO blend.

Tr3smano

Pago de las Bodegas s/n, 47314 Padilla de Duero
Tel.: +34 983 882 103
www.tresmano.com

Tr3smano started life as Proventus, winning respectable scores for the quality of its wines. It restarted in the hands of three well-connected people. The first was José Ramón Ruiz Caso, who bought the property and owns La Europea, the leading importer of Spanish wines into Mexico.

Much of the local expertise came from well-known Rioja producer Fernando Remírez de Ganuza, who had vineyards near Olmedillo. The company now draws on those vineyards as well as some in Gumiel de Izán and from growers within the highly rated La Horra/Roa triangle; there are 30 hectares in total. The trio was completed by Pedro Aibar, founder of the Somontano DO, and of the Blecua winery there. He subsequently ran El Coto in Rioja and runs his family business of Pagos del Moncayo in Campo de Borja.

The project is relatively new, but the results are altogether promising, showing excellent fruit and very fine tannins. It's a great winery, with an excellent choice of vineyards. If I have one quibble it is with the name, which is altogether too tricksy – easy to say but tiresome to write.

VALLADOLID

Valladolid, the gateway to Ribera del Duero, is just under an hour on the high-speed train from Madrid's Chamartin Station (unlike the beautifully restored Atocha, not a station to enjoy lingering in). It's too easy to abandon Valladolid for the vineyards, but be sure to add on a night or two to explore the city, which has an important place in Spain's history. The Catholic Kings, Fernando of Aragón and Isabella of Castile, were married here, thus marking the first stage that would unite their two kingdoms. From the twelfth century to the time of Philip II, and briefly afterwards, it was the capital of Castile and then of the united Spain. But in Philip II lay its decline, because he chose to move the court to Madrid. The symbol of that move today is in Valladolid's imposing cathedral. It was commissioned in 1585 but the architect, the great Juan de Herrera, was called away to build the palace of El Escorial, so it was never finished as he planned. Richard Ford strongly disapproved of the move to Madrid, saying: 'A position on a fine river, in a rich fertile country abounding in fuel and corn, and under a better climate, was abandoned for a mangy desert, exposed to the death-pregnant blast of the Guadarrama [Sierra].'

There are plenty of striking buildings to visit, including the university with its Baroque façade. The university itself was founded in 1346 and is one of the oldest in Spain. The National Sculpture Museum has an exceptional collection of medieval and Baroque works, including glorious creations in polychrome wood. As a footnote, there's a memorial to Christopher Columbus, who died here, and to Miguel Cervantes, author of *Don Quixote*.

Despite the very cold winters and very hot summers, Valladolid likes to live on the streets, and the students (there are two universities and a number of other education institutions) add to the atmosphere. There is plenty of food to enjoy, notably the roast lamb, white asparagus, wild mushrooms and very good bread.

Torres

Del Rosario 56, 47311 Fompedraza
Tel.: +34 938 177 400
www.torres.es

Slow but sure is the Torres way. First come the vineyards, then the wines, then the winery. So there's no visitor experience at this relatively young winery – however their head winery at Vilafranca del Penedès more than compensates in terms of wine tourism. At Fompedraza they make Celeste Crianza and Celeste Roble. The first wine launched was the Crianza 2003, which appeared in 2005. The first Reserva from Ribera del Duero is planned for launch in 2018. This, like many projects here in Ribera del Duero, is still young and needs time to settle.

Valdubón

Antigua Ctra N-1 Km 151, 09460 Milagros
Tel.: +34 947 546 251
www.valdubon.es

The Ferrer family of Freixenet Cava owns Valdubón. Their winemaker is Javier Aladro, a Jerezano who is a long way from the land of Sherry. However he is cheerfully dedicated to Tinto Fino – with a dash of Merlot and Cabernet Sauvignon. He draws on fruit from 155 hectares of vineyards. Freixenet own half, and he works with growers for the rest. Valdubón have the classic categories of wines. The Reserva is boldly aromatic – and a vertical tasting shows how well it ages with time. Top of the range is the Honoris, fermented in French oak vats, and with a fine balance of mocha, cinnamon, liquorice and cedar.

Vega Sicilia

Ctra N-122 Km 323, 47359 Valbuena de Duero
Tel.: +34 983 680 147
www.vega-sicilia.com

Driving to Vega Sicilia is much like driving to find one of Napa's iconic wineries. The journey is simpler with a GPS, but in the old days it was easy to shoot past it, and be forced to hunt for an easy place to do a U-turn. Come from Peñafiel and once you have passed Finca Villacreces you are almost there – it's on your left. The beautifully tended gardens coming up provide a clue. If you get to Arzuaga Navarro, then you have gone too far. It lies discreetly on the N-122. In fact the road neatly bisects the estate, separating winery from hillside vineyards. Unlike some of its neighbours there's no grand structure to signify its stature. Vega Sicilia has no need, since it is Spain's most historic wine icon, to flaunt its magnificence.

The estate is some 890 hectares, of which about a quarter are planted to vine. The rest is carefully managed, including a new plantation of cork oaks. Perhaps one day Vega Sicilia will be able to bottle their wines using their own cork. In early medieval times there was much argument about who owned the rights to this property. In the twelfth century the abbey of Valbuena won its case. Sadly there is no record that the monks planted vines, although it is likely that they and the local population would have done so. The contemporary history of Vega Sicilia begins in 1695, when the property was sold to the first Marquis of Valbuena. It remained in the family for over a century, but in 1817 was put up for sale, after a turbulent period for Spain's economy. Finally, in 1848, a buyer, Toribio Lecanda del Campo, a Basque entrepreneur, came to the rescue. In 1859, Toribio distributed the inheritance to his five children, and the third child, Eloy, received Vega Sicilia, amongst other properties.

Lecanda was clearly a visionary farmer when presented with the estate of field and forest. Amongst his plans was 230 hectares of vines with planting material imported from Bordeaux: Cabernet Sauvignon, Carmenère, Petit Verdot, Malbec and Pinot Noir. (The Pinot Noir did not survive, but Vega Sicilia still has 20 per cent Bordeaux varietals in the vineyards.) The vineyards and bodega were model projects. He received a prize from the Ministry of Public Works, which explained:

The farm called Vega Sicilia y Carrascal, formerly a barren piece of land, partly because of the nature of its soils and partly as a result of its abandonment over a long period, has been transformed by the efforts and financial sacrifices and investment, and the admirable management, of its owner, into an estate of high importance for its excellent yield and agreeable appearance for the quality of the wine produced from its exquisite and varied types of vine…

The story ends sadly: Lecanda was ruined, and had to sell Vega Sicilia soon after, in 1894. This was the year that the entrepreneurial Cosme Palacio founded his eponymous winery in Rioja. As phylloxera began to spread, Palacio decided to seek out isolated, untouched vineyards, which brought him to the Duero valley. His Basque cellar master Txomin Garramiola is credited with taking on Lecanda's vision and making wine to match the exceptional site. The earliest extant label of Vega Sicilia Único is 1915, though the Único may have been made before. In due course Palacio returned to Rioja and Txomin remained. He was the one who recognized that the quality of the fruit meant that the wine could undergo long oak-ageing.

In the 1950s, the winery was sold to PRODES, an agricultural enterprise. The official history comments that the winery and the vineyards suffered under this ownership from lack of investment and poor quality control. An improvement came with the purchase by the Venezuelan industrialist Hans Neumann in the mid-1960s. Here was an owner who bought Vega Sicilia because he loved the wine. Finally in 1982 the Neumanns sold to the Álvarez family, owners of a diversified international service business. Father David Álvarez was not a passionate wine enthusiast, but he recognized the exceptional prestige of the Vega Sicilia estate. The year 1982 was an *annus mirabilis* for Ribera del Duero; the DO was created, and Alejandro Fernández Pesquera was shot to stardom by Robert Parker.

Álvarez' second son Pablo, a considered, thoughtful man, was given gradual responsibility for the estate and became general manager in 1985. Vega Sicilia needed investment, and it has blossomed. The new winery, built under the guidance of former winemaker Javier Ausás, is an exceptional building, with every attention to detail. Given the age of these wines it will take years to see the long-term effects, but they can only be good. In the years since Txomin there have been few in charge of the winery: Jesús Anadón for many years, Martiniano Renedo, Mariano García and Ausás. He was succeeded as technical manager by Gonzálo Iturriaga de Juan.

Vega Sicilia makes three wines, Valbuena 5°, Único and Reserva Especial. There was also a Valbuena 3° but Álvarez stopped this in 1987 to focus on the top three.

Neither Valbuena nor Único is 100 per cent Tempranillo. The former has a little less than 10 per cent of Merlot and Malbec; the latter, a similarly small quantity of Cabernet Sauvignon. Valbuena spends 30 months in barrels and vats of different ages and origins, with a further two years in bottle. Único has ten years of ageing before release, while the Reserva Especial carries on the tradition of blending across three vintages. These are wines built for the long haul.

What about the name? That's a long story – or stories. In the beginning the name Villacreces was used, though that now belongs to another winery. Subsequent usages of Santa Cecilia, Vega de Santa Cecilia and so on finally led to today's version. 'Vega', according to company history, was a medieval term for the lands of the Duero valley, and the hillside slopes. Santa Cecilia is more complicated. This may refer to the Roman saint, or to a religious building on the site. There are suggestions that there is a connection with Sicily. However, Vega's response to this idea is firmly negative. Sicily was ruled intermittently by the Spanish Bourbon kings, but nothing has been found to link the winery on the Duero with the Mediterranean island. Vega de Cecilia first appears in the records in 1525. The 'de' does not disappear from the name until the turn of the nineteenth century. Today Tempos Vega Sicilia is the brand that unites all the Vega Sicilia wineries: Alión (Ribera de Duero), Pintia (Toro), Macán (Rioja, with Benjamin de Rothschild) and Oremus (Tokaji).

Viña Mayor

Ctra Valladolid-Soria Km 325.6, 47350 Quintanilla de Onésimo
Tel.: +34 983 680 461
www.grupobodegaspalacio.es
Viña Mayor is a part of the extensive Bodegas Palacio 1894 group, known until the beginning of 2017 as Hijos de Antonio Barceló. It provides a reliable, drinkable face of Rioja and Ribera del Duero among others.

What's interesting now about Viña Mayor, and worth watching, is that Almudena Alberca was appointed as technical director in 2015. She formerly worked at Dominio de Atauta, and is close to qualifying as a Master of Wine. She is already developing some different styles for Castilla y León, in the range called La Poda. Here she is showing a much more contemporary and fresh expression of wine. There's a Sauvignon Blanc from Rueda, a Tempranillo from Ribera del Duero, and a Tinta de Toro from Toro. A promising future.

Viña Sastre
San Pedro s/n, 09311 La Horra
Tel.: +34 947 542 108
www.vinasastre.com

Sastre likes to describe its wines as rich, dense and weighty, because of the terroir, but insists that this richness is counterbalanced by the freshness of their Tinto Fino in its ideal place. The family business was founded in 1932, and initially they made their wine from their original 23 hectares. Their vineyards are in La Horra at a chilly 800–840 metres, a layout of rolling slopes. Winemaker and viticulturist Jesus Sastre is meticulous in vineyard management, committed to organic farming. In the winery he ferments with the native yeasts. The cold stabilization is done by leaving the vats outside. When it's –15°C outside there's no need to turn on the electricity. Viña Sastre delivers a very honest profile of Ribera del Duero. The wines are in two categories: *vinos de pueblo* and *vinos de parcela*, village wines and single vineyard wines. At the village level, there's a white, a *rosado*, a *roble* and a Crianza.

The white, Flavus, comes from the banks of the Duero. What's interesting about this herby, mineral white is that in a mainly red region where Albillo is the most common white, it is made from Cayetana Blanca. Cayetana is not the most promising of grape varieties, as it is widely planted in southern Spain, and a popular base for distillation into brandy. However Flavus originated from a project to recuperate the older varieties of white grape that were interplanted as was usual with the Tinta del Pais vines. Roble, which Jesus Sastre describes as artisanal in its making, spends less than a year in French and American oak, and like so many Ribera del Duero wines is much the better for it, giving a lively bold expression of fruit. Crianza comes from much older vines, bush vines approaching 60 years in age, and with just 14 months in French and American oak achieves a good balance.

There are four parcel wines. The oldest vines (90 years) go into Regina Vides. These are bush vines from several La Horra vineyards, some yielding less than half a kilogram per vine. They have 18 months in new French oak. Among the parcel wines Pesus is a little different, as it is the only one that is not 100 per cent Tinta del País. There's 15 per cent Cabernet Sauvignon and Merlot in the blend, which makes it perhaps more contemporary. But it also proves that the people at Sastre know what they are doing with their 100 per cent Tinta del País, and that it is just as good without additions.

A DO that keeps on growing

Ribera del Duero has plenty of growing to do. With close to 300 bodegas it is hard to profile them all. I have selected in these pages favourites as well as established names. There are plenty more to discover. So here are highlights. These are names to look out for, each with an interesting story, some of them great value.

The wines at **Abadía de San Quirce** continue to improve. **Cruz de Alba** is a 'boutique' winery owned by Ramón Bilbao from Rioja and **Comenge** is another boutique, founded in 1999 by Jaime Comenge, whose father wrote a classic viticultural text. CVNE from Rioja has purchased a winery, but said at the time of writing that they were not intending to launch in Ribera del Duero imminently. **Dehesa de los Canónigos**, close to Alejandro Fernández in Pesquera, has a new white from Albillo. **Tomás Postigo** produces wines of very high quality, from experience honed in Protos and Pago de Carrovejas; these are excellent value. **Resalte**, founded in 2000 has an Expresión special selection that is particularly refined. **Rolland & Galarreta** is one of the joint projects between Frenchman Michel Rolland and Javier Galarreta. **Tábula** is making polished, modern wines, while those of **Valderiz** are well-made and good value. **Valduero**, one of the earliest wineries in the DO, also has good value wines. **Valtravieso** makes a range of fresh wines, from possibly the highest vineyards in the DO at 920 metres. Finally, at **Verónica Salgado** seek out the great value Viñas Viejas de Autor.

7

RIOJA: A WORLD WITHIN A WORLD

What's the best way to arrive in Rioja? For me, it's coming from Bilbao, taking the road through the mountains and watching Rioja as it unfolds before you. The mountains are majestic, and in between is undulating countryside with rivers running through and hilltop towns spread about. There's a lot to be said for arriving by rail, too. Take the train from Zaragoza. The last section, Logroño–Haro, meanders past the Ebro and vineyards. For the people who lived here in previous centuries Rioja must have seemed a blessed enclave. Any time is good to come: autumn is particularly beautiful; winter brings snow (and sometimes problems driving); in spring there's blossom on the trees and in the summer it's hot, but with plenty of cool places to enjoy wine in the evening. Too many wine regions can be flat monocultures of vines. Come to Rioja, it's altogether more human.

HARO AND THE STATION QUARTER

When phylloxera came to France, the producers cast around for vine-growing land. Spain was conveniently close and with the opening of the railway line from Logroño to Bilbao via Haro in 1880, Rioja was an ideal source. Thus it was that Haro's Barrio de la Estación came into being, with wineries clustered around the railway. The first to arrive was R. López de Heredía y Landeta in 1877, followed by CVNE in 1879, Duque de Montezuma and J. Gómez Cruzado in 1890, La Rioja Alta in 1890 and Bodegas Bilbaínas in 1901. (To complete the contemporary set, Muga moved from Haro town in 1970, and in 1987 came RODA.) In those

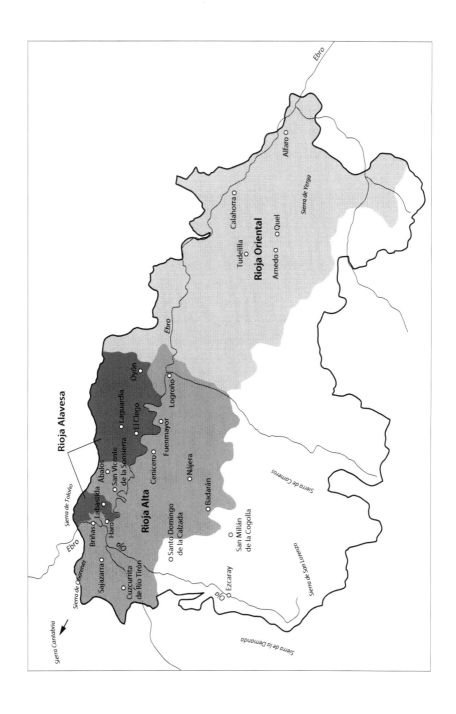

early years the bodegas jostled with factories making brandies, soaps and fertilizers. While some of the Haro bodegas may seem today the epitome of classical wines, Haro was cutting-edge in its day – the first town in Spain to have electric street lighting.

Phylloxera came to Rioja, inevitably, in 1899. The first outbreak was in a vineyard in Sajazarra. The region recovered reasonably quickly as by then the wine world had discovered that the solution was to graft vines onto much more resistant American *labrusca* rootstocks.

For a number of years Rioja continued to define itself like so many parts of the world in terms of French wines, for instance by selling 'cepa Borgoña' (intended to mean 'Burgundy style') wines. The really significant change, after Spain's entrance to Europe, was Rioja's elevation to DOCa status, *denominación de origen calificada*, a first in Spain in 1991. While regulation can be criticized for too much policing and of the wrong kind, it has to be noted that a DOCa should never be about selling any wine at bargain basement prices. The very nature of being a DOCa should protect it from that unsustainable marketing. Yet when the DOCa was introduced it was a generic blanket for all Rioja wines to satisfy all interested parties: grower, small producer, cooperative and multinational. Hence Rioja can be sold too cheaply. Surely the wine world has changed? One size (or type of classification) need not fit all. This takes us right back to the questions raised in the Club Matador Manifesto at the end of this chapter (see p. 266).

LA CATA DEL BARRIO DE LA ESTACIÓN
••• HARO STATION WINE EXPERIENCE •••

It's open house for the seven bodegas at the annual Barrio event.

THE NAMING OF RIOJA

Before we go any further, this is the place to run through the ever-growing list of possibilities behind the naming of the region. There is a River Oja, which surely must be the reason for Rioja's name. But this is a little trickle compared to the grandeur of the Ebro, and its dominance in the landscape. Then there's a possibility it refers to a local tribe called in Latin, *Ruccones*. Another source suggests that the source is *Erriotxa* or a similar spelling, which means 'bread country' in Basque. The US writer Ana Fabiano suggests that it might come from *Rialia*, describing a collection of small tributaries in Rioja Alta around the River Oja. She also speculates that it could come from the Basque *Arrioixa*, or 'land of rocks'. And thus, the debate continues.

DEFINING THE LANDSCAPE

Those who like to define Rioja in terms of Burgundy, will note that in geographical terms there *are* similarities. Imagine Rioja turned upright, clockwise through 45 degrees, and there you have Burgundy. It is approximately 40 kilometres wide by 100 kilometres long, running from north-east to south-west, tucked in between mountain ranges. Administratively it is composed of three provinces: La Rioja (43,885 hectares of vineyards, 118 municipalities), Álava, the southern tip of the Basque country (12,934 hectares, 18 municipalities), and to the east, Navarra (6,774 hectares, 8 municipalities). There is also one bodega to the far west of Rioja that is in Castilla y León. Climatically there are strong differences. Nothing is straightforward about the soils, either, a complex blend of chalky clay, ferrous clay and alluvial types. Add to this the differing aspects and elevations – up to 700 metres, and in a few cases up to 900 metres. Blend in the grape varieties. To finish, there are the decisions of the producers, each serving diverse customer tastes.

The River Ebro, which decants to the Mediterranean, winds through Rioja and into it flow seven significant small rivers – significant in terroir terms, that is, each offering different aspects and soils. All of these come down from the Iberian system of mountains to the south. Starting in the west, the River Oja rises to the south of Rioja in the San Lorenzo mountains and flows down to Haro. The snows and cold of the Sierra Demanda above the river valley have a strong influence on the higher altitude vineyards. Next comes the Najerilla river valley. Again, it rises in the San Lorenzo mountains and comes down to the Ebro with many terraces of vineyards on both sides. The Iregua valley to the east of it flows down to Logroño, creating fertile conditions for plenty of market garden produce and olives. The River Leza joins the Jubera before arriving at Agoncillo by the Ebro, and is distinctive for its cliffs and canyons. Great for walkers, both rivers are distinctive for the difference from the elegant beauty of some of the Rioja Alta landscapes. Finally, the Cidacos valley winds at length down past the Monte Yerga, and the high Garnacha-dominant vineyards of Quel and Arnedo till it comes to the Ebro just after Calahorra.

Rioja's story is all about diversity. As Ana Fabiano notes, Rioja contains 36 per cent of all the plant biodiversity in Spain. Furthermore when vineyard sites range from 300 to 700 metres, the climate really varies, and that's before one takes in considerations of slope, aspect and soil. That's why the vintage assessments beloved of fine wine retailers and auction houses are so difficult. Take the terrible frosts of April 2017. They wiped out 100 per cent of some vineyards, but others escaped completely. In terms of climatic influences, at the north-west end, Rioja is little more than 100 kilometres from the Atlantic, which gives the producers of Rioja Alta a good reason to describe their cooler vintages as Atlantic. The Sierra Cantabria is some protection from the Atlantic extremes. To the south the frequently snow-capped Sierra de la Demanda and the Sierra de Cameros protect the valleys of Rioja from strong winds from the south-west.

A NEW WAY TO UNDERSTAND RIOJA VINEYARDS

The CRDOCa recognizes three distinct viticultural sub-zones. Rioja Alta, where the climate is mainly Atlantic, with soils that are chalky clay, ferrous clay, or alluvial; Rioja Alavesa, where the climate is Atlantic, and the soils are chalky clay, broken up in terraces and small plots; and Rioja Baja, with alluvial and ferrous clay soils, which has a drier, warmer climate, with strong Mediterranean influences. These categories are long established, but are quite crude divisions of such an exceptional wine-producing region. Growers who have worked in Rioja for a long time know the subtleties. To advance the lively debate about if or how Rioja should segment its wines by sub-zone, the consultant Jose 'Pepe' Hidalgo, whose connections with the wines of Rioja are long and deep, has made a very constructive map (see p. 201). He points out that there are too many villages – 144 of them – to permit the sensible naming and management of village wines as Burgundy has done. The problem is compounded if you add in estate or vineyard wines. He advises that the work should begin by recognizing the correct sub-zones, beyond simply the historical ones of Rioja Alta, Rioja Alavesa and Rioja Baja. Now that there is so much understanding of the soils and vineyards, it is time to define them more clearly.

His sketch map identifies nine *comarcas* or zones. Each zone name opposite is written in bold type and the rivers are shown with fine lines. Hidalgo's plan neatly summarizes many actual assumptions about Rioja – Monte Yerga and Alto Najerilla for instance are well-known – while finding a logical pathway through the puzzle of some of the others.

Hidalgo's proposed La Sonsierra is what is currently Rioja Alavesa, as well as the few areas of Rioja Alta which are on the north side of the Ebro and geographically – if not politically – belong to Alavesa. The soils are calcareous clay, and this is practically the only part of Rioja where these soils are found. Rainfall is 400–500 millimetres and the annual average temperature 12–13°C. Moving east from La Sonsierra he identifies Ribera Oriental del Ebro, the eastern bank of the River Ebro, a large section which runs all the way down to Álfaro in the east. What unites this zone are the mainly alluvial soils, with some ferrous clay also. There's less rain, at 300–400 millimetres annually and it's warmer at 13–14°C. The wines from here have higher alcohol levels, and are less fresh, but much more deeply coloured and fruity. To the west is the Ribera Occidental del Ebro, the west bank of the Ebro with the river as its northern boundary. There are three main types of soil here: alluvial by the rivers, red-coloured ferrous clays, and also a smaller amount of calcareous clay. It's a cooler zone, 12–13°C and a little rainier at 400–500 millimetres.

Furthest west Hidalgo proposes Riberas del Oja y Tirón, the banks of the rivers Oja and Tirón. The northern boundaries here are the Ebro and the Obarenes mountains, and the southern is the Sierra de

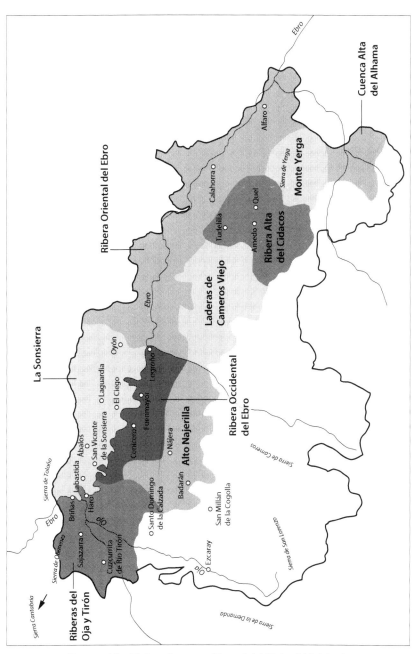

Proposal for Rioja sub-zones (Copyright © José Hidalgo).

la Demanda. There are three types of soil here: on the slopes of the Obarenes mountains it is brown limestone, closer to Haro, Briones and Ollauri it's calcareous clay and in the southernmost part, ferrous clay. It's cooler here, often much cooler, at 11–12°C, and the annual rainfall varies, depending on the site, from 400 to 600 millimetres. The wines are well coloured, perhaps the most Atlantic in style, with greatest potential for long ageing in bottle.

The zone of Alto Najerilla is undoubtedly the freshest and most humid of the DOCa, given its altitude of 700 metres. The Serradero mountain at 1,495 metres looms over it, and the rivers Najerilla and Iregua segment and define it. The climatic data illustrate this well: 10–12°C average temperature and rainfall between 400 and 600 millimetres depending on the site. The riverside soils are alluvial, but the rest are ferrous clay. This is the zone of very pale reds, the *claretes riojanos*, of refreshing reds and some fine Garnachas. The Laderas de Cameros Viejo is altogether different: a mountainous zone at 700–1,000 metres, with average temperatures at 10–13°C and rainfall at 500–600 millimetres. The wines are well-built, full-bodied and long-lasting. The Ribera Alta del Cidacos is the proposed region on the bank of the Upper Cidacos river. This rises from 500 to 1,000 metres, with the peak of Peña Isasa at 1,456 metres. The average temperature falls as the altitude rises, from 13°C to 10°C, while rainfall is 400–500 millimetres. There are alluvial soils by the river, and ferrous clay to the north, with brown limestone in the highest parts. The best wines having long ageing potential.

The eighth proposed region, Monte Yerga, is already well accepted. The Yerga mountain rises to 1,101 metres, and many of the vineyards are clustered at 500 metres, with others rising much further. Monte Yerga has become very fashionable as the popularity of Garnacha has risen, and the vineyards at 600–700 metres and higher are extremely promising. The climate changes with the altitude, with temperatures from 13–11°C and rainfall at 400–500 millimetres. The final suggested zone is Cuenca Alta del Alhama, literally, the high basin of Alhama. Hidalgo comments that it's probably the smallest and least known of Rioja's sub-zones. It's reasonably high at 500–700 metres, with average temperatures of 12–13°C and rainfall at 400–500 millimetres. The brown limestone soils here are excellent for Garnacha and there are some old vine reminders of the Garnachas that once grew here.

Until such time as the CRDOCa introduces a really clear system, this simple sketch map of Hidalgo's is a measured, constructive introduction to the diversity of Rioja. In the meantime, Rioja continues to be divided into Rioja Alta, Rioja Alavesa and Rioja Baja. Álava has always been a special case, as it is part of a separate province with a very strong political identity. As Europe in general becomes more interested in separatism Álava's interest in her differences from the rest of Rioja have also become more acute. It's not just the language that is so obvious on all the road signs the moment you cross into Álava. Nor is it simply the style of winemaking, with a continued tradition in partial or total carbonic maceration for young wines. It's not just the genuine beauty of the region: the villages and towns that stand out against the vineyards, the Ebro, and the Sierras de Toloño and Cantabria. These are special places. The region was always known for the quality of its produce. In 1164 King Sancho el Sabio (the Wise) ordered that vines should be planted in the region, which gave rise to the villages of Labastida, Labraza and Salinillas. They were definitely appreciated by the far-sighted Queen Isabella la Católica who ordered in 1504 that Alavesa wines should be taxed at a lower rate than those from the surrounding regions. The pilgrims in search of sustenance en route to Santiago de Compostela must have been delighted.

INTRODUCING THE VIÑEDO SINGULAR

Fast forward to 2016 and 40 producers came together to propose the creation of Viñedos de Álava. This was not well received in the CRDOCa. They were already having to contain any repercussions from Juan Carlos López de Lacalle having taken the Artadi winery out of the DOCa just a few months earlier. In a flurry of activity in 2017, the CRDOCa managed to restore calm, and the Álava producers withdrew their plan. There are now two new proposals from the Consejo Regulador, which have to be ratified at a governmental level. This will take time, but in essence the proposals are as follows.

For wine to be able to declare that it comes from a Viñedo Singular, the vineyard has to have demonstrable boundaries and ownership for a minimum of ten years. The vineyard must be more than 35 years old, and it can be made up of several plots or vineyards together if they are connected. The yield must be at least 20 per cent below the regional requirement. The vineyards must be well-balanced with limited vigour, hand-harvested, and managed with respect for the environment. In terms of finished wine it must show traceability, undergo quality assessment both initially and before sale, and have an 'Excellent' rating.

Will this be enough to satisfy the critics? One exporter of Spanish wines was blunt: 'I cannot see how it will help the consumer; a shoddy single vineyard wine will still be a shoddy wine but it will now be backed by an official recognition as "something special".' On the other hand Alejandro López, the winemaker at Bilbaínas, is more optimistic: 'Rioja is now in the perfect moment to show all its diversity regarding terroir, knowledge and origin … That's the beauty of this initiative. The conjunction of these two concepts of estate wines versus Reserva and Gran Reserva will depend on the type of wine, the style of the house, the style of the winemaker, but they can be totally complementary.'

At the time of writing there are many owners of famous vineyards who do not seem keen to go to the trouble of registration when their wines are already known. On the other hand there are others who are looking forward to the extra recognition that the label will provide in 2019 or 2020 when the legislation passes.

INTRODUCING VILLAGE WINES

The second decision taken in 2016 was to allow village wines to be declared as such on the label. At last! Rioja is taking the Burgundian route. Not entirely. The critics are unhappy here, too: the CRDOCa requirement is now that the winery must be in the same village as the vineyard. This prevents people with multiple single vineyards in different villages making multiple village wines, unless they go to the expense of constructing a winery for each. These producers argue that nowadays roads are good, and chilling available, that grapes can be brought quickly and safely from one end of Rioja to the other. Adding fuel to the fire of the critics, the new regulation will permit producers to include up to 15 per cent of non-village fruit from neighbouring vineyards outside the village boundary. Critics say that these two decisions play into the hands of the large producers, who have the strongest voices in the DOCa. Is this proposal undermining the very nature of village wine, as they say, or is it merely practical? At this stage these two decisions look as if they have been made in haste, to satisfy producers who were threatening to break away, and may be regretted at leisure. Undoubtedly revisions will be needed.

TO BLEND OR NOT TO BLEND?

There are now so many styles of Rioja – modern, *vino de autor*, single vineyard, carbonic maceration and more – and so many strongly held opinions that it is easy to lose sight of one important quality in many fine Riojas. Namely, that they are blends. There are historical reasons for this. Many producers did not own their own vineyards, and there are commercial brands who still don't. They rely on the growers for supply, growers from right across Rioja. Then there are also producers who wanted to make classical blends of two or more varieties, of Tempranillo with Graciano or Mazuelo, for instance, who own vineyards or buy their grapes from the best places, but not necessarily close to the winery. Rioja Alta producers sourced and still source their Garnacha grapes from Tudelilla in Rioja Baja. This was never an issue, until the debate promoting single vineyard wines became so excessively heated.

There are many kinds of Rioja. Which is better: a cross-DOCa blend of the best grapes, or a single vineyard where perhaps only one variety flourishes? This is the same debate over the merits of Penfold's Grange and Henschke's Hill of Grace in Australia. One is a multi-regional blend, the other a historic single vineyard. Different styles, different consumers, equal pleasure. Everyone has different views: my current notebook is filled with diagrams of Burgundian-style pyramids (Bierzo proposals), interlocking circles (neighbouring village proposals) and criss-crossing rectangles (the CRDOCa vision). Speaking at RODA, director general and all-round viticultural expert Agustín Santolaya pleaded: 'Don't Burgundify Rioja'. RODA is the newbie in the Barrio de la Estación, having only been founded in 1989. Santolaya's mission is to make the best wine from a blend of the best vineyards; the traditional approach, though perhaps in a modern way. Look back at history, he says: 'Traditionally Rioja blended its wines from great vineyards; there were practically no single vineyard wines made.'

HARO'S BATTLE OF WINE

Where does one start explaining this one? There is a real history behind the event which takes place on St Peter's Day, on 29 June. It started life as a pilgrimage to San Felices in Bilibio, where a mass is held in a tiny chapel. (Although another story says that it was an annual ritual to beat the bounds - walking the town boundaries - to make sure that Haro kept its independence.) In time, people making the pilgrimage used to throw wine around liberally. Then in 1949 the local paper named this the Battle of Wine. (Actually, as with all events of this kind, the record varies considerably, so it could be that the name changed in 1965.)

Either way, it's a highlight of the calendar - whether you pile in or book a week away. Plenty of tourists come, but there are plenty of locals too. The plan is to wear a white shirt and a red neckerchief. The 4-mile pilgrimage is led by the Mayor, on horseback, and everyone follows carrying jugs, bottles and wineskins filled with red wine as well as all kinds of pump-action spraying equipment including children's plastic bazookas. Once the mass is over the mayhem begins. The crowd makes its way back in town, absolutely soaked, and Haro parties on. Still keen to take part? Visit www. wine-fight.com.

For a less raucous festival, San Mateo is the one. It's the harvest festival and starts on 21 September. There's a public holiday, processions, inevitably some foot-treading of grapes and generally plenty of feasting and music. It starts with a bang, with the letting off of a rocket, and there's a glorious procession of giant-sized figures - kings and queens and characters from history.

WHITE RIOJA REBORN

A decade ago, perhaps less, white Rioja had a really terrible reputation. The general view was that it was made from only one variety – Viura – and that Viura was flabby and boring. Yet in just a few years white Rioja has returned to favour. It may still only account for some 6–7 per cent of Rioja production but from that low base its market share has been increasing by some 20 per cent year on year. There are a number of reasons for this. They include: climate change, improved distribution, the requirements of export markets and the creativity of individual winemakers, while maintaining respect for the old ways and the classics. The launch of the latest Castillo Ygay 1986 white from Marqués de Murrieta with some 30 years of age hit the fine wine headlines and helped to bolster the profile of white Rioja as something exceptional. Of course, like the Viña Tondonia Gran Reserva white, it is a one-off, an original. In general, today's white Riojas are – many of them – beautifully balanced, with subtle oak, and complex. They could not be further from the oxidized, tired wines of the past.

White Rioja is not just made from Viura – though it remains the dominant variety. Malvasía de Rioja (know in Catalunya as Subirat Parent), with its distinctive reddish, yellowish bunches, plays a small but significant part. Garnacha Blanca again amounts for a tiny percentage of the vineyard, but is making some finely textured wines. The Consejo Regulador wobbled a little when it permitted the introduction of Chardonnay and Sauvignon Blanc to an already fine line-up of varieties. An understandable step, an attempt to give their wines an international appeal, but the future for a DOCa lies in making great terroir wines with local varieties.

New varieties are appearing. Tempranillo Blanco made the headlines first. This is a genetic mutation; a single plant with white grapes was found in 1988 in Rioja, in Murillo del Río Leza. It's a late budding variety, but like the red Tempranillo it ripens early. It can show citrus and floral notes and has been popular because of its relationship to Tempranillo itself. Another of the 'new' varieties is in fact an old variety, rescued and revived. Maturana Blanca is the oldest known grape variety in Rioja, and may have been referred to in 1622. The fact that it is sensitive to botrytis will have helped it fall out of favour. In character it has bright acidity, a tendency to warm alcohol, and a hint of bitterness on the finish. Another 'new' variety is Turruntés de Rioja, no relative of the Galician Turruntés or the Argentine Torrontes. Instead it is similar to Albillo Mayor, found in Castilla y León. It is low in alcohol, with a welcome high acidity, offering crisp apple notes. For a taste of these traditional and new white varieties, look to Abel Mendoza, and to Juan Carlos Sancha, the university lecturer and *bodeguero*, who has also fostered these rarities.

Rioja at a glance

Grape varieties

White: Viura (6.5 per cent of total vineyard, 72.7 per cent of white vineyard), Malvasía, Garnacha Blanca, Tempranillo Blanco, Maturana Blanca, Turruntés, Chardonnay, Sauvignon Blanc, Verdejo.
Red: Tempranillo (79.7 per cent of total vineyard, 87.5 per cent of red vineyard), Garnacha, Graciano, Mazuelo, Maturana Tinta. Ninety per cent of total wine production is red.

Size

Vineyard: 65,012 hectares (La Rioja 68.3 per cent, Álava 21.1 per cent, Navarra 10.6 per cent)
Growers: 16,139
Wineries: 601 (La Rioja 326, Álava 259, Navarra 15)
Total number of 225-litre barrels in Rioja: 1,325,629

Producers

Abel Mendoza Monge

Ctra a Peñacerrada 7, 26338 San Vicente de la Sonsierra
Tel.: +34 941 308 010

For a taste of the traditional white Rioja vineyard, Abel Mendoza is your man. With some 37 parcels around San Vicente de la Sonsierra, he makes fine reds, but also no fewer than five single varietal whites: Viura, Torrontés, Tempranillo Blanco, Garnacha Blanca and Malvasía. I am sure his importers don't find it easy to sell the whole diverse portfolio, but it's a treat for us Rioja lovers.

Mendoza is a *viticultor* through and through, a man who knows his vines personally, and for whom the phrase Single Vineyard could have been designed. His wife Maite Fernández runs the winemaking in the cellar in San Vicente. For red wines, they work mainly with Tempranillo. Jarrarte is a young, joyful, well-liked Crianza, while Guardaviñas, a no-added sulphur wine is made from biodynamically farmed grapes, the Tempranillo Grano a Grano, is as the name suggests destemmed, and selected berry by berry. The result is super-polished in style. Its partner, the Graciano Grano a Grano reveals the purity and power of the variety, and for that reason Mendoza recommends cellaring it for a few years. These are exciting wines.

Alegre & Valgañón

LR 209, 26212 Sajazarra
Tel.: +34 609 886 652
www.alegrevalganon.com

Once upon a time, not so long ago, when Eva Valgañón was a little girl, she helped her family plant a chilly 1.07 hectare plot of vines at 580 metres far to the west end beyond Cuzcurrita de Río Tirón. Today she's married to Oscar Alegre, whom she met when they were studying winemaking in Italy, and that La Calleja plot is part of their project, with 16 hectares of family vineyards in all. Alegre has worked for some of Spain's top producers in export, while Valgañón has worked as a winemaker. They have been making wine together only since 2014. Like their colleagues in the Rioja 'n' Roll marketing group they want to make wines that reflect their vineyards. Hence the white (Viura with 10 per cent Garnacha) is aged for around a year not in barriques but in used demi-muids, and the red (Tempranillo with 25 per cent Garnacha) is fermented in wooden vats with 25 per cent whole bunches, and aged in used French barriques and demi-muids. The business is young, and the wines are very promising.

Both are fans of the great old Riojas. If you are keen to discover the glory of the old vintages then be sure to visit Fine Rioja Wines (www.fineriojawines.com), an online wine merchant Oscar runs with Johnny Hartwright. Mouthwatering.

Amaren

Ctra Villabuena 3, 01307 Samaniego
Tel.: +34 945 175 240
www.bodegasamaren.com

The little baby of the Luis Cañas winery (see p. 237) has turned into a healthy adult. The birth of the new wave *vinos de autor* for Luis Cañas was very adeptly handled. Rather than muddling the brands, as happens commonly elsewhere, with newer and more classical wines, Amaren is a whole different business, but very close physically to the mothership. Amaren (meaning, naturally enough, 'from the mother') sources from 30 hectares, and controls the same quantity again.

Arizcuren

Santa Isabel 10, 26002 Logroño
Tel.: +34 941 233 073
www.arizcurenvinos.com

Architect turned winemaker Javier Arizcuren opened his garage winery in downtown Logroño in 2016. Unlike some other city wineries worldwide this winery uses local grapes – though they are from the other end of La Rioja. His first vintage was in 2016 and used grapes from his family vineyards in Rioja Baja, in Monte Yerga at Quel. The total vineyard holding is 16 hectares but he currently uses only a small part of that. His first wine was Solo Mazuelo, one of the rare single varietal Mazuelos (Cariñena) in Rioja. Mazuelo was always a small part of the traditional Rioja blends. The variety that gives a distinct purple/blue colour is becoming ever more popular, partly perhaps as a result of its excellence in Priorat, but partly also for its lively acidity which makes it ideal for restaurants, and warm evenings. The second wine is Solo Garnacha. He has been working to restore the old bush vine heritage of the region. The third, also Garnacha, is yet to be released at the time of writing but will show more of this commitment to restoring the heritage – from pre-phylloxeric vineyards of around 120 years of age at 750 metres.

The Taller de Arizcuren Vinos – a shop window on winemaking – is open for visits.

Artadi

See page 265.

Artuke Bodegas y Viñedos

La Serna 24, 01307 Baños de Ebro
Tel.: +34 945 623 323
www.artuke.com

La Condenada 'the condemned' is a gloomy name for a vineyard, but what a treasure it is. Just a short drive from the family winery in the middle of Baños de Ebro this little vineyard sits up on the crest of a hill. It is the very essence of what a Viñedo Singular should be about, though I am not altogether sure it is what the Rioja decision-makers had in mind when they created the concept.

Arturo and Kike (hence Artuke) are the sons of Miguel Blanco, who is from a vinegrowing family. In 1991 he decided to stop producing bulk wine and turned to bottling his own. His sons now run the business from the family's 22 hectares of bush vines, which are divided up into 32 plots between Baños de Ebro and the highly rated village of Ábalos. Although the distance covered is not great, there is a diversity of soils, slopes and aspects, which they farm to biodynamic principles. They make two village wines. The first, Artuke, from Baños, is from vines dating back to 1902 at 450 metres on chalky clay soils, fermented using carbonic maceration and keeping the stems. Pies Negros from Ábalos is foot-trodden as its name suggests, and is grown at around 620 metres.

They are members of Rioja 'n' Roll, and like the other seven members of the group, are strongly committed to making wines from individual sites that express their originality. They currently make three single vineyard wines. La Condenada was purchased in 2012, and is a field blend on very poor, sandy soils of the usual suspects of Tempranillo, Garnacha and Graciano, plus the altogether less common Calagreño, a white grape similar to Palomino. Finca Los Locos, named after their grandfather who was thought to be crazy for buying such an apparently poor site, is a wine from a vineyard at 550 metres overlooking the Ebro, with gravelly soil over limestone. The final wine is K4 from an exceptional site planted in 1950 at 650 metres, up in the foothills of the Sierra Cantabria. They call it their Atlantic wine; one that captures a freshness and delicacy of Tempranillo with 20 per cent Graciano. The brothers have their attention on a new site, even higher, stonier and more extreme. These are fine wines.

Baigorri

Ctra Vitoria-Logroño Km 53, 01307 Samaniego
Tel.: +34 945 609 420
www.bodegasbaigorri.com

One of Rioja's modern architectural icons, Baigorri is the impressive glass box that comes up suddenly on the road to Samaniego, at the crest of the hill just as you cross the border into Álava. Suddenly all the other modern constructions of concrete and steel crumble into pretentiousness before the bold clear glass winery with its balancing roof and bold lettering just in case you should be unaware that it is Baigorri. Only the car park in front spoils the design.

The building, dating from 2002, is a memorial to the boom days of construction; they just don't make them like this any more. And indeed the founder had to sell up in the end. Nevertheless the winery has flourished, and the clever design is more than just clever, it continues to produce award-winning wines. This is a scrupulously designed and scrupulously managed winery, a vision in perfectly managed concrete, with some 3,000 barrels to finish the wines. At the outset, Baigorri was better known for the quality of its bodega than its wines. However, the team is turning that around and working hard to raise the quality overall.

Baigorri draws upon 25 hectares of its own vineyards, plus another 100 hectares under contract. It's a bodega that actually uses the term *vino de autor* for the non-Reserva range of wines. The De Garage was the first, and deservedly gained attention, as it continues to do, for its silky, bold expression. Newer to the line-up is Belus, a Mazuelo-dominant wine, with a blend of local varieties, aged in French oak. The Garnacha in the series is bold and inky, with well-handled French oak. B70 is the very top of the range, an ambitious wine, made from old vines, super-selected, fermented in open-top 600-litre vats and matured in new French oak for 22 months.

This is an interesting winery to visit, and not just for wine geeks; make time for the restaurant at the lowest level, which overlooks the vineyards.

Barbarot

Polígono Las Eras, Lonja 5, 26330 Briones
Tel.: +34 610 455 584
www.barbarot-wines.com

Bárbara Palacios López-Montenegro was born into a Rioja wine family. She trained in Bordeaux, and has worked at Chateau Margaux, Mudhouse (New Zealand) and Mondavi (California); as well as in Italy, Chile and Argentina. She launched her own label in 2005, when she first took over a vineyard planted at around 500 metres by her father Antonio. The vineyard is Tempranillo and Merlot, and the combination of clay soils and Merlot was a reminder of her experience of similar soils in St-Emilion. After a few years in borrowed wineries, she set up shop in 2008 in a garage winery, an easy and convenient warehouse in an industrial estate outside Briones. There she makes her Tempranillo with its dash of Merlot.

Bárbara's constant companion is surely Rioja's most famous vineyard dog: Merlot, the golden retriever. He now has his own label, Puppi. This is a juicy, cherry-fruited blend of Tempranillo with 15 per cent Merlot, from young vines, which spends six months in used French oak.

Barón de Ley

Ctra Mendavia-Lodosa Km 5.5, 31587 Mendavia
Tel.: +34 948 694 303
www.barondeley.com

Barón de Ley is an impressive site: a relatively new business (1985) established in a sixteenth-century fortress that later became a Benedictine monastery. The group is big business, too, a publicly quoted company that also owns El Coto in Rioja and Finca Museum (in DO Cigales). The ageing cellar capacity of 4.5 million bottles for Reservas and Gran Reservas indicates the size of the bodega. Vineyards are spread across the Rioja, nearby in Rioja Baja as well as in Rioja Alta, giving the mix of soils and styles to make their blends. Their Reservas and Gran Reservas are modern, with the emphasis on fruit, consistent and reliable. Finca Monasterio is the top-end, *vino de autor* style, estate grown, French-oaked wine. Most interesting are the single varietals, and in particular the 7 Viñas Reserva, blended from Tempranillo, Graciano, Garnacha, Mazuelo, Viura, Malvasía and Garnacha Blanca, a blend from a single vineyard. Four wines are made from the seven varieties, which are then aged in foudre for a year.

AGE BEFORE BEAUTY?

There's a heated argument, and not just in Rioja, about the traditional categories of (the unpronounceable to many) Joven, Crianza (and its impossible to understand friend Semi-Crianza), Reserva and Gran Reserva. These categories were regulated by the authorities to make a systematic practice out of what was already happening. But as with all regulation, it went too far. It forced producers into an exact minimum number of months or years in barrel or bottle, and into using a barrel of a specific size. Other countries (and what the critics really mean is – France) were classifying their vineyards either by the historical quality of the vineyard, or by the commercial recognition of the winery. Rioja, however, only rated its wines by age. But the fact that a wine has spent two years in barrel does not in itself make it better than a wine that has only spent a year. Yet that is what the traditional classification suggested. Gran Reserva had to be better than Reserva and Reserva surely had to be better than Crianza. No matter that a Gran Reserva might be tired out by the time it came to market, because the grapes lacked the initial intensity and the winery had poor oak. No matter that Crianzas can often be a best buy; and no one would call López de Heredia's finely aged Viña Cubillo a callow Crianza.

With the arrival of the trend for *vinos de autor* in the 1990s, producers took the matter into their own hands. They could produce wines which simply declared their vintages under the 'generic' category, and they could age them in French oak barriques for as little or as long as they wanted. Initially too many were over-oaked, overripe, over-extracted and over-alcoholic. It was hard to tell they were even Rioja. Today we are reaching an equilibrium, where many *vinos de autor* are calming down. Meanwhile producers of Gran Reservas have cleaned up their oak. They are also bringing much younger Gran Reservas to market, as soon as they fit the regulations, which muddies the waters in terms of what constitutes 'Gran'. On top of this there's a refreshing trend for wines to be aged in larger sized oak containers, and used containers, and even the occasional ferment in amphora, to reduce the influence of the traditional oak. At last it's possible to find the Tempranillo, and to understand the origin.

While the categories remain in use, here are the definitions of the class system, effective from January 2019:

Joven. Young wines that are usually in the first or second year with 'bright, fruity characteristics'. These may have been oaked. If they have had less than the one year (red) or six months (white) required in the Crianza category, they are listed as Joven.

Crianza. Red wines must spend a minimum of two years in the bodega, of which a minimum of one year is in cask, and one year in bottle. White and *rosado* wines must spend a minimum of six months in cask and six months in bottle before release.

Reserva. Red wines must spend a minimum of three years in the bodega, of which a minimum of one year is in cask and six months in bottle. White and Rosado wines must spend at least two years in the bodega, of which at least six months must be in cask.

Gran Reserva. Red wines must spend a minimum of five years in the bodega, of which a minimum of two years is in oak casks and two years in bottle. White and *rosado* wines must spend a minimum of four years in the bodega, of which a minimum of one year must be in cask.

The size of the casks described here is 225 litres. If you wish to use a larger cask – 500 litres, 1,000 litres – to reduce the influence of oak, the wine will be in the generic category. Regulation section 22.3 states: 'wineries must have a minimum stock of 22,500 litre of maturing wine, of which at least half must be kept in 50 oak barrels of approximate 225 litres category'. This means that small producers cannot make wines in these categories.

Generic wines. An increasingly widespread category, this simply certifies the vintage. The translation sounds terrible in English, but in quality terms it can include exceptional wines. It also includes all the *vinos de autor*, and wines made by producers who want to follow their own oaking and maturation regimes.

Basilio Izquierdo

Ctra Vitoria s/n, El Collado 9, 01300 Laguardia
www.bodegasbasilioizquierdo.com

The delightfully wise Basilio Izquierdo had already had one exceptionally fulfilling career in Rioja, but then in retirement in 2007 embarked on yet another, equally complex and diverse, if on a smaller scale. Izquierdo trained in Bordeaux with Michel Rolland. While Rolland went on to become the much-travelled wine consultant, Izquierdo, who was born in Ciudad Real, eventually became technical director for CVNE for more than three decades (1974–2006). If you have ever loved a great Imperial or Viña Real from those golden years, then raise a glass to Basilio.

It is interesting to see what a person with such experience chooses to do when entirely free from corporate pressures. In 2007 he set up in an awkward space, one that could not be further from the custom-made facilities he had at CVNE. He doesn't own vineyards, but makes blends from the best places. So his B de Basilio blends Tempranillo from Laguardia and Leza, with Tempranillo and Graciano from Haro, and Garnachas from Rioja Baja and Najerilla. This is what the great cross-regional blends were all about in the hands of the skilled master blenders, but no one ever talked about their details to consumers.

His white B de Basilio is mainly Garnacha Blanca, not the Viura one might expect. With less than a year in oak it shows the real potential for white Rioja. His Acodo range includes a lively *rosado*, again unusual for Rioja, made from Garnacha with 30 per cent Garnacha Gris. Most interesting of all are his experimental small batches of original wines made in small vats, barrels and amphorae. And on very special occasions you may be lucky enough to try his blend.

Beronia

Ctra Ollauri-Nájera Km 1.8, 26220 Ollauri
Tel.: +34 941 338 000
www.beronia.es

Beronia has been transformed. González Byass' Rioja property used to produce traditional Riojas with frankly elderly-tasting barrels. In the early 1990s there was a major investment and all the barrels were replaced over a short period. Later, new brooms were brought in to consult on winemaking. The result: Beronia has become a bestseller – and perhaps as important – an award winner. Its Reserva is a model of a well-made modern Reserva.

Like a number of other Rioja wine businesses, the winery was founded by a group of Basque businessmen, in 1973. They belonged to a *txoko*, a society which met to enjoy wine and good food. By 1982 they had sold the majority of shares to the Sherry business. Today's winemaker, Matias Calleja, draws on fruit from some 900 hectares of vineyards, from many growers. These range from a few pre-phylloxeric vineyards more than 100 years old to some that were only planted in 2011. The next step on the quality ladder will be to open the new winery, in time for 2019. This will only be for Reserva, Gran Reserva and special edition wines, such as III a.C. and the single varietal Mazuelo Reserva. In an acknowledgement of the feasting at the heart of its origins, the new winery will have its own *txoko*, for entertaining. Visit the website for up-to-date news of the opening, and opportunities to visit.

There is a full portfolio of wines at the entry level, as well as an organic Rioja. Moving up the age scale, the Crianza and the Reserva are reliable, and the Gran Reserva goes on improving from year to year. The Selección de 198 Barricas is a Reserva wine, a selection from 198 barrels with American oak staves and French oak ends. For those who prefer the more intense, dense character of a *vinos de autor* then III a.C. is a polished choice, a selection of the oldest vineyards, Tempranillo with just 2 per cent Graciano and 2 per cent Mazuelo. And the name? It refers to the Celtic tribe, the Berones, who lived in the area in the third century BC (a.C.: *antes de Cristo*).

WHAT'S IN A NAME?

At the time of writing, the western region of Rioja is still officially known as Rioja Baja. It's a terrible word: *baja* (low) has become pejorative in all sorts of ways. It implies that the vineyards are low in quality, low in status and low in altitude when high altitude is now so fashionable. The new name is to be Rioja Oriental instead. Although it's geographically correct for these eastern vineyards, translated into English I have to say there are incongruous echoes of Chinese takeaways. Still, a change is necessary, and if the producers can get behind it then we will take it on. For the moment though, Rioja Baja it remains. The official word in summer 2017 was that, 'It has been suggested that subzone Rioja Baja could be renamed Rioja Oriental, a proposal which will be explored in the coming months for its legal and commercial viability'.

Bhilar

Ctra de Assa 4, 01309 Elvillar
Tel.: +34 647 157 283
www.bodegasbhilar.es

David Sampedro Gil is a local; the village of Elvillar was his childhood home and it's where he has built his Bhilar (the Basque version of Elvillar) bodega, and where he lives with his wife Melanie Hickman, his children and the family dog. Over the years he has worked as a consultant winemaker elsewhere (working as 'DSG'), but realized that what mattered most was the old vines and the quality of the fruit from the vineyards in the shadow of the Sierra Cantabria. Throughout, his approach is minimum intervention with maximum expression.

The new winery on a promontory overlooking the landscape has been built with the same attention to sustainability, and is solar powered. In the vineyards he works biodynamically and in 2014 replaced tractors with horses. His estate wines are Phincas and Thousand Mils. This is their top white, a blend, and was originally called Thousand Milks, a play on the words *mil leches*. However, the authorities pointed out you can't name a wine after a milk product. Perhaps Mil Leches wasn't the politest choices of words either. He also has a number of single vineyard wines, Phinca Abejera and Phinca Lali, from a vineyard planted in 1910. Phinca La Revilla Sexto Año is a remarkable wine from a hidden vineyard of Viura, which is aged for six years in oak, following the tradition of the great old white Riojas. Sampedro's wife Melanie Hickman owns a further 3.5 hectares of old vines in a terraced vineyard in Laguardia.

Under the Bhilar label, Sampedro also makes Shanela and Costa da Santa Marina in Salnés in Rías Baixas and Phinca Durmiente (Rufete Blanco) and Phinca Encanto (Rufete Tinto) in Salamanca. As DSG he makes Pasolasmonjas and Lagrimas de Garnacha in the San Martín cooperative in Navarra. Full of promise.

Bilbaínas
Estación 3, 26200 Haro
Tel.: +34 941 310 147
www.bodegasbilbainas.com

This giant of the Barrio de la Estación, with its vast brick structure, dominates the station quarter of the town of Haro. Bilbaínas is the only place large enough to hold the annual masterclass tasting for the wine trade at the festival of the Barrio.

This vast project started life as Savignon Frères in 1857, making it the holder of the oldest bottling licence in the Rioja appellation. Savignon was one of the many French producers who left Bordeaux with the arrival of phylloxera, oidium and other problems. The undoubted lure was the railway for shipping wine back to France. Some forty years later they were also among the winery owners who were keen to sell up and return to France once phylloxera had been tamed.

The bodega was purchased by a group of Bilbao businessmen led by José Angel de Aurrecoechea, who worked in shipping bulk wine. In 1901 they founded Bodegas Bilbaínas, building the imposing entrance and bodegas. While the French had simply made wine in vast vats and shipped it, the new business aged and bottled its own wines. The business grew, with bodegas in Elciego, Zaragoza and La Mancha, and the wines were exported. There's a document to show that Winston Churchill was a keen consumer of Viña Pomal, one of Bilbaínas' brands.

The vineyard holdings also grew. But over the years and as happens so often, with the fragmentation of interests within families, quality declined. By the 1990s Bilbaínas urgently needed rescuing. Its neighbour CVNE made a bid for it but it was ultimately rescued by Bilbao businessman, José Luis Urdampilleta. He recruited the well-known consultant José 'Pepe' Hidalgo as technical director and winemaker in 1994 to put out the figurative fires (*bombero-oenologo*, fireman-winemaker was the exact term used!) and restore the quality and reputation. It was a huge task, which required not simply the restoration of the premises and the vineyards, but building and developing a clear strategy, and introducing a new team. In 1997 Codorníu, the Cava company, purchased Bilbaínas and the work continued. In 2007 Diego Pinilla inherited the task of development and refinement. He is now head of wine for the whole Codorníu group, and Bilbaínas is run by his former assistant Alejandro López.

The bodega's brands have been configured around the names of their vineyards: Viña Zaco, Viña Pomal (some 90 hectares), and La Vicalanda. Zaco has been positioned as the entry level wine, with a Rías Baixas Albariño as the white. Viña Pomal has been slowly restored to some of its former glory, with a very clear ladder of classical categories: in particular the finely balanced Reserva, 100 per cent Tempranillo aged in American oak, and the Gran Reserva which has 10 per cent Graciano in the years when it ripens well. The pinnacle of Pomal is Alto de la Caseta, a plot of bush vines planted on a small hill near the Ebro. Also in the Pomal range come the Vinos Singulares, dressed up in versions of very traditional labels. But the wines are anything but traditional, each one an exploration of a single varietal – Garnacha, Graciano, Tempranillo Blanco and Maturana Blanca. Each one of these is a step away from the focus on Tempranillo, and a sign of the growing confidence and independence of the winemaking team.

Finally comes La Vicalanda. This new vineyard project was fostered by Hidalgo back in 1994. The potential seen then is being proved now by the longevity of the wines. This is bush vine Tempranillo with a focus on selection, longer macerations for colour and flavour, and shorter ageing in French oak, all to produce a wine that is more forward and denser in character. There are two wines: a Reserva and a Gran Reserva (produced only in the best years).

An interesting new addition is their 'traditional method' sparkling, Viña Pomal Brut Reserva. It's a *blanc de noirs* from Garnacha, the first of its kind in La Rioja – and not altogether common in Spain. Currently it is classified as Cava, but given its 18 months' ageing it qualifies for the new sparkling wine category which Rioja is producing. The slumbering giant is awake: Bilbaínas is back at last alongside its peers in the Barrio de la Estación.

Campo Viejo

Camino de Lapuebla de Labarca 50, 26006 Logroño
Tel.: +34 941 279 900
www.campoviejo.com

The wines with the cheerful yellow (Tempranillo, Garnacha) and orange (Reserva) labels are many people's first introduction to Rioja, though they may not even realize that they are from the region. That's certainly the case in the UK where it is the best-selling Spanish wine brand (not just Rioja mind, but the whole of Spain).

When it comes to wine branding, then Campo Viejo is Spanish wine. In 2015–16 2.2 million twelve-bottle cases were sold worldwide. It's the leading Rioja brand worldwide, and the leading premium Spanish wine brand globally by volume. This brand success is driven by the expertise of its parent Pernod Ricard. Given the clear, simple messages of the portfolio it's easy to think of Campo Viejo as a simple business.

It's actually rather complicated, more an ocean liner than a yacht. The huge winery outside Logroño, opened in the early part of this century, was designed to hide itself and its barrels and tanks away. Head winemaker Elena Adell is also quick to point out its little clever design details, which she implemented after years of working in a less than perfect space. Adell oversees the vast production project with a female team led by winemakers Clara Canals and Irene Pérez Gutiérrez. Given the size of their production, work is naturally focused on blending and consistency. Adell also drives the innovation, something in which Pernod brands can seem lacking, with their narrow portfolio within each brand.

Adell is a pleasure to taste with, especially when she brings a bag of cherries freshly picked from her garden to share. Here's someone who savours flavour. There's a Garnacha in the line-up now, reflecting the Garnachista trend. The white wine, mainly Viura, also has a proportion of Tempranillo Blanco. Seek out the wine at the top end. Dominio Campo Viejo is Tempranillo with a dash of Graciano and Mazuelo. From five plots, leading to six vinifications of wines, aged for eleven months in casks from two French forests it is altogether an exceptionally dense and polished wine, and a deserved award winner. For some inexplicable reason it is not available to UK consumers, who as a result often fail to see the quality behind the CV label.

Castillo de Cuzcurrita
San Sebastián 1, 26214 Cuzcurrita de Río Tirón
Tel.: +34 941 328 022
www.castillodecuzcurrita.com

Nothing less than a proper castle with a medieval square keep and a walled vineyard greets those who make the journey to the far west of Rioja Alta. It's been beautifully restored – well worth a visit – and the walled vineyard is in equally fine condition. Wine had been made here until the 1980s but the vineyard and winery were then abandoned. Long memories talk of fine wines from the old, old days. The current owners purchased the property in 1999 and brought in the experienced consultant Ana Martín Onzaín to revive and direct the winemaking, with the first vintage in 2000. The new winery was built in 2005.

I have a particular interest in Cuzcurrita, because I came across it at the end of a long day of tasting Spanish wine. I tried it with no idea of what to expect, and it impressed me immediately. As I went on to find out, in a region where there are many large brands blending wines right across Rioja, they offer a welcome purely local focus, showing a cooler more continental style, as well as a single vineyard wine. They own 15 hectares of vineyards in all (of which 7.5 hectares are the enclosed unirrigated Cerrado del Castillo de Cuzcurrita, planted some 40 years ago), and have contracts with a further 10 hectares. In general, the vines are densely planted bush vines. The wines are 100 per cent Tempranillo, and are sold as generics rather than age classified. There are two established labels: Señorío de Cuzcurrita is the larger production, while the registered organic Cerrado del Castillo comes from the walled vineyard and is only available in the best vintages. The wines are clearly aged in French oak, and the Cerrado shows deep and expressive extraction overlaid by perfumed oak.

The new wine in the portfolio is Tilo, named after their century-old lime tree. The vines are more than 70 years old, grown on very poor soil, and aged for 24 months in new and used French oak. The result is a dark, fresh, 'Atlantic' Rioja.

Castillo de Sajazarra

Del Río s/n, 26212 Sajazarra
Tel.: +34 941 320 066
www.castillodesajazarra.com

This terrific castle, just west of Haro, was bought by the Líbano family in the 1960s, and the winery created in 1973. They now own 9 hectares of vineyards in 24 plots around the winery or close to it. The vineyards go up to 680 metres, so there is a clear Atlantic style to some of the wines. The most notable wines in the range are the Castillo de Sajazarra Reserva, which is mainly Tempranillo, and has 24 months in French and American oak, and Digma. This is the top wine, 100 per cent Tempranillo, from the two best vineyards, one with a more Atlantic influence, the other more Mediterranean, with 14 months in New French oak. The style of these wines is to have a clear oak-aged character.

Contador

Ctra Baños de Ebro Km 1, 26338 San Vicente de la Sonsierra
Tel.: +34 941 334 228
www.bodegacontador.com

Contador burst on the scene at the turn of the millennium. The first and loudest arrival of a new generation of winemakers, it earned top scores very quickly. It might have seemed that Benjamin Romeo was new to the business and had had a magically lucky beginning. However he was the winemaker at Artadi for 15 years, until 2000, so he knew exactly what he was doing. His father Andrés, after whom La Viña de Andrés Romeo is named, was a grower in San Vicente de la Sonsierra, and in the process of taking over from his father Romeo bought one of the typical old cellars with which the hillside is riddled, this one just next to the church. The first wine he released – La Cueva del Contador, from the cellar/cave – was 1996, and the first Contador appeared in 1999. The perfect scores for his 2004 and 2005 placed him in the stratosphere. To service the demand he introduced Predicador. His white was first launched as Gallocanta ('cock crow'). However a US wine producer objected, so it is now Que Bonito Cacareaba. This blend of Viura, Malvasía Riojana and Garnacha Blanca is fermented and aged for eight months in new French oak. There's no doubt the oak is bold, but so is the wine. It's a powerful expression that will develop and improve over time.

His vineyards are in San Vicente, as well as in the neighbouring Labastida and Ábalos. He stresses that the journey time at grape harvest from vineyard to winery is no more than half an hour. The vineyards are treated organically and there are more than 50 separate plots, mainly of bush vines. In 2008 he opened a gravity-flow winery at the foot of San Vicente. Fermentation takes place in 10,000 litre tronco-conical French oak, and racking is done on a waning moon.

Look out for the lovely white he makes at a joint project he is involved with in Catalunya, Vins del Massis. Macizo is a silky, complex, impressive Garnacha/Xarel·lo blend.

CVNE

Barrio de la Estación s/n, 26200 Haro
Tel.: +34 941 304 800
www.cvne.com

CVNE and Muga lie at opposite sides of the road into the Barrio de la Estación. But CVNE is by far the older. It was set up by the Real de Asúa brothers, Eusebio and Raimundo, with their friend Isidro Corcuera, and colleagues, in 1879. The Corcuera, Real Asúa y Compañía Sociedad Colectiva Mercantil, as they called themselves to begin with, worked as a negociant, buying and blending wines. Within a few years they had decided to build a bodega and relaunched themselves as a limited company: Compañía Vinícola del Norte de España. Again, not the snappiest of names. In due course, it was pronounced by the world as Coo-nee, and the business now uses the abbreviation CVNE as its brand name. Descendants of the founders still run the business; the fifth generation Victor Urrutia is the managing director.

At the turn of the nineteenth century, Gustave Eiffel built the striking cellar with the apparently unsupported ceiling. He showed himself here and in Jerez in sympathy with the needs of winemakers. (In more recent times, during Rioja's construction boom, there has been at least one occasion in Rioja where the winemakers have had to fit their work around the architect's ambition, rather than the other way.)

In 1915 CVNE launched Monopole, the oldest white wine brand in Spain. Latterly it has not been Rioja's most exciting white but for the centenary they went back to the old style, consulting their retired winemaker Ezekiel García, winemaker at CVNE from the 1940s to the 1970s, and godfather to many great wines (Jesús Madrazo remembers affectionately: ' '54, '58, '62, '64, '78 … great vintages'). The key is that the wine is aged in Sherry butts and finished with a little Manzanilla, from Hidalgo-La Gitana. Apart from the fascination for the consumer, it's a welcome sign that CVNE, despite being a major producer, has an element of playfulness and creativity.

In 1920 the great Imperial appeared on the scene; some of the bottles used were an Imperial pint in volume, hence the name. Today Imperial is a Rioja Alta wine, while its partner, Viña Real, now in its own winery (see p. 262), is entirely from Rioja Alavesa. For a number of years the winemaker Basilio Izquierdo (p. 215) and the viticulturist José Madrazo worked together, making exceptional wines. In the early 1970s Viñedos del Contino (see p. 263) was established with wines made by Izquierdo. Madrazo's son Jesús worked first at CVNE and then took on Contino. In 2005, the Real de Asúa winery was opened inside the CVNE site. Today winemaker Maria Larrea draws on some 440 hectares of vineyards of which CVNE owns 200 hectares.

Dinastía Vivanco

Ctra N-232, 26330 Briones
Tel.: +34 941 322 013 (winery) / +34 941 322 323 (museum and visits)
www.vivancoculturadevino.es

The web address above shows you where Vivanco's enthusiasms lie. 'It's the winery with the museum', anyone who knows it will tell you. However to be fair, the winery came first. Back in 1915, in fact, when the first of the Vivancos made wine, in the traditional fashion for home consumption. His son began to build the business, while *his* son, Pedro Vivanco, born in 1946, built a very successful business in wine and property, in the meantime acquiring a vast collection of wine implements and memorabilia. His dream was to create a foundation, a museum and an education centre. In 1990, having purchased a dominant site at the entrance to Briones, Dinastía Vivanco was launched, and in 2004 the museum was opened by King Juan Carlos.

The winery produces a range of mainstream wines, but the most interesting is certainly the range called Colección Vivanco. This contains varietal wines, Parcelas de Garnacha, Parcelas de Graciano, Parcelas de

Mazuelo, Parcelas de Maturana Tinta, as well as a Dulce de Invierno sweet wine, made from a blend of Tempranillo, Graciano, Garnacha and Mazuelo. The Colección makes a fine complement to the educational and research aspect of the foundation.

Pedro Vivanco was a respected expert on the soils and vineyards of Rioja. He died at the very end of December 2016. His sons, Rafael (the director of winemaking) and Santiago, work in the business and will continue both foundation and winery. This is the most extensive and interesting wine museum in Spain, with a bar and restaurant to revive visitors at the end of a trip.

Exeo
Costanilla del Hospital, 01330 Labastida
Tel.: +34 945 331 257
www.bodegasexeo.com

It's best to drive an automatic – and a small one at that – when making your way to Exeo. It's at the top of Labastida, and as the road gets narrower and steeper the best thing is to shut your eyes (if you're a passenger that is) and hold on tight. It's worth the trip: inside there's a tempting cave of delights – concrete eggs and new oak barrels crammed together, and below there are underground passageways. This is no easy cellar to work in. The wine that lured me here was Cifras, a Garnacha Blanca, finely textured after time in barrel. The brothers Fernández also run Tierra Agrícola Labastida. Exeo, as the name suggests, is a step outside, in a different direction, making Cifras Tinto and Letras. One to watch.

Exopto
Ctra de Elvillar 26, 01300 Laguardia
Tel.: +34 650 213 993
www.exopto.net

Less a garage winery and more an industrial shed, Exopto is in an unlikely position in a small industrial estate at the foot of Laguardia, a contrast with the old town on the hill. But Tom Puyaubert is not one to waste his money unnecessarily, choosing to spend it on the best grapes, vats and vineyards. The brand name expresses his ambition, coming from the Latin for 'to desire eagerly'. Exopto is part of the Rioja 'n' Roll marketing group (see box on p. 234).

Bordelais Puyaubert founded the winery in 2003. He had come to Spain as a salesman for leading French barrel company Saury but his work opened his eyes to Spain's potential and led him to fix on Rioja. He continues to work for Saury, which keeps him up to date with what's happening in the barrel world, as well as with his fellow winemakers. It also helps to stabilize the finances in years such as 2017 when crops are lost to frost.

What he wanted to do is respect the classical tradition of Rioja, and to ensure the wines are fresher, with more fruit, and finer oak. All the wines he produces are blends – Tempranillo with Graciano and Garnacha. Inside the industrial lock-up there is a treasure trove, a glorious collection of concrete and oak vats, and new and used barrels. The juicy Bozeto (Garnacha and Tempranillo dominant) finishes in large vats, while Horizonte and Exopto go into barrel. He plays with fine- and medium-grained French oak, and with different degrees of toast. If you ever want to know anything about barrels, Tom's your man.

He works with around 15 hectares of vineyards, bush vines, divided into micro-parcels. All the Tempranillo vineyards are in the much sought-after town of Ábalos in Rioja Alta. The Garnacha and Graciano come from the slopes of Monte Yerga in the south-east of Rioja. The contrast of the cooler, Atlantic, Rioja Alta works well with the ripeness and Mediterranean warmth of Rioja Baja.

Horizonte is the first wine Puyaubert made in 2003, with the focus on Tempranillo. Horizonte Blanco is a selection of the local whites – Viura, Malvasía and Garnacha Blanca. Exopto is the top of the range, 100 per cent destemmed; with 18 months in new French oak barrels it is juicy, concentrated, spicy and polished.

Faustino

Ctra de Logroño s/n, 01320 Oyón
Tel.: +34 945 622 500
www.bodegasfaustino.com

Faustino is a high-volume producer that inspires impressive loyalty amongst its traditional customers. The frosted Burgundy bottle, the period portraiture, the Gran Reserva, the straightforward numbering of the cuvées from VII to V to I, all contribute to its success. The Gran Reserva is rightfully popular with its midweight style and mellow, vanilla typicity.

The winery was founded by Eleuterio Martínez Arzok who settled in Oyón in the 1860s, and started to make bulk wine, as was the practice of the day. His son Faustino took on the business and was able to begin bottling in the 1920s. It was his son Julio Faustino who launched the first Faustino in honour of his father in 1960. (For something completely different, the winery offers 'dramatized' cellar tours where visitors can meet 'Don Faustino' in costume.)

The business has extensive vineyard holdings – 650 hectares in Laguardia and Oyón. It is also at the heart of the Faustino group of wineries, which includes Bodegas Campillo and Marques de Vitoria in Rioja, Bodegas Portia in Ribera del Duero, Condesa de Leganza in La Mancha, Bodegas Valcarlos in Navarra and the table wines Bodegas Victorianas. In addition it makes a Cava. The statistics impress: its Rioja wineries together hold stock of over 9 million bottles, which are being aged as Reserva or Gran Reserva.

Finca Allende

Plaza Ibarra 1, 26330 Briones
Tel.: +34 941 322 301
www.finca-allende.com

Miguel Ángel de Gregorio is king, or at least prince, of the town of Briones, based as he is in the impressive Palacio de Ibarra on the main square. From the top of the building you can look out towards his single vineyards. That's the point: de Gregorio has been interested since before the rest of the world got excited about the idea, in the flavour of village wines, and single vineyards. His father came from La Mancha to run the vineyards at Murrieta, when de Gregorio was tiny. In the course of time de Gregorio became technical director at Bodegas Breton, and shaped the style of that then new winery.

In 1995, he set up on his own, now well aware of the best sites and small vineyards, and moved to it full time a few years later. His focus was on north, north-east and north-west facing vineyards to guarantee an Atlantic freshness. As he points out, Rioja is only a short distance as the crow flies north from the Atlantic. The Finca Allende red is a juicily fresh Tempranillo, and the white a fine introduction to the potential for white wines in Rioja: Viura with Malvasía, fermented and aged for 14 months in new French oak. There's a Tempranillo with no added sulphur too, with just five months in American oak. It's vividly fresh, a key to its stability, but just in case, it has a best before date.

The elegant Aurus is from old deep gravel plots of Tempranillo and Graciano. The range of single vineyards continues to grow. Calvario, unlike his others, is south-east facing, bush vines planted on a hill of that name in 1945, on stony, iron-rich soils. The biblical-sounding name may be by chance but it is echoed in the grandeur of the wine. A classic, a mainly Tempranillo field blend, it was first made in 1999. It is aged in new French oak for 18 months, and is a wine of great refinement. Mártires was planted on clay soils in 1970 in the location of a former Celtic sanctuary, one of many in the area, where Christians subsequently built a chapel to the Holy Martyrs. The 100 per cent Viura white wine is gloriously fresh, even in a warm vintage. This is one of the great white Riojas of the new generation, with nine months in new French oak.

The special selections keep on coming. Mingortiz is the only Allende wine on limestone, named after its vineyard, planted in 1964. The optically selected 100 per cent Tempranillo delivers a blast of cherry fruit, before the complexity of oak kicks in. Gaminde, meanwhile, dates back to 1942, a site of clay and gravels, delivering an elegant minerality.

A Riojan winemaker who once worked with Miguel Angel de Gregorio told me that they learnt everything from him, because 'he was really obsessive with quality'. That's exactly right: this apparently jovial and easy-going personality could not otherwise produce wines of such clarity and individuality. There are other fine wineries in the town – Miguel Merino, Dinastía Vivanco – but he is the one who has put Briones on the map.

Finca Nueva is Finca Allende's second, separate 'drink-me-now-or-soon' label.

Finca la Emperatriz

Ctra Santo Domingo-Haro 26241 Baños de Rioja
Tel.: +34 941 300 705
www.bodegaslaemperatriz.com

The Empress is perfectly real, no less than María Eugenia Augustina de Palafox y Kirkpatrick, sixteenth Countess of Teba, fifteenth Marchioness of Ardales (or more briefly, Eugénie de Montijo, the wife of Napoleon III and Empress of France). The third and last-ever French empress, in fact. In 1878, a wine from her estate in Rioja won a prize in the Universal Exhibition. In 1996 the estate was purchased by the brothers Eduardo and Victor Hernáiz, and they launched the project to recuperate the vineyards and make quality wines. Two decades later these rank as top quality modern Rioja Altas.

The 101-hectare estate is situated in the north-west part Rioja Alta on a high plateau at 570 metres. The soil is hard and rocky, with boulders from the erosion of the Sierra de la Demanda. The white colour of the rocks increases the solar reflection on the vines. The estate produces three classic blends, as well as four single vineyard wines. Eduardo Hernáiz plans to classify them as Viñedos Singulares now the legislation is finally passed permitting the category in Rioja. Parcela N°1 is a selection of the oldest Tempranillo vines, matured in new French oak. Terruño comes from 20-year-old vines, grown on a trellis, aged in French oak with a touch of American. There are two Cepas Viejas 'old vines' varietals: Garnacha, from one of the stoniest of the vineyards over sand, a cool, fresh Atlantic wine; and the white Viura, from vines some 70 years old, fermented in French oak, and aged for a further ten months.

Finca la Emperatriz is a member of the Bodegas Familiares de Rioja.

Bodegas Familiares de Rioja

www.bodegasderioja.com

Around 20 *viticultores* and small bodegas met in 1991 to form an organization that would defend the interests of family businesses. Today their numbers have doubled, and also include medium-sized bodegas. They say they are the only group of family businesses to represent the whole of Rioja. Their fundamental principles include: owning their own vineyards, commitment to working in Rioja, pride in a family business, investing in their local villages and creating jobs, and sustainable viticulture. They campaign on a number of themes of particular concern to small producers. Notably there is a demand to bring the regulation minimum number of barrels to be held by a stock-holding ageing winery down from 500 barrels – since the current requirement excludes many small producers. Its other issues include banning the use of Rioja brand names in other wine regions (which muddies the water, confusing the consumer and potentially bringing Rioja into disrepute). They have also been involved in recuperating and researching scarce local varieties, and have campaigned for the differentiation of Rioja's sub-zones by origin and quality.

Finca los Arandinos

Ctra LR 137 Km 4.6, 26375 Entrena
Tel.: +34 941 446 126
www.fincalosarandinos.com

The world of wine is a small one. I went to stay at Los Arandinos because I was going to eat (and drink, too) at Venta Moncalvillo, run by Carlos Echapresto, the award-winning sommelier, and his brother, the chef. The very fine wine list of old (and new Riojas) means you want to be an easy taxi drive away. I discovered when I got there that Arandinos is also a winery. And what's more that the achingly trendy, concrete hotel on the hilltop had been designed by the architect Javier Arizcuren, who grows grapes in Quel, and has his own urban winery in Logroño.

Arandinos' grapes come from its own vines, some 20 hectares spread over 20 plots around the town of Entrena. The vines range in age from 4 to 80 years, growing on stony and pebbly soil and facing north-north-east. The range includes Malacapa, a juicy Tempranillo with a note of Mazuelo and oak; and Finca Los Arandinos Reserva which is a modern, bright style. An attractive modern approach to wine tourism in a historical region.

Finca Valpiedra

Término Montecillo s/n, 26360 Fuenmayor
Tel.: +34 941 450 876
www.familiamartinezbujanda.com

Finca Valpiedra is one of Rioja's loveliest vineyards. Romantically positioned in a bend in the River Ebro, this is surely what an estate vineyard should look like. The winery was founded in 1889. It now belongs to Carlos Martínez Bujanda and his sister Pilar, who retained control when the larger family split the business into two in 2007. They also own wineries in other regions (notably Finca Antigua in La Mancha). Their brother Jesús owns Valdemar (see p. 261).

At Valpiedra they produce just two wines: Cantos de Valpiedra is the 'second' wine, which categorizes itself as a Crianza, a bright, approachable Tempranillo. Finca Valpiedra claims no ageing category; it is Tempranillo with 3 per cent Graciano and 5 per cent Maturana Tinta, aged in French oak for 24 months. It's in a modern style, but very approachable and supple without being overstated. In 2009 they opened Viña Bujanda, which offers a range of traditional Riojas.

Finca Valpiedra is Rioja's only member of the Grandes Pagos de España.

Gómez Cruzado

Avda Vizkaya 6, 26200 Haro
Tel.: +34 941 312 502
www.gomezcruzado.com

It's easy to miss Gómez Cruzado, tucked in opposite López de Heredia in Haro's Station Quarter. Yet its history goes back a long way. In 1886, Ángel Gómez de Arteche, an aristocrat, decided to start winemaking. Thirty years later the business was purchased by Ángel and Jesús Gómez Cruzado. Over the years the business has changed hands a number of times. Today, all is calm. The winery is owned by the Baños family, who are from Badarán in western Rioja, and currently live in Mexico. The winery itself is managed by David González and Juan Antonio Leza, who joined in 2008 after a decade working as consultants.

Compared to its neighbours, Gómez Cruzado's production is small, at around 200,000 bottles annually. In terms of its kit, it's probably the most up-to-date: the concrete eggs are certainly a novelty in the Barrio. The grapes are sourced from three regions: at 750 metres in the Sierra Cantabria, from the distinctly warmer zone of Bajo Najerilla at around 500 metres and close to the Sierra de la Demanda in Alto Najerilla, where they farm at 750 metres, with bush vines aged more than 80 years.

They make a standard classical range. Of particular interest are the 'generic' wines: Honorable, Pancrudo, a very fashionable 100 per cent Garnacha from a north-facing site in Alto Najerilla, Cerro las Cuevas and Montes Obarenes, a Viura with a little Tempranillo Blanco.

Hacienda el Ternero

Finca El Ternero s/n, 26212 Ternero
Tel.: +34 941 320 021
www.elternero.com

The Hacienda's wines have been turning up in trendy London wine bars recently. It's the label that does it. Ternero means 'calf', hence the engraving of the extremely large bull-like calf on the label. With that packaging it looks like the Rioja you can drink while looking cool. In fact there are plenty of reasons to want to go behind the label. The Hacienda is, for instance, the only Castilla y León winery that is DOCa

Rioja. It's also on a site that dates back to the eleventh century, when it belonged to a local monastery providing shelter to the pilgrims on the Camino de Santiago. The wine is made in the monastery buildings: a white, two Tempranillos and two senior Tempranillo blends both with a dash of Mazuelo from their own vineyards. All are Atlantic wines, cool and fresh in style.

Herederos de Marqués de Riscal

Torrea 1, 01340 Elciego
+34 945 606 000
www.marquesderiscal.com

How should one best enjoy a visit to Marqués de Riscal? There's a lot to be said for booking into the Frank Gehry-designed, titanium-roofed hotel and enjoying a glass of the wine in the Michelin-starred restaurant. Especially if you can indulge in a fine old bottle from their cellar, which the sommelier will decapitate in front of you with heated tongs, rather than risk the crumble of the cork and the shaking up of the sediment.

The old wines *are* in the cellar; Riscal has a full collection dating back to the very beginning, and in 2015 held a complete vertical tasting. Well, almost complete; starting from the first bottling in 1862 there were only eleven vintages missing. The tasting was a revealing and brave exercise. It demonstrated when Rioja was hit by phylloxera, when the vines – and wines – weakened at the turn of the nineteenth century, only being replaced and finally bouncing back in the 1920s. The ones to look for are the 1922, the 1945 and the 1964.

The history of the two key Marqueses of Rioja runs in parallel. Both Murrieta and Riscal came back to Rioja and started winemaking at more or less the same time. Camilo Hurtado de Amézaga, Marqués de Riscal de Alegre, Barón del Castillo de Chirel and Conde de Castronuevo, was a liberal writer who, since 1836, had been living in Bordeaux to avoid the political upheavals of the time. He recognized that Bordeaux winemaking, and particularly the use of oak, would be valuable in Rioja. He founded Riscal in 1858. In due course he recruited the Frenchman, Jean Cadiche Pineau, the winemaker at Chateau Lanessan, who had been consulting without great success for the Rioja authorities, to guide the winemaking. Riscal persisted with the oak, but most of the Riojan growers rejected his innovation because it meant that they had to keep the wine longer before they could sell it.

Riscal built a Bordeaux-style cellar and bottled his first wine in 1862. He brought in a wide selection of French varieties on the advice of Pineau, though in due course most were supplanted, except for the Cabernet Sauvignon. The wines rapidly went on to win awards at the French exhibitions. The Cabernet Sauvignon was given experimental status by the authorities, though it was the significant part of the renowned 1945 vintage Cuvée Médoc. Today the Cabernet Sauvignon has such a long history in the vineyard and is so well adapted it should not be called 'experimental'.

In the 1970s Riscal took a pioneering step in the search for a white wine. The current Marqués, Francisco 'Paco' Hurtado de Amézaga, working with the influential French oenologist Émile Peynaud, identified Rueda. Historically the region had been growing Palomino, a variety best known for Sherry, in Jerez, and making its own oxidative Amontillados and Olorosos. The Riscal white was an eye opener at a time of tired white Riojas. Today Riscal owns the largest vineyard area in the DO with 230 hectares of Verdejo and Sauvignon Blanc, and controls another 250 hectares, as well as vineyards in VT Castilla y León.

Barón de Chirel arrived in 1986, a Tempranillo blend with 'other grapes', for which read Cabernet Sauvignon. This was a *vino de autor*, individual, modern, new-French oaked. However the combination of Cabernet and Tempranillo sets the wine apart from so many of the others; Tempranillo can lack acid, and the Cabernet here gives splendid backbone. A Chirel white, Viñas Centenarias, launched much more recently with the 2014 vintage, was made, as the label indicates, from 100-year-old Verdejo. The difference from Rueda Verdejo is that it comes from ungrafted pre-phylloxeric bush vines, of which there are isolated pockets in the region. While Rueda suffers from overproduction and vines that are too young, Chirel is one of the rare Verdejos that shows real quality. It is polished, with eight months on lees in 3,000-litre foudres and 600-litre barriques.

Riscal owns almost 500 hectares of vineyards and controls another 950 hectares, all of them in Elciego and Laguardia. The family is still in charge: Hurtado de Amézaga has guided many years of innovation, while being a guardian of its history, and his son Luis is also in the business. The 'regular' Riscal Reserva is recognized everywhere, though it has been inconsistent. Look out for the more recent Finca Torrea, a Tempranillo–Graciano blend from the vineyards next to the winery, and the fine, old, classic Gran Reserva.

Juan Carlos Sancha

Finca Fuentelacazuela, Camino de las Barreras s/n, 26320 Baños de Río Tobía
Tel.: +34 941 232 160
www.juancarlossancha.com

Juan Carlos Sancha's business is a perfect example of theory into practice. A professor of oenology at the University of La Rioja, with a research interest in the rare grape varieties of the DOCa, he used to be winemaker at Viña Ijalba, which was well known for being one of the earliest to revive Graciano. Now he produces a range of organically farmed wines from scarce varieties including Tempranillo Blanco, Maturana Tinta and Maturana Blanca and the very rare Monastel [sic], which he says is the only wine from that variety. Most widely available are his Ad Libitum white and red.

His winery is in Baños de Río Tobía in the Alto Najerilla valley, close up to the Sierra de la Demanda, with cold winters and cold nights. Hence the name of his Garnacha Peña el Gato – the cat's rock – on the basis that it was so cold even cats did not go up to the 95-year-old vineyard at 650 metres. He uses old vine Garnachas in the area, working with local growers. Each of the growers' wines has a label hanging round the neck identifying the producer. A winery to watch.

RIOJA 'N' ROLL

What a great name! It's a loose marketing umbrella for eight Rioja wineries, created in 2015, each deadly serious about what they do, but all ready to come together to party to promote their wines. No need for white tablecloths, sharpened pencils and silence when they present their wines, serious though their wines are. The members of the group are Oscar Alegre and Eva Valgañón of Alegre & Valgañón, Arturo and Kike de Miguel of Artuke, Bárbara Palacios of Barbarot, Tom Puyaubert of Exopto, Olivier Rivière of Ganko, Bryan MacRobert and Clara Canals of MacRobert & Canals, Roberto Oliván of Tentenublo and Sandra Bravo of Sierra de Toloño. Five of them are Spanish and descendants of *viticultors*; while Puyaubert and Rivière are French, and MacRobert is South African by birth. Their aim is 'to defend wines made by actual people; wines made in specific villages and vineyards; wines that are free and are not boxed into a category; wines which reflect our personality and the vineyards that we work in Rioja'.

> These are people who spend their lives in the vineyard, observing, working, communicating. They are also a tremendous force for good. Rioja needs a new generation. And in a region where big business and wine blends have dominated production, they are a force for change and diversification. They are not the only ones by any means, but with their disco nights they are not afraid to make a bit of noise about it.

López de Heredia Viña Tondonia

Avda Vizcaya 3, 26200 Haro
Tel.: +34 941 310 244
www.tondonia.com

Here's the winery of the Barrio de la Estación that represents the very essence of the grandeur of old Rioja. However there's nothing aged or grand about the team in charge, led by the unstoppable María-José, her siblings and her husband. This is a family business, with a deep sense of history. Anyone interested in the original Rioja boom, should start here. The family are living another boom now, as the wine world demands access to the remarkable long-aged Gran Reservas which have become such a cult.

Age is rightly venerated in Rioja. Yet José Luis Ripa, María-José's husband, reminds me that this was not always the case. 'Don't forget everyone used to make Riojan "Sauternes" and Riojan "Bordeaux". Residual sugar was more important than age in those days. There would be a "demi-sec" and a "botrytis".' Fashions – and wine labelling regulations – change. (Their Rioja Graves became Gravonia with the change in the law in 1954.)

The glory of a visit to 'Tondonia' as it is more often and easily called is the way that age and youth jostle each other, just as the energy of María-José and the family contrast with the tradition and history of the cellar. The red painted Swiss chalet style roof and watchtower (known by its Basque name, *txori toki*, or bird house) catch the eye. At ground level there's an unexpectedly radical visitors' entrance, designed by the late Zaha Hadid, yet containing a little traditional shop inside. (The Hadid building was a pavilion at the 2002 Alimentaria Fair in Barcelona; the traditional shop was used in a Brussels exhibition in the early twentieth century.) Deep underground are the cobwebby cellars, leading to a very hospitable round table at the heart. Up above, the offices are stainless steel and glass. This juxtaposition of styles is a shock to the system, and reflects something of the shock of the daily demands facing the team as the cult-hunters of the wine world step up to place their orders. At a wine tasting it's usual to see the largest crowd of people round their table as María-José and José Luis struggle to keep up with the bottle opening. He comments in frustration: 'I say to people, why don't they appreciate our Tondonia [their classic red Reserva]; it's not just about tasting only the Gran Reserva'.

The founder of this remarkable enterprise was Rafael López de Heredia y Landeta. He decided to follow the lead of the French negociants who had recognized the quality of Rioja, earlier in the century, when phylloxera hit Bordeaux. The family date the construction of the bodega to around 1877, making it the oldest in Haro, and one of the first three in Rioja. He bought together the vineyards that created Viña Tondonia, over 100 hectares, where Don Rafael had originally planned to build an Arabic-style castle. Their other vineyards, in total 170 hectares, make wines that have become famous to wine lovers: Bosconia, Cubillo and Zaconia (the home of Gravonia). Thanks to his foresight, the business now has a solid foundation of local vineyards. They are planted with the usual varieties including Garnacho (the local name for Garnacha).

The winery is a remarkable visit, notable for its oak vats, sourced from forests in Cantabria, Bosnia and Allier as well as the USA. It's the size as well as the age that impresses: from 60 hectolitres (for whites) to 240 hectolitres. There was no way of bringing them in on a cart; they had to be constructed and maintained on site. The wines are aged in barrel – as they say 'ageing wines should be seen as a pedagogic act; the wine is "educated" and hence should never be rushed through speeded-up improvisations'. An important detail of the winemaking is the search for consistency across vintages; so that the more 'commercial' wines are a blend of vintages to retain the style. The Gran Reservas, however, are not blended.

Until the early 1980s, you would see the year of the harvest shown on the label as '6° año', indicating that the bottle on sale had been harvested six years before.

Cubillo, from the Cubillas vineyard, is the youngest, a cherry-red, youthful Crianza, yet its quality and age set it apart from typical

Crianzas. Bosconia, from the El Bosque vineyard, was originally the Burgundy-style wine, made with Pinot Noir. Today the Reserva is earthy, almost rustic, with a burst of strawberry and balsamic energy. Its big brother, in exceptional years, is the Gran Reserva, which is aged for a minimum of eight years, followed by ten years in bottle in the cellar. Just before bottling any of the Gran Reservas, three members of the family will decide whether the wine has the qualities to be rated 'Gran Reserva' and aged further. Tondonia, the Tinto Reserva, is anything but a simple Reserva, given its Gran Reserva ageing of six years in barrel. Yet stylistically it has the forward, brighter, cherryish polish of a modern Reserva. The Tondonia family also contains a white Reserva and the three very remarkable, cult Gran Reservas, the red, the white and the *rosado*. The latter is an instantly recognizable wine for its evolved, ethereal, oxidative character. With 60 per cent Garnacho, 30 per cent Tempranillo and the rest Viura, it's a complete original.

Luis Cañas

Ctra Samaniego 10, 01307 Villabuena
Tel.: +34 945 623 373
www.luiscanas.com

This is a winery that appeared to burst onto the scene fully formed in the early 1990s. In fact it was actually founded long before, working, like so many others, in one of the underground cellars which populate the area. What made the difference was the arrival of the entrepreneurial Juan Luis, who had taken over from his father at the end of the previous decade. His restructuring of the business was assisted by the demand for new wave Riojas, and *vinos de autor*. Cañas was able to supply them all. Today the family owns or manages around 400 hectares of vineyards and makes the classic categories of Rioja. One of the most regularly successful is the Selección Familiar, a blend of 85 per cent Tempranillo with other grapes, aged in French and American oak. A popular, comfortable style. The top of the range is Hiru 3 Racimos (*racimos* means 'bunches', and in Basque *hiru* means three). This is a classic *vino de autor*, using bunches from vines aged over 60 years that typically produce three small-berried bunches or fewer, each weighing no more than 250g. This creates a concentrated, dense wine, which is a blend of Tempranillo with 10 per cent Graciano. Amaren is the sister winery, entirely focused on *vinos de autor* styles.

Macán/Benjamin de Rothschild & Vega Sicilia

Camino de los Caños s/n, Paraje de San Millán, 01307 Samaniego
Tel.: +34 983 680 147
www.vegasicilia.com

The first commercial bottling of Macán was the 2009, but the project dates back to the early 2000s and a meeting between Benjamin de Rothschild and Pablo Álvarez of Vega Sicilia. Rothschild wanted to invest and Álvarez sensibly proposed a joint venture. The only difficulty is that with a marriage of historic names such as these, expectations are excessively high. The owners fixed on San Vicente de la Sonsierra and former winemaker Javier Ausás went about seeking out parcels of vineyard, looking for vines with a minimum age of 40 years. He took his time – ten years – and the work was done with as much secrecy as possible, if for no other reason than to keep the prices down.

There are two wines: Macán and Macán Clásico. The wines are 100 per cent Tempranillo, and show their French influence, including naturally enough their maturation in French oak. Year by year Macán becomes more clearly the Grand Vin, as was originally intended, with the fruit denser and darker. Both wines are firmly oaked, following the character of the Vega Sicilia parent. I referred above to the high expectations. The team spent a number of years making wine and working on the styles. It's possible, given their reputations, that they should have waited a little longer before exposing them to scrutiny. Certainly the first vintages felt like a work in progress. Now, though, the wines are growing comfortably into themselves. It illustrates that moving from Tinto Fino (Tempranillo) in Ribera del Duero to Tempranillo in the very different soil and climate of Rioja is not straightforward; just as those from Rioja who have done the reverse trip to Ribera del Duero have learned. There is the potential for success, but success is not guaranteed.

MacRobert & Canals

Polígono Cantabria, Calle Soto Galo 12, 26006 Logroño
www.laventurawines.com

This is the project of (South African winemaker) Bryan MacRobert and his partner Clara Canals (a winemaker at Campo Viejo). MacRobert studied viticulture and oenology at Stellenbosch University. The next few years were spent working two vintages in the same year between Priorat and Swartland, while setting up his own project in South Africa (which he still pursues).

The Rioja venture is called Laventura, which is a play on *aventura* and *ventura*, adventure and venture, roughly translated as 'nothing ventured, nothing won'. The first vintage was in 2013, using bought-in grapes, in rented premises. Since then he has acquired some vineyards of his own. The range has grown, including two individual, original whites, a Viura and a Malvasía, which is something of an orange wine, given the time it spends on its skins – like a red wine. This is a wine that's all about texture, not fruit. Of the reds, Lanave is a juicy blend (Garnacha–Tempranillo), and there is a Tempranillo and a Garnacha. All of these wines show his keenness to uncover the qualities of his vineyards. In the winery this means cement tanks and larger oak barrels so as not to disguise the fruit.

Marqués de Cáceres

Avda de Fuenmayor 11, 26350 Cenicero
Tel.: +34 941 454 000
www.marquesdecaceres.com

The Marqueses have had a great part to play in Rioja's history: Murrieta, Riscal and Cáceres. The story at Cáceres is that as a result of the Civil War, Enrique Forner spent some years in exile in Bordeaux, where he owned two chateaux. In the 1960s, wishing to return to Rioja and use grapes from local growers, he took the advice of his friend, the great Bordelais expert Professor Émile Peynaud, about location and approach. Forner's arrival is always regarded as a significant marker in terms of the new wave of winemaking to Rioja.

The bodega which Forner built in Cenicero had the good fortune to launch with the outstanding 1970 vintage. Even today those early vintages can taste remarkably vivid. The growers became shareholders, hence the formal name of the business as a Union Viti-Vinícola. The first vintages were very striking wines, benefiting especially from the purity of oak, and Peynaud's importation of winemaking.

Forner's daughter Cristina has taken on her late father's mantle and is a great campaigner for the wines. The brand is an established classic, and its traditional labels a favourite with some consumers. At times the classics have wobbled, with inconsistent results in tastings. The Excellens Reserva is a younger, fresher, often more successful style. The more recent range in *vino de autor* style shows good potential. MC is the second wine, and Gaudium the top wine – a powerful, dense and firmly oaked wine built for cellaring. They also make Rueda, and have the brand Deusa Nai in Rías Baixas.

And the Marqués de Cáceres name? An old friend of Enrique Forner – Don Vicente Noguera de los Monteros, Marqués de Cáceres y Grande de España – allowed him to use the title, in return for the payment of a royalty to charity. The original title was granted in the eighteenth century to the first Marqués, for outstanding services to the crown in the War of the Kingdom of the Two Sicilies. His descendant, Don Juan Noguera, continues the connection with the bodega today.

Marqués de Murrieta
Ctra N232/LO-20 Logroño-Zaragoza (Salida 0), 26006 Logroño
Tel.: +34 941 271 370
www.marquesdemurrieta.com

Take a look at the address of the bodega. It's not straightforward spotting that Exit 0 on the highway. On my first visit I ended up in a building site at the end of an unmade road. When you do finally arrive, it's worth the U-turns and squealing tyres. The Murrieta bodega is stacked up grandly against the hillside like a wedding cake. The sweeping driveway is manicured, the new winery perfect. What's more this isn't all about the grandeur. The wines that come out of the winery are really good, and with the new winery should be getting ever better.

The founder, Luciano Murrieta, born in Peru, had a career in the military during the Wars of the Spanish Succession. In the early 1870s King Amadeo I (a short-lived king from Italy) made him Marquis of Murrieta, and Murrieta purchased Finca Ygay and established a bodega. He had been much influenced by winemaking practices in Bordeaux. The winery remained with different branches of the family until it was purchased in 1983 by the current owners, who already owned the lovely Pazo de Barrantes estate and bodega in Rías Baixas. It's been run since 1996 by Vicente Dalmau Cebrián-Sagarriga, who took on the business at a young age on the early death of his father. Cebrían is Conde de Creixell in his own right.

There's an 'is it?/isn't it?' debate around the winery. Was it the first Rioja winery or did Riscal get there first, as the first to produce wines 'following the Bordeaux method'? Each has evidence, though Murrieta looks to have the edge. At an early stage in her career, aged 29, winemaker Maria Vargas joined with Vicente Dalmau in taking the project on. Their progress has been nothing less than impressive. Murrieta only uses its own estate grapes from the 300 hectares of vineyards that surround the winery. The Reserva benefits from a classic blend and is a reliable, polished style, aged in American oak. The Gran Reserva, too, has the classic blend of grapes and the regulation 24 months in barrel (American oak) and is then released after due time in bottle. Like all the Murrieta wines, it has a distinct, fleshy richness, a signature from the soils of the estate. While ready to drink, it's still a very vibrant style with plenty of life ahead. The summit of the classics is the Castillo Ygay Gran Reserva Especial, with a distinctive line of Mazuelo in the blend (some 14 per cent). The juice is fermented in stainless steel and aged in barriques for 28 months, at the outset in new oak. The Tempranillo is in American, the Mazuelo in French. After blending and settling, the wine spends three years in bottle. It's released so much younger than the Ygay white (below) and has plenty of years left for cellaring, if you can hold back from drinking it now.

Dalmau is a real contrast, though the quality of the fruit and the oak is equally good. Inevitably it has something of the *vino de autor* about it. Part of that is to do with its 19 months in new French oak. The other factor is that in addition to the 70 per cent Tempranillo and 15 per cent Graciano there's 15 per cent Cabernet Sauvignon. The fruit comes from an old vineyard called Canajas with a clay-chalk soil and stony topsoil. The grapes are destemmed and fermented separately. All these details could conspire to make it exceptionally overdone, but it is actually superbly well finished. Winemaker Maria Vargas is a great interpreter of her vineyard.

The latest innovation makes intriguing use of the Mazuelo. It joins the small group of pale Provençal-coloured *rosados* coming out of Rioja at high prices. The Murrieta has a striking ribbed bottle to add to the glamour. However for a rosé drinker what is so fascinating is the fact that it is 100 per cent Mazuelo, a rare style. The bright, brilliantly fresh wine is finely aromatic, with an allure given by Mazuelo's typical blueish tinge. Pehaps it's still finding its way, but it is certainly promising.

For lovers of white Rioja, Murrieta must be on the list. Capellanía is one of the pre-eminent new generation white Riojas. It's a single vineyard 100 per cent Viura, planted in 1945 at the highest point of the estate (485 metres). Aged for just over a year in new French oak, by which it is certainly marked, it is nevertheless superbly complex and layered. Capellanía, though, comes second to the Castillo Ygay. This is a rare case where a white wine is even more famous than its partner red. Only López de Heredia's Viña Tondonia can match Murrieta with its venerable Gran Reservas (and the former also has a *rosado*). The white Ygay Gran Reserva Especial 1986, the latest release, comes from the same Capellanía vineyard. There's 3 per cent Malvasía Riojana in the wine, which was fermented in American oak and then aged for 252 months in American oak barriques and 67 months in concrete tanks. It was bottled (8,125 bottles) at the end of January 2014, and aged for a further three years before release. Some wines were bottled in 1992 and then released in 1995, but the majority was kept under wraps. There's nothing of fruit, or oak, in this wine, the character is to do with savoury notes, a tight freshness and a palate that leads you to talk about minerals. It's a wine to go back to, to watch how it develops over time. It may be 30 years old at release but there's life ahead.

Ygay and its Tondonia cousin are wines beyond fashion, wines that speak of a historical past as few others in Europe do. In Spain, there are wines in Jerez in the same category. Sadly, the fortified wines of Fondillon from Alicante are in a much more precarious position.

Medrano Irazu

San Pedro 14, 01309 Elvillar
Tel.: +34 945 604 066
www.medranoirazu.com

The business was founded in 1984, and son Amador took over from father Luis in 2001. He has begun to extend the range with elegant single varietal Graciano and Tempranillo. Parcela 14.8 is a powerful, juicy wine made from 8 rows, 14 rows inside the parcel. The quantities are small – just 2–3 barriques.

Miguel Merino

Ctra de Logroño 16, 26330 Briones
Tel.: +34 941 322 263
www.miguelmerino.com

Miguel Merino is an old friend of the wine trade in the UK, amongst others, given his years working as an export manager, notably for Javier

Ochoa, of Ochoa in Navarra. Finally he fulfilled his dream of making 'a few bottles of wine of the best quality possible' in Rioja. He found and restored a nineteenth-century house in Briones, and located old vine Tempranillos with Atlantic influences. The first vintage was in 1994. His most interesting wine today is the Mazuelo de la Quinta Cruz, one of the very few 100 per cent Mazuelo wines in Rioja, aged half in American and half in French oak. It provides a rare opportunity to discover the variety in this region.

Montecillo

Bodegas San Cristóbal 34, 26360 Fuenmayor
Tel.: +34 941 440 125
www.bodegasmontecillo.com

Montecillo goes back a long way, as it was founded by Celestino Navajas in 1874. The influences were French: his sons studied in Bordeaux and his grandson José Luis, who really grew the business, studied in Beaune, in Burgundy. It was in 1947 that the business was named Montecillo after the little hilltop outside Fuenmayor. When the last Navajas died without heirs in 1973 the business was sold to Osborne – though Sherry was surviving, far-sighted Sherry houses realized they needed to invest in other parts of the drinks world in Spain. The winery has no vineyards of its own, so buys from 800 parcels in La Rioja Alta.

For many years the winemaker was the redoubtable María Martínez, the only woman in her class at university, and a fighter for her career and her wines. It's still possible to taste some of her wines in the historic vintages range that the winery sells. Her successor is Mercedes García whose role is to take the style of Montecillo forward. Under the Montecillo brand she is also making Godello in Valdeorras and Albariño in Rías Baixas.

Muga

Barrio de la Estación s/n, 26200 Haro
Tel.: +34 941 311 825
www.bodegasmuga.com

One of the most significant items in Rioja's history sits outside the winery by the roundabout at the entrance to the Barrio de la Estación. It's an elongated barrel, a foudre. The text reads 'French oak vat used during the period of PHYLLOXERA (1877–1903) to transport wine from the region of HARO to BORDEAUX.' It's the perfect illustration of how closely

Haro's station quarter was tied to the fortunes of Bordeaux. In fact, the Muga bodega, beside which the vintage shipping container stands, did not exist in those phylloxeric days.

The business was founded in 1932 by the current team's grandfather, Isaac Muga Martínez and wife Aurora Caño, a woman with a lifelong expertise in wine. It was not a promising time, in terms of global and domestic economics and politics. Yet the business grew, and with it Muga's aspirations to find suitable premises. Finally in the late 1960s they were able to move from Haro to take on the historic property in the Barrio de la Estación, but Isaac died before he could enjoy the transformation. His two sons Manuel and Isacín managed the process, and the business is run today by the founder's grandchildren, a remarkable set of brothers and cousins. Isacín's sons Jorge and Isaac are in charge of the vineyard and the winemaking respectively, while Manuel's sons, Manu, Juan and Eduardo ('Edu'), run the communications and marketing. Singly and together they stand out in every wine tasting, not only for the quality of their wines, but for their height. They would make an ideal in-house basketball team.

Muga today owns 250 hectares in La Rioja Alta and has contracts over another 150 hectares. This enables Jorge to bring into the winery fruit with varying Atlantic and Mediterranean influences. Though one of the younger wineries in the Barrio, their materials are entirely traditional. Ninety vast wooden vats for fermentation, 14,000 barrels, all of them maintained by the in-house coopers and barrel-maker. Even the clarification is done with egg whites, using a delightful machine to separate yolks from whites. It's a textbook visit to understand the processes of a traditional winery.

And visits are something at which the Mugas excel. As a family business, they retain a warmth that is missing from many other big brands. Wangle an invitation to lunch and you will enjoy traditional home cooking – chickpea soups, meat stews, deliciously sticky *torrijas*, in a room warmed by an open fire. Potential students for the Masters of Wine programme, who attend a two-day masterclass at Muga each year, really appreciate the home cooking in the midst of their intense study sessions. (These courses are run by the Institute of Masters of Wine and supported by the members of the Fundación para la Cultura del Vino:

Muga, La Rioja Alta, Herederos del Marqués de Riscal, Terras Gauda, Vega Sicilia and the Ministry of Agriculture.)

The masterclasses are held in the excellent modern tasting rooms with fine views beside the distinctive tower. When Manuel and Isacín moved in and transformed the existing bodega, they extended the bodega in also sorts of useful ways. I'm less certain about the tower, which is a significant landmark but with much less charm than the wines, though it has lent its name to a wine, of which more below.

Muga offers a classic series of wines from its classical cellar: Crianza, Reserva, Reserva Selección Especial (a selection of vines, in the best vintages) and Prado Enea (in the Burgundy bottle) which is the Gran Reserva. Prado Enea is one of Rioja Alta's great Gran Reservas, with fruit sourced from some of Rioja Alta's highest vineyards, at Sajazarra. It is aged for a year in 16,000-litre vats, with a minimum of three years in oak barrels and three years in bottle. No question of rough edges there. It has a real refinement, and a purity that persists over long ageing.

Despite the classicism in the cellar, Muga also offers wines in the *vinos de autor* category: Torre Muga (that tower) and Aro. The first commercial vintage of Torre Muga was 1991, a project of Manuel, though the style didn't settle till later in the decade. It was a radical change, with more overt fruit from Villalba, and 18 months in new French oak barrels. Aro is the pinnacle of that style, named in homage to Haro without the 'H'. The wine is a blend of fruit from canes selected from the top Tempranillo vines from Torre Muga, grafted to form new vineyards. It has 30 per cent Graciano and spends 18 months in new French oak, creating a dense, polished, savoury wine.

Muga is also known for its *rosados*. Rosado is an established blend of Garnacha with Viura and Tempranillo, a relatively pale fresh wine. However they too have joined the fashion for Provençal *rosados*, and launched Flor de Muga in 2016. It's 100 per cent Garnacha, very pale, with blue highlights, aromatic, and has a delicate, well-structured palate. Finally, it's important not to forget the Muga Cava. When the Cava DO was created it included more zones than just Penedès, and Muga's is probably the best known Riojan Cava. At the time of writing DOCa Rioja has announced that it proposes to authorize 'traditional method' sparkling wine within the appellation. So perhaps future bottles of sparkling Muga will carry the Rioja DOCa instead.

Ojuel

Sojuela 26376
Tel.: +34 669 923 267
www.ojuelwine.com

This is an organic producer in Sojuela, committed to the traditional ways of winegrowing and winemaking, with vineyards at 550–800 metres. They are in the Sierra de Moncalvillo, only 20 kilometres south of Logroño but in an area that seems geographically isolated from Rioja, as well as philosophically distant from the regular image of the wines. Miguel Martínez farms 9 hectares of vines, and in addition to making white and red Rioja in 2012 revived the local tradition of *supurao*, a naturally sweet wine from raisined grapes, traditionally made for special occasions. He dries the grapes in a hayloft, then ferments them in stainless steel, followed by two months in barrel before bottling. He makes a red and a white *supurao* – though initially it took two years for the CRDOCa to admit the wines into the DOCa.

In addition he makes white wines with Garnacha Blanca and Tempranillo Blanco, and reds with Maturana, Tempranillo, Mazuelo and Garnacha.

Olivier Rivière

www.olivier-riviere.com

Although the only thing that matters is the quality of the liquid in the bottle, there are times when the label design cannot help but draw you in and soften you up to like the wine even before you drink it. Olivier Rivière's wine labels, with their distinctive black and white typography, have this effect on me.

Rivière is from Cognac. He studied in France before moving to Spain in search of wine. He worked for a time for Telmo Rodríguez, but soon was tempted to seek out grapes and vineyards of his own. His first vintage was 2006, and the developing quality and excitement of his wines comes from his access to ever-better vines. Today he is one of a small group of producers working in DO Arlanza and bringing that formerly forgotten area to international attention. He owns or rents some 25 hectares across Rioja and Arlanza, nearly all of them either organically or biodynamically farmed.

His work is about discovering the terroir and expressing that using whole bunches or partially destemming them. In his minimal intervention approach he also uses indigenous yeasts and moderate oak. I met Jequitibá, his white blend, in a wine bar in Perth, Australia, and she grabbed my attention with her dried flower and mineral character, and gentle spiciness. As a Sherry lover I had to track down Mirando al Sur, which is Viura made in Sherry butts – nothing about fruit, but full of character. Ganko is a perfectly fresh red, a 50–50 blend of Garnacha and Mazuelo, from Cárdenas, in the south-west part of Rioja Alta, expressing the cool character of Alto Najerilla.

Palacio

San Lázaro 1, 01300 Laguardia
Tel.: +34 945 600 151
www.bodegaspalacio.com

Bodegas Palacio is all about history; and followers of Rioja talk lovingly about older vintages. But Palacio's historical significance lies beyond Rioja, too. Founder Cosme Palacio rented a winery in Ribera del Duero when phylloxera struck Rioja. In due course his winemaker there, Txomin Garramiola, made the wine which became Vega Sicilia. Fast-forward almost 100 years and Palacio hit wine headlines again when winemaking consultant Michel Rolland was brought in to make a juicy Rioja in French oak.

The business produces two lines: Glorioso and Cosme Palacio; the latter's 1894 brand commemorates the founding of the winery. In recent years the ownership of the winery has changed several times. It was sold to Domecq and Seagram, from whence it went to a French management buy-out (and hence the connection with Michel Rolland). Now it's part of the huge Hijos de Antonio Barceló, with properties in Castilla y León, Ribera del Duero, Toro and Rueda, and is owned by the Acciona group.

Palacios Remondo & Álvaro Palacios, Álfaro

Avda Zaragoza 8, 26540 Álfaro
Tel.: +34 941 180 207
info@alvaropalacios.com

When I first started studying wine, I was given the impression that Rioja Baja was the poor relation of Rioja; not just low in name but low in quality. How things have changed, right up to the very sensible proposal to change its name to Rioja Oriental (though personally I'd prefer Mediterranea, as Oriental translates poorly in English). The changes have been driven by Álvaro Palacios, who has shown in Priorat, and again in Bierzo with his nephew Ricardo Pérez, that his insistence on quality and terroir can build the global reputation of a whole region. There are other producers whose role is significant in Rioja Baja, but none more so than Palacios.

Álfaro is practically as far east as you can go without falling off the edge of Rioja; it's certainly the last important town. It's also the largest production town in La Rioja (twice as large as its neighbour Aldeanueva de Ebro). Palacios' father José and his wife Carmen established a wine business in 1945, and in 1970 a hotel in the town next to the bodega. They also had nine children, four of whom became winemakers, along with two of their grandchildren. When José died, Álvaro ultimately took the reins. What we enjoy today is the result of the focus on the vineyard, which is producing ever more diverse and interesting wines.

A distinctive contribution at the outset was made by his brother Rafael, with Plácet Valtomelloso (from the Latin, meaning agreement but also pleasure). From a 4-hectare plot of Viura in La Montesa vineyard it showed the much maligned grape's potential. The oak is subtle, from time spent in 2,000-litre *tinas*, and the wine complex. Rafael Palacios in due course moved to establish his own winery in Valdeorras, where it is no surprise to find that he makes one of the very best white wines in Spain.

Rioja Baja is a further misnomer for the Palacios project since the essence of the wines stems from vineyards on the slopes of the Monte Yerga at around 550 metres, and in its rain shadow, with rain falling around the 360-metre mark. The process was to transform the family's business from the usual Tempranillo, to predominantly Garnacha and from trellises to mostly bush vines, using massal selection for new plantings. The general aim was a move from the 'modern' back to more traditional methods.

The entry-level wine is La Vendimia. It is followed by La Montesa, which every year is becoming a clearer and more defined expression of its origins. It may seem that Palacios is just transferring his enthusiasm for Garnacha grown on slate in Priorat to the very different soils of Rioja. But the poor, stony, chalky limestone soils deliver a ringingly pure Garnacha, when grown at altitude. Propriedad is almost completely Garnacha, grown at the limit at 650 metres, fermented in large vats and matured in large French oak – it is not produced every year.

The latest release is Quiñón de Valmira, sold under the label of Álvaro Palacios Álfaro. Pure Garnacha from vines grown at 615 metres, it is delicate, very refined, with a Pinot-like character far from the grape's usual juicy-charmer profile. The geology is 'austere', with just 20 centimetres of soil over calcium carbonate, which gives rise to scarce and small berries. Palacios notes that the Garnacha grapes, 'also influenced by the freshness of the mountain, offer a soft wine with a thousand details, a smooth liquid full of vitality, pleasure and undecipherable mysteries.' I'd just add that it is a remarkably lovely wine, and a welcome step away from Rioja's *vinos de autor*, and the days of concentration and extraction.

Pujanza

Ctra de Elvillar s/n, 01300 Laguardia
www.bodegaspujanza.com

Carlos San Pedro is one of the more well-connected wine people you could hope to meet in Rioja. His original wines were simply known as Pujanza and Pujanza Norte, but the range has reshuffled itself. Pujanza is now named after its main vineyard, Finca Valdepoleo. This fine Tempranillo is fresh and medium bodied from its 600 metres altitude. Pujanza Norte still retains its name, taken from the El Norte vineyard, which is towards the limit of vinegrowing in Rioja Alavesa. Cisma is a tiny production wine, finely made but with a price to match, from an 0.8-hectare vineyard his grandfather planted in 1925. All in all, excellent modern Riojas.

Ramón Bilbao

Avda Santo Domingo 34, 26200 Haro
Tel.: +34 941 310 316
www.bodegasramonbilbao.es

Back in 1896, Ramón Bilbao Murga was a wine merchant in Haro. He sold wines under his own name and also Viña Turzaballa. Almost three decades later, in 1924, he established a bodega which remained in the family until the death of the last family member in 1966. It's still possible to find Viña Turzaballa in the market, a fine old Gran Reserva style from Rioja Alta. In 1999 the business, by then established in a larger bodega outside Haro, was purchased by the huge Diego Zamora drinks group. The secret to their deep pockets is Licor 43, Spain's best-selling liqueur, a golden, vanilla scented blend of 43 herbs and spices. This enables investment and innovation.

The winery owns 180 hectares in Riojas Alta and Baja and works with another 818 hectares under contract. Wine MD and chief winemaker Rodolfo Bastida, who joined in 1999, manages an impressive output, while maintaining consistent quality. In the Ramón Bilbao range, the wines focus on Rioja Alta vineyards from Cuzcurrita in the west to San Vicente in the East, offering the traditional Crianza, Reserva and Gran Reserva categories, and with an increasing emphasis on fresh fruit alongside American oak influences.

Bastida has established a *vino de autor*, Mirto, using old-vine Tempranillos, fermenting them in French oak vats, and then giving them 24 months to age in new French oak barrels. The brand was launched in 1999 and has improved over time. The fruit is dense and powerful, standing up well to the oak. These need time to settle in the bottle, but are structured for long ageing.

In 2015, the business purchased 90 hectares in Monte Yerga in Rioja Baja, planted with Tempranillo and Garnacha. This has prompted a plot-by-plot study, and a focus on high altitude in Rioja. The first result was Lalomba, from a vineyard at 720 metres. It's a new wave Garnacha *rosado*: Provence-style and Vinolok-stoppered in a Burgundy bottle, it ticks all the fashionable boxes and has a price to match. Despite the pale colour, there is a good level of quince and berry fruit. The Monte Yerga wines have a new winery of their own with fermentation in concrete vats.

Ramón Bilbao also has a winery in Rueda, in a project that is relatively new; Mar de Frades is the Diego Zamora winery in Rías Baixas, and there is Cruz de Alba in Ribera del Duero. Their other businesses include Texas-based Yellow Rose whiskey, Villa Massa limoncello, and Lolea sangría.

Remelluri, Telmo Rodríguez

Ctra Rivas de Tereso s/n, 01330 Labastida
Tel.: +34 945 331 801
www.remelluri.com

See Compañía de Vinos Telmo Rodríguez, p. 251.

Remírez de Ganuza

Constitución 1, 01307 Samaniego
+34 945 609 022
www.remirezdeganuza.com

Today's winery owners have had plenty of different previous careers: some inherited vineyards, of course, and others have made the natural move from winemaker, but among them we also find barrel salesman, export manager, pharmacist, and plenty more besides. For a new entrant to the business, however, Fernando Remírez de Ganuza surely had the best training. In the late 1970s and 1980s he was buying and selling vineyards for his clients. He specialized in putting together tiny vineyards – some 2,400 deals in all – to create larger ones, and a number of his enlarged vineyards were bought by famous Rioja names.

Thus it was that when he decided to set up his own business, he knew exactly where to look: he now has vineyards in Samaniego, Leza, Elciego, San Vicente, Laguardia and Ábalos. The business was established in 1989, but the winery looks as if it is far older, for the new structures were faced with old stone blocks, giving the appearance of a seventeenth- or eighteenth-century hamlet, with a stream running through the middle. What was perhaps surprising is that he also knew what he wanted to do when it came to winemaking, how to achieve it and what to invent to bring about the desired result.

The range consists of the classic wine, named after the winery, which is made only from the shoulders of the best bunches. The tips go into the Erre Punto (which can be read in Spanish as 'R full stop'), a juicy youngster made using carbonic maceration, and a textbook example of the Alavesa tradition of domestic winemaking. Trasnocho reflects the inventions of the owner. It's made from the shoulders of each bunch, but the must is extracted from the grapes by inflating a PVC bag to press them gently. Fincas de Ganuza uses a selection of top grapes, the shoulders destemmed, and aged in French and American oak. Finally, there is an excellent white, the Remírez de Ganuza, which is 70 per cent Viura with a collection of other varieties. It has oak, and needs time, but it will develop well.

Compañía de Vinos Telmo Rodríguez

El Monte, 01308 Lanciego
Tel.: +34 945 628 315
www.telmorodriguez.com

Telmo Rodríguez has already packed two careers into his life, and is now well advanced on the third. I first went to Remelluri, the estate near Labastida in the foothills of the Sierra de Toloño that his father bought in 1967, in the 1990s. I have memories of a magical place, with a medieval carved necropolis for adults and little children in the grounds, a roaring fire in the kitchen, an old chapel, and a very fine white wine. The wine was made from some nine varieties, a really radical departure for Rioja in those days – and even today – and an indicator that the winemaker was worth following.

That winemaker, Telmo, is one of those rare people in the wine world who is known by his first name, like Álvaro (Palacios), and also figures such as Warren (Winiarski), Randall (Grahm), Egon (Müller) and Jean-Charles (Boisset). It takes a strong personality and fine wine, as well as a memorable name, to reach that position. It's in the second phase of his working life that he built that reputation and lost his surname. At a time when flying winemakers were all the rage in the New World, Rodríguez was Spain's homegrown version. He would undoubtedly dislike the epithet, which suggests simply waving a magic wand over a vineyard or winery. But in many ways the Compañía de Vinos Telmo Rodríguez did just that. He formed the business in 1994 with his good friend from student days in Bordeaux, Pablo Eguzkiza.

The roll of honour of the vineyards they discovered and the wines they made together, is impressive. Old vine Garnacha in Navarra, Molino Real, a mountain wine in Málaga (a recuperation of an almost defunct wine style), Garnacha on slate in Gredos before it became known, and then work in Alicante, Ribera del Duero, Rueda, Toro and Rioja. I recall a trip where I met him in a vineyard of old bush vines, and learnt from him the practice of layering. They were recuperating old bush vines, and filling the empty spaces by burying the tip of a long cane from the adjoining bush.

One of the stars from the Compañía must be As Caborcas. Although it is in the DO Valdeorras, to all intents and purposes it could be from Ribeira Sacra just across the Bibei river. It's a superbly fresh, cherry-delicate blend of local red varieties. In Rioja meanwhile, in Lanciego, he built a bodega for LZ, Lanzaga and Altos de Lanzaga, wines whose labels come as close as he could get within the regulations to naming the village.

Then in 2010 he returned to Remelluri with his sister Amaya. It seemed that this would bring a neat end to the story. But it has proved to be only a beginning. Close to the estate Rodríguez purchased a remarkable 1.9 hectare vineyard with the appropriate, blessed name of Las Beatas (literally, blessed ones). One could not have chosen better. It is a tiny site, its slopes covered with a traditional, typical field blend. The wine itself is fermented in 1,000-litre casks, and aged in French oak. It's made in a traditional old underground cellar or *calado* in Ollauri that once belonged to the grand old Rioja name of Paternina. Las Beatas' neighbour is Tabuerniga, a superbly floral, elegant wine, another single vineyard. So the third adventure begins, with Pablo and Telmo working across the many projects, and having the occasional opportunity to break away from work to enjoy great wines, and great food beneath the chilly rocks of the Sierra. Rodríguez' determination to make the case for real Rioja is stronger than ever, and was articulated in 2016 in the Matador Manifesto (see box, p. 266).

La Rioja Alta

Avda Vizcaya 8, 26200 Haro
Tel.: +34 941 310 346
www.gruporiojalta.com

La Rioja Alta's Instagram handle is lariojaaltasa. Not the easiest to type or to recognize. It's the 'sa' at the end that's important. For La Rioja Alta carries the same name as the sub-region it sits in. But the bodega registered its logo in 1916 well before the region was formally recognized ('SA' stands for *sociedad anonima* or public limited company). So wherever it matters you'll find the winery carries the 'SA' on the end. Amongst wine lovers it's just Rioja Alta. The logo has stood the passage of the years: it shows the River Oja with four trees, and the brand name is spelled out in italic script.

The Sociedad Vinícola de La Rioja Alta was founded on 10 July 1890 by five families from Rioja and the Basque country with an initial capital of 112,500 pesetas. The first president was Doña Saturnina García Cid y Garate: an unusual move for the times, and even today while there are plenty of women winemakers in Rioja, there are still few women at the top of Rioja's big bodegas. Two of the founding families are still shareholders. The majority is held by the Alberdi family, which joined in 1910, and today's chairman Guillermo de Aranzabal is a member of that family. There are also other private individual investors. Rioja Alta, one of the occupants of the Barrio de la Estación, has a clear identity: classic styles and American oak, both supported by constant improvement. The wines have changed and moved with the times. So has the marketing. Their Club de Cosecheros created in 1980 was a smart move at the time to build a member network with special privileges, including the opportunity to buy a barrel of wine made exclusively for the club. It's common now but was a real innovation then. Rioja Alta has continued to purchase vineyards, and built an extensive winery in Laguardia to 1996, to manage the growth.

Julio Sáenz is technical director and winemaker; with the help of investment he has continued to renew and develop the wines. He joined the business in 1996, his first job after his MSc, and was promoted to his current role in 2005. He oversees several tiers of brands, each of which has its loyal fans. Alberdi, launched in 1978, is the first rung, entry level, but nevertheless a Reserva, with two years in American oak. Even at this level the traditions are observed – the wine is racked by candle to ensure no sediment gets into the clean wine. Arana, the next tier up, launched in 1974, spends 4–5 years in barrel but is also ranked a Reserva. The 5 per cent of Mazuelo adds a lift to the Tempranillo. Arana was launched as Rioja Alta's six year old, and was traditionally called a Rioja claret style.

Next comes Ardanza, for many fans the best and most loved of La Rioja Alta's output. Ardanza was launched in 1942 as a 'Burgundy-style' wine, hence the burgundy bottle. Typically it's a blend of varieties and plots, married with American oak. The Tempranillo comes from Fuenmayor and Cenicero. The Garnacha which makes 20 per cent of the blend has, since the 2008 vintage, come from the new vineyard in Tudelilla, La Pedriza. Tudelilla is a reliable home for Garnacha, and this gives extra character to the wine. So since 2008, Ardanza has been made 100 per cent with Rioja Alta's own fruit. The Tempranillo spends three years in older American oak; the Garnacha a little less. A silky, mid-weight, classical Rioja, it has plenty of lively modern highlights to set against the cigar smoke. The great vintages for Ardanza were 1964 and 1973; in 2001 the style was polished to deliver brighter colour and bolder aromatics.

Now follow the two great Gran Reservas. The first is 904, which was named in honour of the year 1904 when one of the founders, Alfredo Ardanza, proposed a merger with his own winery, Ardanza. Inevitably the wine lost its initial digit as the years passed, to avoid confusion with vintages. The 904 is a lovely, traditional Rioja, all from vineyards in the Rioja Alta region with 10 per cent Graciano to provide a line of savoury freshness. The wine spent four years in four-year-old American oak (there's no new oak here), before bottling and further ageing.

As the 904 lost its first digit, so too did the 890, originally named 1890 to commemorate the founding of the winery. The 890 is 95 per cent Tempranillo and 5 per cent Mazuelo from Briñas, Labastida and Villalba, with 3 per cent of Graciano from the Montecillo vineyard. The vintage on sale usually seems almost too young, even with all its years of ageing in the cellar. This is a wine to enjoy as the bright garnet fades gently to ochre, and the tertiary aromas build in the glass. A wine for leather armchairs and long evenings with the curtains drawn. The 2005 vintage has been declared a Selección Especial, as was 2001 – the only two Selección Especial wines since 1890. Surely this is just marketing? 'Not at all,' said Sáenz in 2018, 'we have done this because 2005 was an exceptional vintage. And because we can see with twelve years ageing it is still so young that it is going to have a great ageing capacity. It will keep on developing over the next 15 to 20 years.'

What has been wonderful about La Rioja Alta in recent times is its consistency. Whichever wine you enjoy – and can afford – then, allowing for occasional difficult vintages, you will be able to stay with it. (See also Torre de Oña, p. 261, Áster, p. 167 and Lagar de Cervera, p. 48.)

THE CHANGING LANDSCAPE

Across Spain the countryside lights up in the spring with the delicate pale blossoms of the almond trees. But the beauty of these trees obscures a more complex reality. Until recently EU subsidies were available for those willing to grub up bush vines. These old, low yielding, difficult to handle plants, in inaccessible places, were Spain's viticultural heritage but much was uprooted. In many places, growers chose to plant almonds instead – much less trouble, they were a cash crop at a time when California's supply of almonds was under threat. Such had been the case with La Rioja Alta's La Pedriza vineyard. In the 1990s the winery was looking to acquire its own Garnacha vines in the quality zone of Tudelilla. The current estate manager's father advised them to purchase La Pedriza, 67 hectares of it. Formerly good Garnacha land, with its stony soils, the site had been replanted to almonds. Today the trees are gone, and the vines are back, providing glorious colour in autumn rather than the spring.

Riojanas

Avda Don Ricardo Ruiz de Azcárraga 1, 26350 Cenicero
Tel.: +34 941 454 050
www.bodegasriojanas.com

Riojanas is the home to two great old Riojas, Monte Real and Albina. Of particular interest is the Monte Real, in the style the Italians call *vini di meditazioni*, soft and supple from its time in American oak. I have fond memories of a wonderful vertical tasting going into vintages way back before I was born. Very unfortunately, the current wines don't live up to the reputation of their predecessors. Look out for the older wines on specialist lists, especially the 1964, but check they have been stored properly first. Riojanas, founded in 1890, is one of the historic brands of Rioja. Riojanas also owns Viore in Rueda, Vega Naum in Rías Baixas and Torreduero in Toro.

RODA

Avda Vizcaya 5, 26200 Haro
Tel.: +34 941 303 001
www.roda.es

For a long time RODA was the new kid on the block in the Barrio de la Estación, the modern winery right up at the end. The one with the odd name which made just two wines, only from Tempranillo, from plots all over Rioja rather than just a few local vineyards. But now, with 30 years under its belt, RODA has grown up into a modern classic. Its focus still remains narrow, though it now has four wines, with the addition at the bottom of a junior wine and a wine at the top of the range too.

Catalan businessman Mario Rotllant and his partner Carmen Daurella gave the first initials of their names to the business. With a background in drinks distribution, they cast about in Spain for a top-quality site: 'I wanted a wine to enjoy now, but that could live longer, and that was complex. Bordeaux was too tannic.' Catalunya and Ribera del Duero were both candidates but in the end Rotllant selected Rioja, and the heart of Haro. They were able to buy the exceptional old cellar, which was tunnelled out in the rock below the Barrio (and is well worth a visit). On top, they their built their modern cellar. Rotllant wanted to choose the best place, and the best vines to create his wines. He also wanted to choose a new, young team who 'were experienced but not conditioned by Rioja'. Furthermore, 'we were looking for perfection. I never wanted them to take a decision thinking about the cost.' Rotllant did the sums, and out of that fixed the prices. Every year 7 per cent of gross turnover goes back into research. RODA became known for its Tempranillo seed bank, which has identified over 500 morphotypes in Rioja. Now the Familia RODA 107 collection gives growers internationally access to better plant material.

At the outset young viticulturist Agustín Santolaya and his colleague Isidro Palacios were charged with the secret project of finding the best old vineyards in Rioja Alta on which to base the project. From that research came 17 sites, which are vinified separately as single vineyards before the blend is made. RODA has not chosen to follow the single vineyard fashion, preferring as Santolaya puts it 'to reflect the panorama'. In 1998 Santolaya joined as general manager, a position he retains.

The first vintage of RODA I and RODA II was 1992. In 2002 the wines changed their names to RODA and RODA I, to head off the common assumption that RODA II is a second wine. The difference between the two is explained as RODA being red fruit, and RODA I being black fruit. It's an excellent, straightforward, consumer friendly model, but I must confess that it only rarely works for me. If I'm told there are red fruit I will find them, but if tasting blind I can't always be sure. Cirsion was the next to arrive, with the 1998 vintage. This is a supremely polished wine, only produced in the best years. It's a selection in the vineyard of the grapes with the ripest tannins. A decade later, Rotllant finally introduced Sela. He says he never wanted to make a blend to build volume – that wasn't in his model. But the bright, cheerful Sela fits in nicely, with fruit from 15–30 year old vines, which will one day be used for the senior brands.

Rotllant knows how to manage successful businesses and is proud to say that since RODA became profitable in 1998 it has not made a loss. Given the viability of the company he finally made it to Ribera del Duero in the end and set up Bodegas La Horra in 2009, also with Santolaya at the helm, in the very desirable village of La Horra. Last and just as important, he owns an estate in Mallorca which produces the exceptional olive oil, Aubocassa. Snap it up if you are visiting RODA.

El Sacramento

www.elsacramento.com

Viñas Leizaola bought the El Sacramento estate in 2011. It's a glorious extension of land, on a promontory close to Laguardia, with bush vines planted in 1986. Etienne Cordonnier, the owner, is a fine wine broker in Belgium. His roots in the Basque country go deep: his grandfather was President of the Basque Government in exile in the 1960s. Jesús de Madrazo Mateo (formerly of Contino, and a significant figure in the world of Rioja) is the winemaker and a minority shareholder – and also shares the marketing role. Madrazo's inside knowledge of Rioja has undoubtedly enabled Cordonnier to go further and faster than he might otherwise have done. The wines are classically made, with the first commercial vintage being 2011. The impressive winery in the heart of the estate welcomes visitors, from May 2018.

Sierra Cantabria

Amorebieta 3, 26338 San Vicente de la Sonsierra
Tel.: +34 941 338 040
www.sierracantabria.com

Whichever way you choose to enter the Sierra Cantabria group of wineries you are sure to be delighted. The Eguren family are growers, now in their fifth generation, and their wines have a determined sense of place. The group divides up now into Sierra Cantabria, and the Viñedos Sierra Cantabria, which is the upper range of wines, Viñedos de Páganos (see p. 264), Señorío de San Vicente, Teso la Monja in Toro (see p. 134), and Dominio de Eguren, a value line from Manchuela.

Sierra Cantabria was established in 1957 in the Eguren home territory of the lovely and historic hilltop town of San Vicente de la Sonsierra. Today's winemaker is the much-awarded Marcos Eguren, devoted to his vineyards and his wines. Sierra Cantabria is well-known for continuing to make the historic local style, *cosechero*, the wine of the harvest. It's a carbonic maceration red, Murmurón. In this winery he also makes the classic Crianza and higher categories.

The creation of Viñedos Sierra Cantabria is a more recent development. It has enabled Eguren to unite all the single vineyard and top wines of Sierra Cantabria. They have purchased a former winery, with deep cellars, outside San Vicente. The wines in this collection include Organza, one of his few whites, a blend of Viura with Malvasía and Garnacha Blanca, rich, a little spicy, with a lift of citrus. The reds are showcases for Tempranillo, all of them with the purity and freshness that is a keynote of the Eguren style. Colección Privada is a 50–50 wine in its making: 50 per cent carbonic maceration, 50 per cent traditional; 50 per cent French oak, 50 per cent American, ripe but with controlled freshness. Finca El Bosque is the result of exhaustive selection in the vineyard and the winery, punchdown during fermentation by foot rather than machine for gentler extraction and handling of every barrel separately during its maturation in the cellar. Amancio, its partner, is made from very low-yielding old vines, with just two bunches or fewer, and undergoes similar treatment, spending 24 months in oak. Powerful, it is built for the long haul.

At the San Vicente winery, the Egurens produce Señorio de San Vicente. As they put it, 'one winery from one vineyard using one grape variety'. The winery was founded in 1991 to showcase the Tempranillo of Sonsierra, a version known as Tempranillo Peludo or 'hairy' Tempranillo from the hairy character of the underside of the leaves. The wine comes from their La Canoca vineyard, and so is one of the many wines across Rioja that deserves the title of Single Vineyard. Says Eguren, 'Peludo is not a single clone, it's a massal selection of three or four. What's distinctive is that it has a small berry and an intense aroma. In the old vineyards of Sonsierra there was plenty of Tempranillo Peludo, everyone had it. Finally people are interested again, and they are collecting cuttings. And it really expresses Sonsierra and our vision of the vineyards'. The family did their own massal selection and planted La Canoca in 1985; the planting is more dense than usual, as they are looking for a lower yield – less than 1 kilogramme per vine.

Sierra de Toloño

Calle la Lleca s/n, 01307 Villabuena de Álava
Tel.: +34 626 233 085
www.sierradetolono.com

Sandra Bravo is well worth a visit, though take a coat if you go to the vineyards. For as her brand name suggests they are up in the Sierra at 650 metres, and it gets cold (though fortunately her vineyards were high enough to sit above the disastrous frosts of 2017). The bonus is that the fruit she harvests makes for wines with bags of freshness and elegance. In a few years Bravo has packed in plenty of experience –from Bordeaux, Chianti and Marlborough to Priorat. So although the project is just a few years old (2012 was her first vintage), the wines show impressive confidence.

Her total production is small at around 40,000 bottles, but the vast old winery in which she works gives her plenty of room for growth and experimentation. You'll spot the amphorae, which she is starting to use for her white wine Rives de Tereso. Her 'regular' Rioja tinto is deliciously fleshy with aniseed and herbs. As a sign of her success in careful innovation, the white Nahi (pronounced nai, and meaning desire) is a co-fermented blend of biodynamically-farmed old-vine Viura, Malvasía, Calagrana and Rojal, fermented in 500-litre French oak, round and mouth-filling. These are wines to watch (and taste).

Tentenublo

La Fuente 52–54, 01308 Lanciego
Tel.: +34 699 236 468
www.tentenublo.com

The photo on the holding page of Roberto Oliván's website is a striking image: apparently a bucolic shot of a man in a vineyard beneath a tree. On closer examination he is preparing to put his head in a noose. Is this how he feels about the agonies of being a producer today, having to be on top of web design and social media as well as corks and bottles and regulations? Or perhaps it's the result of the frost in April 2017, or the press demanding visits and barrel samples?

Certainly Oliván has become one of the darlings of the new generation of producers. The winery is named after the word for the ringing of bells to ward off hailstorms. Oliván is a Rioja local, working with some 10 hectares of his mother's family's vines plus those he has acquired around Lanciego and the little village of Vinaspres, some of them up to 100 years old. The tapestry of tiny plots is interwoven with field blends of some scarce old varieties. Hence his Tentenublo white is a blend of Calagrano with Malvasía Riojana and Viura. His is a low intervention style, and he ferments the wine in large oak vats. The range of wines is growing constantly, all in small production, and all of them worth looking out for.

Torre de Oña

Finca San Martín s/n, Páganos, 01309 Laguardia
+ 34 945 621 254
www.torredeona.com

The La Rioja Alta winery bought this estate in 1995. There is a distinct change of air and style from the parent business to Torre de Oña, located as it is in Laguardia, and thus in Rioja Alavesa. A model of a château estate, it has its own house amid the vineyards. The team, led by technical director Julio Sáenz, has had to get to grips with managing and differentiating its 46 hectares. There have therefore been more than two decades of research into soil types and viticulture. The first two wines released were Torre de Oña itself (Tempranillo with a dash of Mazuelo, 40,000 bottles), followed by Finca San Martín (100 per cent Tempranillo, 125,000 bottles). The newest wine, launched in 2017, is Martelo. This comes from vines of over 60 years of age at some 580 metres, mainly Tempranillo with some other varieties, field blends. There is plenty of limestone in the soil. With these wines, and particularly Martelo, La Rioja Alta has created an estate with wines that are different but complementary in quality. This has proved a much better venture than simply making a *vino de autor*.

Valdemar and Inspiración Valdemar

Camino Viejo 24, 01320 Oyón
Tel.: +34 945 622 188
www.valdemar.es

Valdemar is owned by Jesús Martínez Bujanda, who set up his own business in 2007, separating from his brother Carlos and sister Pilar, who retained Finca Valpiedra (see p. 230). Valdemar has extensive vineyard holdings in Rioja, mainly in Rioja Alavesa. Conde Valdemar is its established brand, offering the regular ladder of Riojas, typically aged in American oak, in addition to a Garnacha and a single vineyard white, Finca Alto Cantabria, which was the first barrel-fermented white in the DOCa. The Finca del Marquesado property produces a Crianza from its 135 hectares.

In contrast, Inspiración Valdemar was launched in the white heat of the *vinos de autor* revolution. Founded in 2000, the winery is next door to Valdemar, and as impressively polished as the wines. This winery is all about careful selection and micro-fermentations, with a resulting greater ripeness and lighter alcohol than the Conde Valdemar wines. There are six wines, all single vineyard, five reds (including a varietal Maturana and a varietal Graciano) and a white, a Tempranillo Blanco.

They have also launched in Ribera del Duero, with the Fincas Valdemar label.

Valenciso

Ctra LR-313 Ollauri-Nájera Km 0.4, 26220 Ollauri
Tel.: +34 941 304 724
www.valenciso.com

One of the first of Rioja's 'garage' wineries, this was founded by Luis Valentín and Carmen Enciso. They had long been known from their work at Bodegas Palacio, and set off on their own when Palacio was sold on to a new owner, launching in 1998. They started with just 24,000 bottles in that first vintage, and from the very beginning had their wine exactly right. In due course they moved from a warehouse to a purpose-built winery. They make just one red, Valenciso Reserva, Tempranillo from a selection of vineyards all in Rioja Alta. It's delicate without being old-fashioned, polished without being anonymous or international, altogether just right. Their white wine, which came later, a Viura–Garnacha Blanca blend, has nine months of barrel ageing. There are occasional special releases.

Viña Real

Ctra Logroño-Laguardia Km 4.8, 01300 Laguardia
Tel.: +34 945 625 255
www.cvne.com

Viña Real is fully integrated into the CVNE group, but as it has its own winery, it has its own entry here. Viña Real used to be made in the main winery in the Barrio de la Estación in Haro. But as space began to run out even in the extensive buildings in Haro, the decision was taken to create a new home for Viña Real. Its new site is just over the border in Rioja Alavesa, enabling Viña Real to be 100 per cent Alavesa grown Alavesa made wines. Inevitably there have been those who have told me that it was also a politically judicious step. This way CVNE kept a foot in both (political) camps, La Rioja and Rioja Alavesa, and was able to benefit from financial advantages accruing to Álava wineries from the Basque government.

Be that as it may, the investment CVNE chose to make created a remarkable winery built into the hill of Cerro de la Mesa above the road to Laguardia. It looks like a giant oak fermentation vat, low and round, and the fermentation tanks inside are ranked around the outside walls. The first vintage was made in 2002. Undoubtedly, having the single winery for the brand has improved the identity of the wines. The Crianza and Reserva are regular choices; but the Gran Reserva is a fine example of a new generation Gran Reserva from Álava fruit. The top wine is Pagos de Viña Real, made from their own vineyards around the winery. Tempranillo, with malolactic fermentation in new French oak barrels, gives the wine its confident, modern profile. The latest arrival is one of the new generation of ultra-pale rosados, mainly Viura with just 15 per cent Tempranillo.

Viñedos del Contino

Finca San Rafael s/n, 01321 Laserna
Tel.: +34 945 600 201
www.cvne.com

In recent years Contino, like Viña Real, has come firmly back into the CVNE management system – hence the corporate web address. Yet Contino's glory was its individuality, with a remarkable vineyard at the bend in the river, managed with scrupulous attention by a member of the CVNE family. It was the first winery I ever visited in Rioja, and Jesús de Madrazo was the first technical director I ever encountered in the region.

I visited Contino on a Sunday afternoon near the end of the harvest, with a vision of golden leaves in the vineyard, a meander of the Ebro in the distance, and a few magisterial trees dotted about (I learnt later that it was 62 hectares on calcareous clay). Contino has always been about excellence. For those of us who enjoy the Contino wines it has also been about discovery. Jesús de Madrazo was important in revealing the potential of Riojan Graciano, a wine he called Contino's Sleeping Beauty. That's because of the time it needed to spend in bottle before it could reveal its glory. Once upon a time the variety was hardly known, and today it seems there is more claimed in wines than there can possibly be planted. His influence was not just with Graciano, but also in developing his own approach to Garnacha, a *blanco* (a blend of Viura with Malvasía and Garnacha Blanca) and a fine *rosado* from Garnacha and Graciano with a dash of Viura. These wines were originally made for visitors and friends, but now they are available for a wider audience.

De Madrazo makes friends wherever he goes, all of them struck by his deep knowledge of Rioja and his generosity. After 18 years at Contino he moved on after harvest in 2017 to join El Sacramento (p. 258). He in turn had taken over from Basilio Izquierdo (see p. 215). His successor is consultant winemaker, keen cyclist and all-round enthusiast Jorge Navascués, from a winemaking family in Aragón. Jorge will continue the tradition of Contino and refresh it. As he comes from Garnacha country, we can be sure to see a focus on that variety. I wish him an equally long and happy tenancy.

Viñedos de Páganos

Ctra de Navaridas s/n, 01307 Páganos
Tel.: +34 902 334 080
www.eguren.com

An impressive winery, carved into the hillside, this is the home of the Eguren family's single vineyard wines, El Puntido and La Nieta. La Nieta comes from fewer than 2 hectares, planted in 1975 on extremely poor soils, from which only around 4,000 bottles are produced. The wines are fermented in large oak vats and aged in new French oak for something over a year. La Nieta is intense when young, but develops with great elegance. El Puntido (note that neither Nieta nor Puntido, nor any of the other top wines carries a Rioja age classification; the Eguren wines eschew these) is the big brother in size. It comes from a 25 hectare vineyard of Tempranillo and is therefore the much more accessible (in availability at least) of the two. Try them both: it's a personal choice in the end and La Nieta is my favourite.

Ysios

Camino de la Hoya s/n, 01300 Laguardia
Tel.: +34 945 600 640
www.ysios.com

There's hardly any need to have a specific address for Ysios. Take the northern exit from Laguardia and it's fewer than 5 minutes from the roundabout at the foot of the town. Just aim for the Sierra Cantabria and Ysios will be in front of you. For Ysios is the winery with the spectacular undulating roof designed by Santiago Calatrava. Like some other of

Calatrava's buildings (notably in Valencia) the stupendous design has subsequently led to maintenance complications for the owners. In this case the owners are Pernod Ricard, and the very competent winemaker in charge is Elena Adell of Campo Viejo (see p. 220). Clearly it's not the easiest building to work or to fit tanks in, especially at the bottom of each undulation, where the roof is lower. Cleaning the windows must be a nightmare too.

Although for architecture fans this winery is a must visit – at least to walk around the outside – up until now the wines have never quite fulfilled the building's promise. The best pick is the 100 per cent Tempranillo Edición Limitada.

Artadi

Ctra de Logroño s/n, 01300 Laguardia
Tel.: +34 945 600 119
www.artadi.com

Artadi dates back to 1985, when it was founded by a group of winegrowers keen to come together to make wines from Álava. This small cooperative transformed itself into the hugely successful Artadi, and went on to develop projects in Navarra (Artazu) and Alicante (El Sequé). At the end of 2015, Juan Carlos López de Lacalle decided to leave the DOCa Rioja. The event was a surprise, and crystallized a range of discontents which producers who focus on single vineyards have with wineries who blend across the DOCa, as many do. It was also part of a larger sense of dissatisfaction with regulators across Spain, which was expressed in the Club Matador Manifesto (see box, p. 266). In a similar move, producers in Cava had left to create a separate quality grouping, DO Clàssic Penedès (100 per cent organic farming, 100 per cent Penedès, 100 per cent Reserva wines) and Pep Raventós of Raventós i Blanc left the Cava DO to create his own Conca del Ríu Anoia. López de Lacalle remains committed to the soils of Rioja Alavesa, if not its regulatory body, so for that reason he keeps a place in the Rioja chapter, but out of alphabetical order. The labels on his wines now declare 'Bodegas y Viñedos Artadi de Laguardia S.A., Álava, España'.

From the beginning Artadi made a *cosechero* wine, a wine of the vintage, using traditional carbonic maceration. The Joven is still that wine, more or less, and made with the conspicuous care that distinguishes Artadi wines. In the early years Artadi's winemaker was

Benjamín Romeo, who eventually left to found Contador (see p. 222). Viñas de Gaín has become an established success as a village wine. The single vineyards are especially interesting: Valdeginés, La Poza de Ballesteros and El Carretil. Each one of these expresses a different soil, with a distinct and different character. The top wine is El Pisón, from a 2.8-hectare vineyard dating from 1945. It is Tempranillo with a little Garnacha and Graciano, which came from his grandfather, and is owned by the business he shares with his wife Pilar, Viñedos Lacalle y Laorden. It's a gloriously aromatic wine, but needs time to grow and develop in the bottle. A favourite among high-scoring critics, but deservedly so.

On the radar – VT Valles de Sadacia

This young IGP is named after the Sadacia valley in the south-west of Rioja, between the valleys of the Sadacia and Cidacos rivers. It's a category for wines made from Moscatel Riojana, which dwindled away to almost nothing after phylloxera. It is used to make dry wines, as well as sweet ones.

THE CLUB MATADOR MANIFESTO

In November 2016, a group of leading wine producers, wine merchants and wine writers met at Madrid's Club Matador to debate the need for full-scale renewal of the Spanish DO system, and to sign the Manifesto below in defence of terroir. Leading Rioja producer Artadi had already left the Rioja DOCa at the end of 2015, and criticism of traditional classification systems was growing strongly. The meeting was organized by Telmo Rodríguez, and the Manifesto gathered some 150 signatures. Since then CRDOCa Rioja has felt the need to come out with some rapid changes, not all of them generally praised, while Bierzo has declared the clearest pyramid of *crus* proposals. The Manifesto captured a moment of intensity of feeling and its ripples will continue to spread.

Spain boasts the richest biodiversity and the most varied landscapes in Europe but it also faces the greatest challenges in terms of environmental awareness and conservation. The world of wine is no exception.

The Spanish wine appellation system has proved effective in protecting geographical names and origin, but it has been oblivious to soil differentiation and levels of quality. Efforts have been aimed at turning our vineyards into the world's biggest, not the best.

However, we have the history, the places and also the passion needed to make the most out of our exceptional crus and vineyards.

Deep changes are needed to boost our wine heritage and bring a sense of self-worth to Spanish wine. It must be a global change for everyone involved, from producers to the authorities.

All the great wines in the world come from exceptional vineyards. That's why the most revered wine regions have passed laws to defend and protect those unique sites.

We firmly believe that the best way to identify wines based on their origin, quality, identity and authenticity is by means of a pyramid-like structure. Wines made anywhere in the region would be at the base; village wines would be a step above while single-vineyard wines would be at the very top.

All producers will benefit from such a structure. Only by raising the bar and demanding more from ourselves, will we be able to improve quality and explain Spain's wine reality more accurately. It will also help to sell all kinds of wine better.

Therefore, we call upon the Regulatory Boards to be sensitive to the new wine reality that is emerging all over Spain and to approach a classification of the land in terms of quality. We are certain that establishing such distinctions is the first step towards excellence. Beyond emerging as an unstoppable trend, terroir wines are the best way to improve the quality of Spanish wines and achieve international recognition.

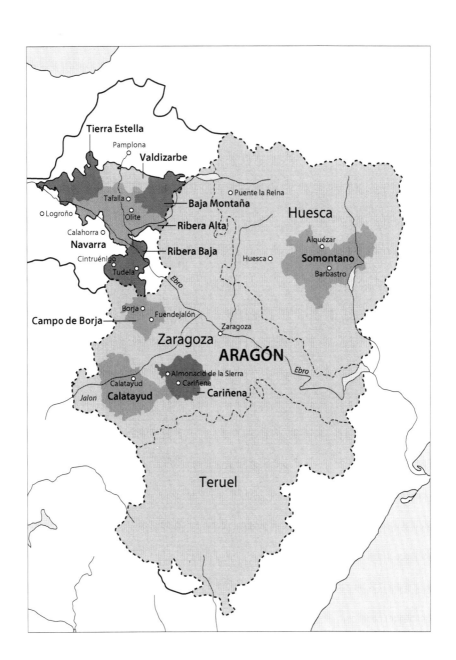

Tierra Estella

Pamplona ○

Valdizarbe

○ Puente la Reina

Tafalla ○

Baja Montaña

Huesca

○ Logroño

Olite

Ribera Alta

Calahorra ○

Navarra

Ribera Baja

Huesca ○

Alquézar ○

Somontano

Cintruénigo

Barbastro

Tudela

Ebro

Campo de Borja

Borja ○

Fuendejalón ○

Zaragoza ○

Zaragoza

ARAGÓN

Ebro

Almonacid de la Sierra

Calatayud ○

Cariñena ○

Calatayud

Cariñena

Jalon

Teruel

8

NAVARRA AND ARAGÓN: LAND OF KINGS AND GARNACHISTAS

NAVARRA

A good wine is made near Puente de la Reina, where several streams meet in the plain.

Richard Ford

Strictly speaking, Navarra is the Kingdom of Navarra. The first inhabitants of Navarra were the Basque forerunners, the Vascones, and Basque heritage remains important for the region's inhabitants. Navarra was an independent kingdom until it signed over its independence to King Ferdinand in 1512 in return for certain rights or *fueros*. There hasn't been a King of Navarra since 1791. At that time Navarra was a French territory, and Louis XVI was the last *Roi de France et Navarre*.

Navarra's wine trade was for centuries as glorious as its kings. A significant route to Santiago de Compostela passed through the top of the region – from Pamplona to Puente la Reina and Estella and into Rioja. The wines were popular with the pilgrims, and by the fifteenth century an export trade to France was well established, including *rosado* wine. Exports to the New World followed in due course.

At the outbreak of oidium and phylloxera in France, Navarra operated a cross-border business until the diseases reached its own

269

vineyards. In the twentieth century Navarra wobbled. The growth of cooperatives fostered vine growing but did not restore the quality or the marketing that Navarra has enjoyed centuries earlier. Gradually its neighbour Rioja overshadowed Navarra. In the 1970s the decision was taken to promote Tempranillo, even though Navarra lacked the soils to make it sing. The subsequent decision to authorize Cabernet Sauvignon and Merlot, as well as Chardonnay, can be seen in retrospect as a mistake.

The authors of *The Finest Wines of Rioja and Northern Spain* comment:

The British wine press, in the 1980s and '90s, led the chorus of plaudits for the new Navarra. This so-called modernization was generally considered positive, as gurus painted a picture of a world wine market with an unquenchable thirst for Cabernet and Chardonnay. It didn't pan out for Navarra, though, as a new generation of overcropped, highly technological, international wines failed to convince international buyers that they were any better than Australian Chardonnays or Chilean Cabernets; while in Spain, the region's negative image as 'poor man's Rioja' proved very difficult to dislodge. Worse still, thousands of hectares of the region's distinctive, native treasure – Garnacha – were ripped up in favour of imported varieties.

Spot on! Writing in 2011, they were highlighting that change was on the way. And so it has proved. Navarra is on the move, and Garnacha is an important part of that. Garnacha was 90 per cent of the vineyard at the beginning of the 1980s and although the number of vines was reduced, it is climbing back. There are still issues – Navarra was always the place for *rosado* in Spain, and had an international reputation. The demand for pale-coloured pink wines internationally has been damaging. Rioja has been faster to produce pale wines. Local winemakers argue that the flavour is lost when the wines are paler. They may be right, but the consumer is against them.

> ## Navarra at a glance
>
> ### Grape varieties
> **White**: Chardonnay, Garnacha Blanca, Malvasía, Moscatel de Grano Menudo, Viura, Sauvignon Blanc
> **Red**: Cabernet Sauvignon (9%), Garnacha Tinta (42%), Graciano, Mazuelo, Merlot, Tempranillo (29%), Syrah, Pinot Noir. Red varieties make up 91 per cent of plantings.
>
> ### Size
> **Vineyard**: 11,027 hectares
> **Growers**: 2,378
> **Wineries**: 96

The Navarra DO (created in 1975) is a huge region shaped like an inverted triangle stretching south from Pamplona for 100 kilometres, covering a range of climates and soils, bounded by the Pyrenees and Iberian systems of mountains. To the north towards the Pyrenees the climate is cooler and damper, in the centre the climate is more continental, and further south there are Mediterranean influences. The Bardenas Reales national park in the south-east is a semi-desert. A small part of Navarra province is in the Rioja DOCa.

The DO is divided into five zones:

- **Baja Montaña** (13 per cent of the vineyards). This is red wine country in the north-east of Navarra; it borders on Aragón, with spectacular views and extensive pasture. This is the place for old bush vine Garnacha. The rainfall varies between 470 and 760 millimetres.
- **Tierra Estella** (15 per cent of the vineyards). A sub-zone alongside the Camino de Santiago, with wonderful old castles and churches en route. The hills of Tierra Estella have the highest limestone content.
- **Valdizarbe** (8 per cent of the vineyards). The smallest of the sub-zones, this is south of Pamplona. The soils here are more chalky.

- **Ribera Alta** (35 per cent of the vineyards). The very mid-point of Navarra, this surrounds the town of Olite. The climate here is transitional; Lerín to the east is semi-arid.
- **Ribera Baja** (29 per cent of the vineyards). The southern tip of Navarra. In Ribera Alta and Ribera Baja the soils are poorer and sandier. A fine source of sweet Muscats, as well as reds. The driest part of the DO.

Producers

Arínzano

Ctra NA-132 Km 3.1, 31264 Aberin
Tel.: +34 948 555 285
www.arinzano.com

What a beautiful estate! Wines have been made on this property since the eleventh century. In 1988, the Chivite family purchased the 335-hectare estate and set about relaunching the wines and rebuilding the winery. Today there are 135 hectares of vineyard. The late Denis Dubourdieu was the consultant here and made an excellent start. Sadly the Chivites were not able to continue the work and were forced to sell the jewel of their family interests in 2015. The owners are now the SPI group, owners of Stolichnaya vodka, whose other vinous interests are Achával-Ferrer in Argentina, with minority shares in three Frescobaldi wineries in Tuscany.

The winemaker is none other than the thoughtful, skilful Manuel Louzada, formerly of Numanthia, so the future looks bright. A Vino de Pago, the first in Navarra, has been produced since 2007.

Artazu

Mayor s/n, 31109 Artazu
Tel.: +34 945 600 119
www.artadi.com

The arrival of Artadi in Navarra 1996 put the spotlight on a particularly forgotten world: Navarra's Garnachas, a great heritage that had been sadly disregarded. At that time Navarra was all about the international varieties, as it still is, to a certain extent. Today many Garnachistas have found their way to Navarra, making terrific wines, but it's important to remember that their arrival has been relatively recent.

The Artazu vineyards are up in Valdizarbe, a cool, higher altitude zone, where they work with brown limestone and calcareous clay, altogether poor and stony soils, farming organically. Their first investment was 10 hectares of 60-year-old vines, and their first vintage was 2000. Pasos de San Martín was first produced in 2011 with grapes from the village of San Martín de Unx, one of the centres of Navarran Garnacha. From 13 hectares of vineyard at 600 metres, the wine is matured for a year in lightly toasted 500-litre French oak. Everything about the treatment is subtle. The same goes for the winemaking in the top wine, Santa Cruz de Artazu, which is Artadi's village wine from Artazu, after which the winery is named.

The Artazu project covers all bases, also producing three young wines, a *tinto*, a *blanco* and a *rosado* all from Garnacha. All three are fermented in stainless steel to keep their direct, pure fruit. In addition Artadi have taken on the Monasterio de la Oliva, and are making a Garnacha blend with Tempranillo, Cabernet Sauvignon and Merlot.

Baja Montaña

Ctra Jaca s/n, 31487 Liédena
Tel.: +34 914 430 293

A relatively new project from winemaker Fernando Chivite, formerly of Chivite (see p. 274), working in the cooperative at Liédena. Arbayún is his new wave *rosado*, a real wine rather than a pink drink, made from Garnacha. It's made its way directly to the top of the list of Spain's *rosados*.

La Calandria. Pura Garnacha

Tel.: +34 609 476 387 (Javier Continente)
www.puragarnacha.com

I first encountered the wines in a blind tasting of Navarra wines. The top four – La Calandria. Pura Garnacha included – were all Garnachas, which is what opened my eyes to the changes afoot in the Kingdom. The winery is in Murchante and its sole focus is old vine Garnacha, sourced from Cintruénigo and Tierga. Launched by Luis Fernández and Javier Continente, with the first vintage in 2007, it's now run by Continente with Luis Remacha. The current portfolio also includes Cientruénos (no sulphites); Tierga, aged in clay amphorae; Sonrojo, a 'lightly oxidative' *rosado*; and Niño Perdido, a new project of *rancio* wines, following the traditional methods.

Camilo Castilla

Santa Bárbara 40, 31591 Corella
Tel.: +34 948 780 006
www.bodegascamilocastilla.com

What a treat – Navarra does have some exceptional treasures! Particularly good are its sweet wines from Moscatel a Grano Menudo, Muscat à Petits Grains, and Camilo Castilla has a particular beauty. Not all the wines produced here are loveable, but it's worth the tasting when you finally reach the stars.

This is Navarra's oldest winery, a bodega founded in 1856 by Camilo Castilla Alzugaray, which made its name for sweet wines. The Beltran family bought the business in 1987, and today owns 50 hectares of Moscatel vineyards on clay–limestone soils at 370 metres. The business used to make a full range of dry wines, red and white, under the brands Montecristo and K Identity, but they are wisely focusing on the Moscatels, and have repackaged them, updating the look just a little. There are dry Moscatels, but the interest is particularly in the sweet wines. Although there are straightforward clean, sweet, simple Moscatels, the stars are the two 'Goya' wines. The Moscatel de Goya was fortified to 15% abv and aged for two years in vast oak vats; it has 200 g/l of residual sugar. It shows a lovely balance between bright acidity, floral Moscatel aromas, and nutty development. The Capricho d'Goya is anything but a caprice. It has been aged for three years in glass demijohns and oak casks in the open air, through rain, sun and – yes – snow. It spends four years in wooden vats. The result is that it develops a rich, deep, dark brown colour, with wonderfully complex aromas of toffee, roasted nuts and sweet spices, with just a note of citrus. Superbly sweet at 230 g/l of residual sugar, it is figgy and raisined, but at the same time fresh. For its age and originality this remains exceptionally good value.

Camilo Castilla belongs to the A&B Bodegas group, which also includes Finca Egomei in Rioja and Peinado brandy.

J. Chivite Family Estates

Ctra NA-132, Km 3.1, 31132 Villatuerta
Tel.: +34 948 811 000
www.bodegaschivite.com

Chivite is not only a great name in Navarran wine, it's also the oldest. The first mention of the Chivite family linking them with wine was in

1647. In a legal document, Juan Chivite Frias and his sister-in-law are requesting a mortgage for 100 ducats on the estate, which is described in these terms: '… the winery owns up to one hundred and fifty wine vats and is situated adjacent to the house of Pedro Ximénez on the one side and Calle Real and Camino de la Carrera, a quantity of timber and a vineyard with thirty labourers along the road to Cascante …'

There's every reason to believe that the Chivites continued to grow wine. In the mid-nineteenth century the Chivites, located so close to France, benefited greatly when oidium and then phylloxera hit the French vineyards. Claudio Chivite was able to establish a solid export business, with a triangular trade route of Cintruénigo–Bayonne–Bordeaux. In 1872, the building of the new bodega started, establishing the next phase of the winery expansion, which was to continue well into the twentieth century. The family home was also converted into a posting inn for travellers, which spread the name and reputation of Chivite wines further. In 1930 Claudio's grandson Julián Chivite Marco inherited the business and was one of the founders of the Consejo Regulador of Navarra in 1967. From then on the business grew rapidly, developing a well thought out portfolio of brands. Gran Feudo was launched in 1975, a range of young wines, using international varieties, providing a fresh, modern look for Navarra. The *rosado* became particularly famous, with the bright, cherry red colour of Navarra *rosados*, a colour which was still fashionable. In those days, Navarra was the place in Spain for *rosado*, and had a strong international appeal.

In 1985, to commemorate 125 years since the first exports of Chivite wine, the winery launched Colección 125. The Chardonnay in this collection has ranked amongst the top white wines in Spain, though it has to be admitted that competition is hotting up. The long-term consultant on these wines was the much-respected Bordeaux winemaker, Professor Denis Dubourdieu. For a long time he said he chose to be the '*oenologue caché*', but in 2011 he finally went public. He said his contribution to Chivite was to add finesse and ageability to the wine, which has certainly been proved by a number of the old Colección 125 Chardonnays.

In 1988 the family acquired the exceptionally beautifully estate of Señorío de Arínzano (see p. 272). The architect Rafael Moneo, who has subsequently built very fine wineries for Álvaro Palacios and Ricardo Pérez Palacios, made a glorious job of the conversion. Ten years later the Chivite business acquired Viña Salceda in Rioja, followed soon after by the purchase of 50 hectares of land in La Horra in Ribera del Duero. In 2009, Chivite moved into Rueda, and launched Baluarte. Under new management, in 2013 Chivite introduced three new Navarran wines from the Tierra Estella zone, in Finca Villatuerta. Two years later Julián Chivite launched one of the very early pale coloured *rosados*, Las Fincas, which was made in collaboration with the renowned San Sebastian chef, Juan Marí Arzak.

At a vertical tasting of his Colección 125 Chardonnays in Madrid in 2012, Denis Dubourdieu observed of the growth of Chardonnay in Navarra that, 'I was always sure good wines were made in difficult conditions. Just as with people, difficulty strengthens the individual.' As with vineyards, so with people indeed. The Chivite family went through some hard times. Julián *padre* had died in the 1990s. In the twenty-first century the next generation has been afflicted by illness and dispute. In 2011 son Fernando was ousted from the family board, and his brother Julián took over in 2012. By 2016, the business had become complicated, and Chivite had to sell the precious jewel of Arínzano (see p. 272) to a group of Russian investors. Finally, Catalan company Castillo Perelada purchased 80 per cent of the business in the autumn of 2017. This brings Chivite into a group which also includes Priorat (Casa Gran del Siurana), as well as Empordà and Cava. At the time of writing it's hard to read the runes. But Castillo Perelada has certainly acquired some vineyard gems, and brands for which many consumers have great affection. This could be a step towards a positive new future after so much change at the top.

Bodega Emilio Valerio - Laderas de Montejurra
Paraje de Argonga, 31263 Dicastillo
www.laderasdemontejurra.com

This is another of the key names in the recovery of Garnacha. Valerio has 25 hectares of vineyards over 15 plots in the Tierra Estella region, which are farmed biodynamically. The soils are poor with limestone and sandstone, and the rainfall varies from 200 to 1,000 millimetres, as the altitudes of the parcels vary from 400 to 1,000 metres. Various of the vineyards date back to land used for vines by the Benedictines and the Knights Templar. Each vineyard is fermented separately in oak vats or concrete tanks, and only French oak is used for ageing, with a small percentage of new wood. The wines are named after the specific terroirs. Emilio Valerio is the flagship, a blend of red varieties, fresh and elegant.

Domaines Lupier

Monseñor Justo González 4, 31495 San Martín de Unx
Tel.: +34 639 622 111
www.domaineslupier.com

Domaines Lupier arrived like a thunderclap. Suddenly it seemed, from apparently nowhere, a brand new business was producing two stupendous Garnachas – and in Navarra of all places. Over recent years Navarra has become something of a poor relation in the wine world, and the remarkable heritage of Garnacha vines from Navarra had been overlooked, seen as simply serviceable for *rosados*.

Elisa Úcar and Enrique Basarte had met in another part of the Spanish wine world and decided to set out on their own. They fixed on Spain's old vine heritage of Garnacha, and finally decided on Navarra's forgotten old bush vines around San Martín de Unx. Bit by bit they purchased parcels, 27 in all, at 400–750 metres, with different soils and orientations, and the oldest vines dating back to 1903.

They launched their wines in 2008, and the fact that they still make just the two – La Dama and El Terroir – indicates their clarity of purpose, and attention to detail. Since Domaines Lupier started out, others have joined the Navarra Garnacha trail. But Elisa and Enrique remain focused on their own excellence.

Máximo Abete/Vinos Guerinda

Ctra Estella-Sangüesa, Km 43.5, 31495 San Martín de Unx
Ctra Cadreita-Villafranca s/n, 31515 Cadreita
Tel.: +34 948 738 120
www.bodegasmaximoabete.com

Another small project in San Martín de Unx, again full of promise for seekers after Navarran Garnacha. The family winery on the main road does not look in the least promising but once the family takes you into the vineyards, hidden amongst forests, you begin to see where the magic comes from. The bodega is run by the late Máximo's daughters María and Yoanna, and Juanma, Yoanna's husband. Their grapes used to be sold to the cooperative, but since 2011 they have been making their own wines. They make a selection of wines from Chardonnay, Garnacha, Cabernet Sauvignon and Merlot. Their Graciano Navasentero 3+1, and La Abejera from their oldest bush vine Garnachas are particularly worth seeking out.

Nekeas

Las Huertas s/n, 31154 Añorbe
Tel.: +34 948 350 296
www.nekeas.com

This is a cooperative business run by several families, founded in 1992. Their vineyards are at 350–600 metres, on a complex variety of stony soils, and are protected from the Pyrenees by the Sierra de Perdón. They focus on export, and their winemaker, the enthusiastic Concha Vecino, creates wines with strong international appeal. She has ensured the successful transformation to Garnacha. The Cepa x Cepa Garnacha has been produced by grafting Garnacha, 'vine by vine' over other varieties. El Chaparral, full of cherry fruit and dark plums, is from their oldest Garnacha vines, aged between 70 and 100 years.

Ochoa Viñedos y Bodegas

Miranda de Arga 35, 31390 Olite
Tel.: +34 948 74 00 06
www.bodegasochoa.com

Ochoa *is* Navarran wine, or at least was, for many years. A former director of EVENA (Navarra's research centre for viticulture and oenology), Javier Ochoa pioneered research and development in Navarra, as well as leading his eponymous winery, which was founded in 1845. The family – all of them delightful – have 143 hectares of vineyard, and in addition to the classic portfolio of wines also pioneered fresh, late harvest Moscatel. It's the best in the region, and consistently one of the best in Spain.

As true Navarrans you will find three generations of the family, father and mother, daughters and grandchildren, all in white shirts and red neckerchiefs at Pamplona for the festival of San Fermín. Sixth generation daughter Adriana is now in charge of winemaking, aided by her sister Beatriz in sales and marketing. Adriana's innovations include reviving the neat 8A logo for her wines, used by their grandfather, as it's an abbreviation of the Spanish '*ocho-a*' and a play on the number 8. A favourite of mine, making use of their ready supply of Moscatel de Grano Menudo is her 8A MdO, Moscato de Ochoa, her version of Moscato d'Asti.

Otazu

Señorio de Otazu s/n, 31174 Etxauri
Tel.: +34 948 329 353
www.otazu.com

This glorious property just outside Pamplona is very well worth a visit if you are intending to go bull-running, or just enjoy the San Fermín festivities. The estate, dating back to the twelfth century, is impressive. It is managed by Guillermo Penso, whose father, a Pamplonan by birth, emigrated to Venezuela and purchased the property in 1989. At the time there were no vines. Today there are 110 hectares of vineyards, in 30 parcels, mainly sand and gravel over clay, planted to Tempranillo, Merlot, Cabernet Sauvignon and Chardonnay. The estate is in a cool, northerly part of Navarra, which is sometimes complicated climatically, but generally avoids baked fruit in the wines. These are polished wines, with plenty of good oak. At my last visit they were planning the launch of Vitral, their top wine, at a price of €2,000.

The bodega is an impressive, no expense spared conversion of a warehouse originally built in 1840. What adds to the interest of the visit is the art collection. Wineries the world over have collections of art, not all of them absorbing. The modern art and sculpture here, as well as the restored buildings, are worth visiting. Another of Navarra's Vinos de Pago.

Pago de Cirsus

Ctra Ablitas-Ribaforada Km 5, 31523 Ablitas
Tel.: +34 948 386 427
www.pagodecirsus.com

Basque film producer Iñaki Núñez is the man behind this glamorous project, both hotel and winery. It's an impressive building with a film-set tower recalling the days of King Sancho. He has invested seriously in the winery with temperature controlled oak fermentation vats for the top wines. These are polished, well-made wines, with strong international appeal. That's not surprising as the consultant winemaker here since

2003 has been Bordeaux-born Jean-Marc Sauboua, who has long been the winemaker for UK company Direct Wines, making wine around the world. A Vino de Pago.

Pago de Larrainzar
Camino de la Corona s/n, 31240 Ayegui
Tel.: +34 948 550 421
www.pagodelarrainzar.com

This is one of Navarra's loveliest wineries, next door to the monastery of Irache alongside the Camino de Santiago. The estate had been in the Larrainzar family for some 150 years, but the business of wine had been abandoned over time. In 2001 Navarra businessman Miguel Canalejo took on the project of launching a winery. There are plenty of factors that would make it as eligible for Vino de Pago status as Navarra's other Pagos: the walled vineyard, the estate wines, and the consistent quality. However that's not a path they have (yet) chosen. Their Reserva Especial is the blend of their best grapes: Merlot, Cabernet Sauvignon, Tempranillo and Garnacha. In that respect it reflects the modern approach of Navarra, which it achieves in style. Within the range there are also single varietals: Cabernet Sauvignon and Merlot.

San Martín
Ctra Sangüesa s/n, 31495 San Martín de Unx
Tel.: +34 948 738 294
www.bodegasanmartin.com

This is the village cooperative, founded 1904. In my recent tastings their Garnachas have come out with very high scores, endorsing the craggy medieval village of San Martín de Unx (population 436) as a remarkable zone for very fine old Garnacha. The cooperative manages some 600 hectares of dry-farmed vineyards, one-third bush vines, and have Tempranillo, Viura, Macabeo and Cabernet Sauvignon. But it is the Garnacha that shines, notably Alma de Unx, from the oldest parcels. The wine undergoes malolactic in cask and then spends ten months in casks made from Navarran oak, *Quercus petraea*. My note says 'Dominantly oaked nose. Powerful mid-palate laden with impressively ripe fruit. Bold, glossy statement of Garnacha.' Gonzalo Celayeta is the Garnacha guide here (see p. 284). A cooperative with some wines worth following.

Señorio de Sarría

Señorio de Sarría s/n, 31100 Puente la Reina
Tel.: +34 948 202 200
www.bodegadesarria.com

The Senorio has had its ups and downs, to put it mildly. The vast estate is worth a visit on its own account, with the winery tucked away in its woodland fastness. History records that the Lord of Sarria joined King Sancho the Strong in battle in 1212 but it really owes its place in history to the fact that Juan de Azpilicueta, Lord of Sarría, was the brother of Saint Francis Xavier, who founded the Jesuits. Azpilicueta funded his brother's studies in Paris with income from the estate. The chapel on the property has lifesize mosaic portraits of the pair.

The winery was established in 1953. In the late 1990s the winery had to be entirely rebuilt. The wines are yet to impress. Probably the most successful is the *rosado*.

VINOS DE PAGO

This is a much-discussed classification, created in 2003. Pago means vineyard, and a Vino de Pago is intended to be a single estate which can prove a specific terroir and excellence over a number of years. Vino de Pago means that the winery is its own denomination, and can set its own rules regarding varieties, viticulture, vinification and ageing. It's much discussed because it was always intended to be the first and highest level of quality. There are currently 17 Vinos de Pago, in Aragón, La Mancha, Comunidad Valenciana and Navarra – areas which do not have the highest reputation for fine wine. This is the heart of the matter: a winery wanting to make a statement in these lesser regions would choose to apply for Vino de Pago status to set themselves above the rest. The problem is that these are patently not all the best wines. Some are excellent, but others are mainstream. Navarra has been a particular offender in this regard, authorizing no less than four Vinos de Pago: Pago Finca Bolandín (Pago de Cirsus), Pago Prado de Irache, Pago de Otazu and Pago Señorío de Arinzano.

There is a separate organization called Grandes Pagos de España. This is a country-wide marketing network of 30 family estates which produce single estate wines. The two are easily and often confused.

It is part of the Palacio de Bornos group in Rueda, which also has bodegas in Rioja, Toro and Ribera del Duero.

Tandem

Ctra Pamplona-Logroño, Km 35.9, 31292 Lácar
Tel.: +34 948 536 031
www.tandem.es

Visit Tandem and you will notice a fairly regular flow of pilgrims walking – or on occasion cycling – on the Camino down below the winery. Tandem is an architectural study in concrete. The concrete vats inside also ensure the lively, fruity character of many of Alicia Eyaralar's wines, and the screwtop closures on the majority of the wines only enhance this. They also highlight Tandem's energetic focus on export sales, in markets open to their modern, stylish packaging.

Viña Zorzal

Ctra del Villar s/n, 31591 Corella
Tel.: +34 948 780 617
www.vinazorzalwines.com

In a decade the brothers Sanz – Xavier, Iñaki and Mikel – have transformed their family wine business, and consequently made the Viña Zorzal table one of the more enjoyable stopping-off points at a wine show. The front man is Xavier – Xabi – who travels the world building the profile of the wines and sampling, sampling, sampling. It's so much more than marketing, though. The heart of the business is old Garnacha vines in the Corella and Fitero districts. They have around 40 hectares, which also includes Tempranillo and Graciano. It was the latter that caught my eye first, a lively liquorice and black fruit youngster, an original for the area, and indeed not that common in Spain. They work with Rafael Redagera, and their consultant is their good friend Jorge Navascués, the Garnacha specialist from Aragón, who was appointed in 2017 to Contino.

The Graciano is exceptionally good value, as are all their entry-level wines. More recently they have started to produce smaller quantities of Garnachas based on their very old vineyards, and to tease out the differences. The bush vines are up on a windy plateau outside the town, scattered between sites where vines have clearly been abandoned by other owners. Malayeto is at around 520 metres on sandy clay soils, while Corral de los Altos has a more stony origin. Señora de las Alturas is a selection of the oldest vines with a dash of Graciano. Father Antonio founded the business in 1989, and he planted the Graciano. Hence the sons have launched Cuatro del Cuatro, a top end Graciano in his honour.

In recent times the long-ignored Garnachas of Navarra are finally being recognized for their excellence. This change has been driven by the Garnachas coming from the north of the DO, from St Martín de Unx, such as Domaines Lupier. What's notable about Viña Zorzal is that they could not be further away, much closer to Alfaro in Rioja. Indeed they have now expanded, naturally enough, into Rioja. Their chosen area is between Labastida and San Vicente de la Sonsierra, working with 40-year-old Tempranillo and a small amount of Garnacha at 555 metres. They deserve to do well with their very keen commercial sense, marrying the finances between single vineyard bottlings and larger branded wines. The project is new and the single vineyard bottlings even newer; a winery to follow as it develops. And a final word of clarification: the Zorzal bird of the label is a thrush. The business is Viña Zorzal. Not to be confused with Zorzal, the equally interesting family business of brothers working in Mendoza, Argentina.

PACHARÁN

Navarra is the home of one of Spain's great liqueurs, otherwise spelled as Patxarán. The name comes from *pattar* (drink) and *aran* (sloes). It's an anise-flavoured drink, pink or reddish-pink in colour, very aromatic, 25–30% abv, drunk as a digestif or over ice. In contrast with sloe gin, where the sloes are macerated with gin, for Pacharán the sloes are macerated for a number of months in an anise-flavoured spirit. Sometimes a roasted coffee bean, cinnamon stick or a bay leaf is added. Both sweet and dry versions are produced.

Various versions of Pacharán can be found across northern Spain but it's proudly Navarran. Records of the drink date back to 1441, when Queen Blanca I took it for its medicinal properties. It's had its own Consejo Regulador del Pacharán Navarro since 1988. The most famous commercial brand is Zoco, which was launched in 1956, though the Velasco family had been making the drink since 1816. Don't just keep it in the fridge or on the shelf. It has culinary uses, too: try it as an unexpectedly good glaze for roasted carrots, and then let your creativity loose.

On the radar in Navarra

Gonzalo Celayeta

www.gonzalocelayetawines.com

Look out for Celayeta's wines. This is his private project, in addition to his consultancies and work at the San Martín de Unx. A definite Garnachista.

> ### An IGP to watch – 3 Riberas
>
> This IGP was created in 2008, linking together the three valleys of the rivers Arga, Ega and Aragón in Navarra. It authorizes a wide range of varieties, typical of a younger IGP. The whites are Chardonnay, Moscatel de Grano Menudo, Garnacha Blanca, Sauvignon Blanc, Viura, Malvasía, Xarel·lo, Parellada, Riesling, Gewürztraminer, Maturana Blanca, Tempranillo Blanco, Verdejo and Albillo Mayor.

ARAGÓN

> *Arragon, a disagreeable province, is inhabited by a disagreeable people, who are as hard headed, hearted, and bowelled as the rocks of the Pyrenees, while for stubborn granite prejudices there is no place like Zaragoza. Obstinacy, indeed, is the characteristic of the testarudo [hard-headed, stubborn] Arragonese, who are said to drive nails into walls with their heads ... They have however a certain serious Spartan simplicity, and are fine, vigorous, active men, warlike, courageous, and enduring to the last.*
>
> Richard Ford

Aragón is made up of three provinces, from north to south: Huesca, Zaragoza and Teruel. The Somontano DO is in Huesca, while the Calatayud, Campo de Borja and Cariñena DOs are in Zaragoza. It stands at a crossroads, to the Mediterranean and Catalunya, to the Pyrenees and France, and to the Basque country, La Rioja and Navarra. It stretches from the foothills of the Pyrenees to arid, almost desert land.

In the time of Ferdinand and Isabella, Aragón was a region to be reckoned with. It was a cradle of kings, and a centre of trade. Eventually though Aragón lost its way. Much later, oidium and phylloxera wreaked their damage. In the twentieth century Aragón suffered a long period of unexciting wines governed by cooperatives out of step with changing tastes. In the twenty-first century it is a promising wine region with energetic and committed producers recuperating vineyards and making characterful wines. It has built a reputation for excellent value and bargain basement prices. Its task now is to continue the quality and escape the cheap as chips reputation.

CALATAYUD

Calatayud at a glance

Grape varieties

White: Macabeo, Malvasía, Moscatel de Alejandría, Garnacha Blanca, Sauvignon Blanc, Gewürztraminer, Chardonnay

Red: Garnacha Tinta, Tempranillo, Syrah, Mazuela, Monastrell, Cabernet Sauvignon, Merlot, Bobal

Size

Vineyard area: 3,200 hectares
Growers: 612
Wineries: 16

Near the town of Calatayud is an extensive Roman city, Bilbilis. The fact that the Roman poet Martial was born – and died – here is testament to the middle and upper class Roman society that flourished here, certainly in the first century. At the important Celtiberian city of Segeda near Miedes de Aragón, a wine press was found in 2002, and amphorae and pots with traces of tartrates and seeds indicate that winegrowing was well-established as long ago as 153 BC. The name of Calatayud itself came later, probably from the time of a Moorish governor, who had a castle (*qalat*), and whose name was *Ayub*. Well, probably. At least, that is how popular history tells it.

The Calatayud DO was founded in 1990. The River Jalón runs through the DO to the Ebro, but despite this cooling influence the region is hot and dry with rainfall at just 300 to 550 millimetres. However the heat is counteracted by the altitude of the vineyards at 500–900 metres. The soils have a high limestone content, as well as reddish clay. There are very old high-altitude, dry-grown vineyards with slate and quartzite soils, where the climate is extremely dry and the temperature contrasts are also extreme. There is therefore a serious risk of frost damage.

This description of the terroir reveals that it is ideal Garnacha country. This is what has been driving the success of the DO and slowly enabling producers to push up their prices. Calatayud is not yet a name that falls easily from the lips of consumers but it becomes more interesting year by year. Nevertheless it remains too firmly established along with other Aragón DOs as supermarket bargain-basement wine, albeit with an excellent quality–price ratio.

Producers

Ateca

Ctra N II s/n, 50200 Ateca
Tel.: +34 968 435 022
www.orowines.com

One of the projects of the Gil Family, whose home base is Jumilla, this was founded in 2005, drawing on old vine Garnachas grown on slate. The Atteca is a ripe Garnacha, balanced with some toasty oak. Atteca Armas is the top wine, with 18 months in French oak and is full, very ripe and bold.

El Escocés Volante

Barrio La Rosa Bajo 16, 50300 Calatayud
Tel.: +34 637 511 133
www.escocesvolante.com

The flying Scotsman of the name, Norrel Robertson MW, was born in Scotland, and like the famous train of the same name, has travelled far and fast: the world in general and Spain in particular, making wine. His first degree was in politics and his next qualification in winemaking, before he gained the MW. He settled in Calatayud in 2003, where he focuses on the heritage of old bush vine Garnachas in the region. He is gradually purchasing more parcels of vineyards and currently owns around 13 hectares.

His range of wine is growing. I say 'range' advisedly because there is always something new on the horizon. La Multa (named after the speeding fines he was always getting as he 'flew' between vineyards) was one of the early ones, a good value bush vine Garnacha, and El Puño is a very distinctive 100 per cent Garnacha. Dos Dedos de Frente is a Syrah with a dash of Viognier, though as it's not a permitted variety here (see box, p. 285) he can't declare it. There are plenty more wines to discover in the cellar, all with his clear signature. In addition he is increasingly working with less oak, and more concrete, and using egg-shaped fermenters.

More recent projects include El Mondongo from four Garnacha vineyards, which also has added presence from the field blend of Bobal, Garnacha Blanca and Moristel, plus 11 per cent of Syrah from another vineyard. Mondongo has been fermented and aged in egg-shaped vats; there's no oak here to interfere with the style of the fruit. El Cismático is a massal selection of 75–85 year old Garnacha grown on red clay and limestone, fermented in cement vats with 12 months in French oak. This is the first in an intended range of single vineyard wines. Not all of his wines from the region come from DO Calatayud; this is to do partly with the blends he uses and partly with the DO regulations.

Beyond Calatayud, he makes two whites under the Cup & Rings labels: an Albariño in Rías Baixas at Adegas Galegas and a Godello at Terras do Cigarron. There's plenty to come from this flying Scotsman.

San Alejandro

Ctra Calatayud-Cariñena-Calatayud Km 16.4, 50330 Miedes de Aragón
Tel.: +34 976 892 205
www.san-alejandro.com

This lively cooperative was founded in 1962, and has a current production of 3 million bottles. Like other co-ops it is a good source of great value wines. They do good business in export, with US clients including E & J Gallo and Eric Solomon. The Gracián Garnachas are juicy, well-made wines.

CAMPO DE BORJA

Campo de Borja at a glance

White: Macabeo, Garnacha Blanca, Moscatel, Chardonnay, Sauvignon Blanc, Verdejo

Red: Garnacha, Tempranillo, Mazuela, Cabernet Sauvignon, Merlot, Syrah

Size

Vineyard area: 6,810 hectares

Growers: 1,653

Wineries: 16

The empire of Garnacha

In Campo de Borja, they proclaim themselves the 'Empire of Garnacha', reasonably enough given the heritage of the their old-vine Garnachas. The DO takes its name from the Borgias. Alfons de Borja (1378–1458) was an adviser to King Alfonso V of Aragón. A scholarly, pious man, he was elected pope in 1455 and took the name Callistus III. The Borgias – having Italianized their names – clearly went downhill after him.

The DO (created 1980) is at the southern tip of Navarra, between the mountains of the Iberian system and the Ebro valley. The climate is extreme continental, with the typical cold, dry north wind, the Cierzo, and with 350–450 millimetres of rainfall a year. Its vineyards range over the valley and the hillside slopes, between 350 and 700 metres. The soils are poor, well-drained loam over limestone, with some chalk and iron-rich clay, and slate on the slopes of the Moncayo mountain; the best vines are the dry-farmed Garnachas. It delivers arguably the best quality wine at the lowest prices in Spain, possibly in Europe. Its juicy, plump Garnachas give plenty of drinking pleasure and are still very cheap. Although that's a great selling proposition, it is not a sustainable market position. As elsewhere in Aragón, cooperatives dominate, delivering 96 per cent of production. Only 60 growers own any more than 20 hectares.

Producers

Alto Moncayo

Ctra Borja-El Buste CV 606, Km 1700, 50540 Borja

Tel.: +34 976 868 098

www.bodegasaltomoncayo.com

This impressive joint venture, all about Garnacha (or nearly), founded in 2001 by Bodegas Borsao, Jorge Ordóñez and winemakers Chris Ringland and Dan Phillips, among others, has been developing very nicely. They draw on Garnacha bush vines, grown on clay and slate at altitude, some dating backing to 1910, and stress that their Garnacha differs from that of the rest of the DO because of their selection of old clones. Alto Moncayo is the flagship, a polished, well-oaked approach. Aquilón is a textbook bold, spicy, concentrated Garnacha; Veraton a more accessible, youthful style. A new winery coming on stream promises plenty more of interest from the team.

Aragonesas

Magallón s/n, 50529 Fuendejalón

Tel.: +34 976 862 153

www.bodegasaragonesas.com

Founded in 1984, Aragonesas genuinely has something for everyone, and that's because production runs to 10 million bottles a year – they have plenty of material to draw from (3,700 hectares in all). Coto de Hayas is probably their best-known brand, a reliable selection of varietal wines. It is jointly owned by two key cooperatives and an Aragón government agency.

Borsao

Ctra N 122 Km 63, 50540 Borja

Tel.: +34 976 867 116

www.bodegasborsao.com

Formed in 2001 from the amalgamation of three cooperatives, Borsao now has 375 winegrowers, with 2,260 hectares of vineyards between them. To put it another way, that's one third of the DO's vineyards. The business has been a leader in brand building and export. Tres Picos is a brambly, super-ripe, full-flavoured Garnacha which quickly became a flagship for them, Berola is a Garnacha with 20 per cent Syrah, and Zarihs is, well, Shiraz. I may grumble about the name but the liquid is indeed a joyous bright Shiraz. They call it Shiraz, rather than Syrah, because it was made in conjunction with the Australian winemaker Chris Ringland from an Australian clone planted in 2002.

Cuevas de Arom

Afueras s/n, 50570 Ainzón

The team from Bodegas Frontonio has recently started up a small project in a corner of the Santo Cristo winery: Cuevas de Arom. Fernando Mora MW is part of the team, and Arom, as a play on words with aroma, is his surname backwards. The connection with Santo Cristo comes with Mario López, a partner in Frontonio, who is winemaker for the cooperative. What's distinctive is that the wines are stylistically more elegant and less powerful than is typical of Garnachas in Campo de Borja. They are working with a range of materials and sizes, from cement vats and concrete eggs through to foudres. There are currently three wines: As Ladeiras, Os Cantals and Pedraforca. There will certainly be more to come from this project. Why the caves – *cuevas* – in the brand name? They use an 800-year-old cave for cellaring.

This is part of a new image for Aragón alongside Norrel Robertson MW at El Escocés Volante (see p. 286) and Jorge Navascués, new winemaker at Contino, who has his own project, Enología Navascués (see p. 291).

Santo Cristo

Ctra de Tabuenca s/n, 50570 Ainzón
Tel.: +34 976 869 696
www.bodegas-santo-cristo.com

Santo Cristo is a cooperative founded in 1956 to bring together growers across four towns. It produces a range of wines, notably Cayus and Terrazas del Moncayo, both Garnachas.

CARIÑENA

The earliest of Aragón's DOs, this was founded in 1960. More recently it has been overtaken in international profile by the others. The remarkable thing about a DO called Cariñena is just how little of the variety there is here. You need to hop over to Priorat to discover the variety in its full glory.

> ## Cariñena at a glance
>
> ### Grape varieties
>
> **White**: Macabeo, Garnacha Blanca, Moscatel Romano, Parellada, Chardonnay
>
> **Red**: Garnacha Tinta, Tempranillo, Mazuela (Cariñena), Juan Ibáñez, Cabernet Sauvignon, Syrah, Monastrell, Vidadillo, Merlot
>
> ### Size
>
> **Vineyard area**: 14,459 hectares
> **Growers**: 1,587
> **Wineries**: 34

Cariñena's climate is continental and dry, with cold winters and hot summers, and influenced by the cold north wind, the Cierzo. The vineyards spread across the valley and up the hillsides from 400 to 800 metres. The soils are limestone and chalk, with some alluvial soils at lower levels. As in Calatayud and Campo de Borja, cooperative bodegas are significant here.

Producers

Enología Navascués

Avda Ejército 32 Bajo B, 50400 Cariñena
Tel.: +34 651 845 176
www.cutio.es

How does Jorge Navascués Haba do it: consulting for wineries, making his own wines, cycling whenever he can, enjoying life with his family and generally being an all-round lovely person? And now he has taken on the responsibility of single-handedly raising the reputation of Aragón winemaking to an international level by being appointed to Contino in Rioja. Navascués is the third generation working in wine: his paternal grandfather was the winemaker for a Campo de Borja cooperative, and his father is a well-known winemaker, while his mother's family have been growers in Utiel-Requena for generations.

Navascués' client list has also included Pago Aylés in Cariñena, Viña Zorzal in Navarra, and bodegas Somontano, Tacoronte-Acentejo and more. Cariñena is still a favourite: 'In my view, Cariñena is the best region in the world, it's like a mini paradise filled with incredible vineyards. It's one of the oldest vine regions in Spain and it has a history we need to make the most of.' In the DO he makes the juicy, lively Garnacha, called Cutio, as well as a Macabeo of the same name. See page 299 for his wines in VT Valdejalón.

Pago Aylés

Finca Aylés Ctra A 1101 Km 24, 50152 Mezalocha
Tel.: +34 976 140 473
www.pagoayles.com

This is Aragón's only Vino de Pago, or estate with its own DO, awarded in 2011. It's a remarkable property of 3,100 hectares. Jorge Navascués consults here and has developed a range of wines named after the individual letters of AYLES. The Garnacha is 'S', the Merlot blend 'A' and so on. Outside that range, 3 de TresMil is a successful polished blend of Garnacha, Cabernet Sauvignon and Merlot.

SOMONTANO

There are regions where the wineries themselves open the door to the geography and spirit of the land – in Spain, most notably Priorat, Rías Baixas, Jerez. Somontano is a different case. The bodegas are relatively new buildings relatively close together. Nothing in their architecture reveals the history of this region 'at the foot of the mountain' of the Pyrenees. It's easy to leave a visit to Somontano in Huesca province disappointed, with a feeling that you have not got under the skin of the place.

Yet there's history aplenty here. The Somontano wine brand Secastilla references the seven important defensive castles which once protected the region during the time of the Moors. The best way to get a sense of the impressive character of Somontano is by staying a night or two in the romantic old town of Alquézar. Dominated by its twelfth-century castle, with golden bricks, it gives a great sense of the majesty of the kingdom of Aragón. Another distinctive, though less attractive building, dominates one end of the Embalse de El Grado, the long, narrow reservoir between the hills. It's the Sanctuary of Torrecuidad, opened in 1975 on the site of a ninth-century shrine to the Virgin Mary. What makes it significant, and a focus for pilgrims, is that it was set up by Josemaría Escrivá de Balaguer, the founder of Opus Dei. Escrivá was born in Barbastro, the capital of Huesca.

As elsewhere, it was the Church, and the many monasteries in the region, that had fostered vine growing over the centuries. The relationship with France, just over the mountains, became ever closer and by the end of the nineteenth century, with the coming of phylloxera in France, exports were particularly important. That business came to an inevitable end as France recovered. Later, in the twentieth century the cooperative, the Comarcal de Somontano, was important in reviving and developing wine production. Finally in 1985 the DO Somontano was formed. External investors turned Somontano round. The first was CoViSa, whose investment in soils and technology pointed the way, and later not one but two Sherry companies: Barbadillo (with Pirineos) and González Byass (the Viñas del Vero, Blecua and Secastilla brands).

Yet Somontano still feels like a work in progress. That first international recognition has not continued to grow. The wineries give the impression that they are still finding their way. It's notable that the DO permits a broad range of varieties. The upside of this is that producers have great flexibility; the downside is that they lack clarity for the outside world. One of the regular medal winners in competitions is Gewürztraminer – identifiable because it's an atypical variety in Spain, and because it's well done and clearly varietal. It may not taste of Somontano – that has to be the next step for viticulturists and winemakers – but you can recognize the origin from the variety. The difficulty for Somontano is that today's trend is to make wines from indigenous varieties. Merlot and Cabernet Sauvignon have been here long enough to be local, but why would anyone want to buy a Cabernet Sauvignon from here when they could buy it from France, Chile or South Africa? That might explain some of the (too) old vintages still in the market. Somontano's story is still waiting to be told. While we wait, what you can be sure to find is polished, clean, modern wines.

The climate in Somontano is continental as it lies between the Ebro valley and the Pyrenees. This gives it good diurnal temperature variations, plus cold winters and hot summers, with sharp seasonal changes in spring and autumn. The proximity to the mountains means the rainfall, at around 500 millimetres, is higher than is typical for Aragón. The soils are mainly clay and sandstone, and the vineyards range from 350 to

650 metres. There are some old bush vine Garnachas left, but in general there is new planting on trellises. What is promising is that there are some vineyard sites at higher altitudes, where cooler climates are being sought to grow varieties such as Riesling.

You can eat well in Somontano, and it is particularly well-known for its fruits and vegetables. Don't miss the *tomate rosa* of Barbastro. These rugged-looking, thin-skinned, lightly-seeded, juicy tomatoes can weigh over a kilo and are a delightful speciality. Finish any meal with an almond-based sweet treat. As across so much of Spain, many growers took the subsidy to uproot their vines, and preferred to plant almonds. The countryside has changed; as the golden autumnal vineyards began to disappear, the pale pink almond blossom took over to charm in springtime.

Somontano at a glance

Grape varieties

White: Macabeo, Garnacha Blanca, Alcañón, Chardonnay, Riesling, Sauvignon Blanc, Gewürztraminer
Red: Tempranillo, Garnacha Tinta, Cabernet Sauvignon, Merlot, Moristel, Parraleta, Pinot Noir, Syrah

Size

Vineyard: 4,040 hectares
Growers: 412
Wineries: 30

Producers

Enate

Avda de las Artes 1, 22314 Salas Bajas
Tel.: +34 974 302 580
www.enate.es

Enate (En-ah-tay) was launched in 1992 with a vision to be both winery and contemporary art collection. The labels are each painted by an artist from the collection. In the vineyard, the focus from the beginning was on quality and low yields. They continue to stress their respect for the environment, their precision viticulture, and the short distance at harvest between vineyard and winery.

From the 400 hectares of vineyards, they produce a range of polished wines; mainly single varietal, from Chardonnay and Gewürztraminer, Cabernet Sauvignon, Merlot and Tempranillo.

Lalanne
Ctra Barbastro-Naval 3.8Km, 22300 Barbastro
Tel.: +34 974 310 689
www.bodegaslalanne.es

Somontano's oldest winery by a long distance, this was founded in 1842. The Bordelais owners relocated to Spain at the end of the nineteenth century with the onset of the vine pest phylloxera in their vineyards – it's a familiar story. In due course the property gained the nickname of the 'American's Tower', so the story goes, because of the American rootstocks the Lalannes imported. Their contribution to Somontano's later history was to import the first Bordeaux varieties to the region. The Lalanne family is still in charge today.

The bodega lies in the golden half-mile along the A1232 just outside Barbastro, one that starts with Blecua on a slight hill on the right, Pirineos opposite on the left, Viñas del Vero a little further up on the right, and Lalanne next door. The bodega celebrates its history, and has a museum of early winemaking implements. In addition to wines from Bordeaux varietals, they also make a brut nature sparkling.

Pirineos
Ctra Barbastro-Naval Km 3.5, 22300 Barbastro
Tel.: +34 974 311 289
www.barbadillo.com

As the website suggests, this is a property of Barbadillo, the leading producer of Manzanilla, based in Sanlúcar de Barrameda's upper town. It dates back to 1993, and is a joint venture with the cooperative Comarcal de Somontano, which was part of the initial drive for the new Somontano. Barbadillo has 74 per cent of the shares, and the co-op the rest. The history of the co-op means that Pirineos – named after the mountains – has access to some of the oldest vines in the DO.

The production is around 4 million bottles. The bodega uses international and local varieties. Fans of less common grape varieties should look out for the Joven Moristel, unoaked so it's possible to understand the variety. It's a welcome contrast to some of the more traditional wines that used to come from the DO. Punchy and fresh, moderate alcohol, a young wine to drink young. An original, and one which adds character to the portfolio of Somontano styles.

Viñas del Vero

Ctra Barbastro-Naval 3.7 Km, 22300 Barbastro
Tel.: +34 974 302 216
www.vinasdelvero.com

Viñas del Vero takes its name from the river of the same name, which has some picturesque gorges and ravines. The winery was established in 1986, with the purchase of 550 hectares of land, which was planted the next year. Its first wines were made in an experimental winery and released in 1990. In 1993, they moved into today's winery. González Byass bought the business in 2008, recognizing the still unfulfilled potential of Somontano's largest producer (currently 40 per cent of total production).

Viñas del Vero now owns 515 hectares of vineyard and controls a further 500. They grow 14 of the permitted 15 varieties, across 125 different parcels, with a mixture of sandy and rocky soils, mainly south facing, mostly on slopes. The majority are clustered near the winery and the river, at around 410 metres, with a smaller selection up in the Secastilla valley at 600–710 metres, much closer to the mountains. In the highest of these vineyards they have bush vines with an older heritage.

At the end of the first decade of ownership, the portfolio suggests that González Byass is beginning to get to grips with the project. Did they have the right varieties? Were they planted in the right places? It's been a slow process of discovery. The Gewürztraminer is well established; a newer arrival is the Pinot Noir Rosado, which again shows more imagination, making a wine that is not common in Spain – and making it successfully. Nearer the top of the range is Clarión, an unoaked blend of a number of the white varieties in the vineyards. Gran Vos is a classical red blend, aged in French oak.

Under the Viñas del Vero umbrella are two other brands. The first is Blecua, which has its own separate bodega, a nineteenth-century villa, next door to the mothership. The winery was launched in 2000 to make a wine of the highest quality. Known locally as Blecua Tower, it dates back to the eleventh century when there was a retreat for Benedictine monks. There's just one wine made here, a *vino de autor*, from 'triple selected' bunches, fermented in 180-hectolitre Allier vats, and matured for some 20 months in Allier barriques from four different coopers. It's a powerful Bordeaux blend, with the addition of Garnacha and Tempranillo, but is only released in the best years, so the selection of the blend may vary slightly.

The third brand is Secastilla, the wildest part of the Somontano portfolio for González Byass, from vineyards at 700 metres, a drive up towards the mountains, with birds of prey and wild boar at home in the landscape. Secastilla's heart is Garnacha, so it is a valuable property for González Byass now that old vine Garnacha has become important in Spain with the recent search for heritage and tradition in the vineyard. One of the rocky, wind-blown vineyards has bush vines that were planted in the 1940s, with a field blend of reds (Garnacha Tinta, Mandón, Royal, Trepat, Vidadillo) and whites (Alcañón and Moscatel de Secastilla). In another vineyard, Garnacha was planted in 2000. Three wines are produced. La Miranda Garnacha Blanca has ten months in Allier barrels, La Miranda is the red version, with less time in oak, and the flagship Secastilla is a powerful, muscular Garnacha with a little Syrah and Parraleta, aged for eight months in French oak. The concept of Secastilla is full of promise; the vineyards and their wild isolation should deliver good things. As a sign of González Byass' ambition for this brand, Secastilla (not Blecua or Viñas del Vero) is a member of the Grandes Pagos de España, a network of leading family-owned estates in Spain.

ON THE RADAR: ARAGÓN'S IGPS

Bajo Aragón

This IGP enjoys strong Mediterranean influences. There are four sub-regions: Bajo Aragón, Bajo Martín, Campo de Belchite and Matarraña.

Grape varieties

White: Chardonnay, Garnacha Blanca

Red: Cabernet Sauvignon, Garnacha, Merlot, Syrah.

Ribera de Gállego-Cinco Villas

This lies, as its name suggests, on the banks of the river Gállego, close to Zaragoza. Macabeo is the predominant white variety; for the reds, Garnacha and Tempranillo dominate, with Cabernet Sauvignon and Merlot.

Ribera del Jiloca

There are five bodegas in this IGP. Its slate soils and altitude give it strong potential for quality wine. The wines are mainly Garnachas; where white is made Macabeo is used.

Ribera del Queiles

This red-wine only IGP takes in 16 municipalities, spread between Navarra and Zaragoza. The varieties available are Cabernet Sauvignon, Garnacha, Graciano, Merlot, Tempranillo and Syrah. Its best-known winery is **Guelbenzu** (www.guelbenzu.com).

Valdejalón

Another promising IGP, taking in 36 municipalities.

Varieties

White: Macabeo, Garnacha Blanca, Moscatel, Airén

Red: Garnacha and Tempranillo, plus Cabernet Sauvignon, Syrah, Monastrell and Merlot.

Frontonio

Tel.: +34 976 322 361

www.bodegasfrontonio.com

Valdejalón - where? At a time of up-and-coming regions for Garnacha in Aragón, Valdejalón is surely the least well known. The people behind this project were also unknown but have built a strong profile since their first vintage in 2010. Part of the reason for this is Fernando Mora who became a Master of Wine in 2017. He was formerly an engineer, but caught the wine bug, and made his first vintage from his own vines in the bath, using a temperature-control kit. Things have moved on since then. He gave up his job in 2013 and now works full time with his partners, oenologist Mario López and lawyer Francisco Latasa.

They have 25 hectares and also buy in some grapes. The vines are at 300 metres, on clay-limestone soils, and at 600 metres on red slate. The vines are, of course, Garnacha, and the team are Garnachistas through and through. It is no surprise then that one of them uses 'Garnacha Samurai' as a social media handle.

The entry level Botijo range is good value, if rustic. A step up is Microcósmico, with a juicy Garnacha and also a Macabeo. Next comes Telescópico, with a Garnacha, a fresh, bold Cariñena and a particularly interesting and individual Garnacha–Macabeo–Viognier blend. The top end is the tiny production of Las Alas de Frontonio, Garnacha (10 per cent whole bunch), aged for seven months in 300-litre Allier oak barrels. Labelled 'natural', it has no added sulphites.

From this energetic beginning, focused strongly on international sales, more will surely come. In the meantime take a look at Santo Cristo in Campo de Borja (p. 290), where they make Cuevas de Arom wines.

Navascués Enología

50400 Cariñena
Tel.: +34 651 845 176
www.cutio.es

This is a family project from Jorge Navascués (see Cariñena, p. 291). The focus is old bush vine Garnacha growing at some 800 metres. The wines made here are called Mancuso – the name of a gold coin used in Aragón under King Sancho. Mas de Mancuso is a vibrant cherry and mocha wine, with a tang of bright acidity. Very promising.

Valle del Cinca

Nudging the border with Catalunya, this IGP uses Macabeo and Chardonnay; the reds are Garnacha Tinta, Tempranillo, Cabernet Sauvignon and Merlot.

9

WHERE TO EAT, DRINK AND STAY

All my travels in Spain have been punctuated by memorable cooking. Sometimes simple tapas from the very best *jamon de bellota*, cured ham from acorn-fed pigs; fine sheep's milk cheeses; salted almonds; anchovies; tortilla and croquetas. These last two can be a bit riskier. There's nothing worse than a dry, thoroughly-cooked tortilla that has been sitting on the counter for hours, except perhaps a greasy croqueta. As always, take a look at what others are eating before you decide. If you didn't enjoy the tapa, then move on.

Some of my memorable meals have been in wineries, and others in restaurants. Right across the regions in this book you can be sure to find traditional home cooking, with the best ingredients simply cooked. In Galicia, the seafood is of the very freshest and needs no complicated saucing. Should you tire of the seafood, then tuck into an *empanada*, the flat pasty-like pie, often filled with sardines or anchovies with tomato. Asturias, apart from its cider, has very fine cheeses, as well as *fabada asturiana*, the quintessential Spanish white bean stew jam-packed with chorizo, morcilla (black pudding), pork shoulder and more. Txakoli country is clustered with internationally famous restaurants, and terrific tiny bars with *pintxos*, small bites, of every category. In Navarra, Rioja, Ribera del Duero and Castilla y León roast lamb is the perfect match to the local wine. Even the vegetables are something special, particularly the white asparagus, the peppers, the artichokes, the potatoes (especially with chorizo) and the autumnal mushroom bounty. Aragón shares much of this bounty, and also has very good *longaniza* (spicy pork sausage), *lomo* (cured loin of pork), *cecina* (air-dried beef), vegetables galore and that most pricy of ingredients in Spanish cooking, saffron.

In every region, it's worth planning in an extra day's stay so that you can enjoy the food as well as the wine, and explore the countryside. Book ahead when you can. A few of these restaurants are in the world's top 10, and a visit to them will require serious planning. Many others also need to be booked ahead of time.

A note on timing: lunch usually starts around 2.30 p.m.; and dinner at 9 p.m., later in the summer. But by all means have tapa or two at 12; and a snack after siesta. Don't turn up early; the chef may not even have arrived, and there's nothing gloomier than sitting in an empty dining room waiting for the action.

This list is not exhaustive. It's a selection of restaurants and bars where I have enjoyed good food and wine; you will discover your own favourites to add to the list.

GALICIA

Abastos 2.0
Praza de Abastos, Rua das Ameas 13-18, 15703 Santiago de Compostela
Tel.: +34 981 576 145
Located just by the food market, Abastos has the freshest food. The cooking is modern, with plenty of seafood and a really interesting selection of wines and vermouths.

Casa Aurora
Madrid 20, 36960 Sanxenxo
+ 34 630 767 981
From the outside, this looks like just another of the modern waterfront bars, but the welcome is very warm, and the seafood excellent.

D'berto
Teniente Domínguez 84, 36980 O Grove
Tel.: +34 986 733 447
www.dberto.com
This Michelin-starred eatery is a terrific site for indulging in the seafood and shellfish of Galicia. There's a scary fish tank in the window but inside

at the back is a fine selection of local wines. A good place to explore the 'traditional method' sparkling wines from Albariño.

Mesón a Curva
Rúa Rafael Pico 56, Portonovo, 36970 Sanxenxo
Tel.: +34 620 252 573
Excellent, fresh seafood simply cooked, with a fine wine selection in a waterfront location.

Restaurant Pepe Vieira
Camiño da Sierpe s/n, 36992 Raxó
Tel.: +34 986 741 378
www.pepevieira.com
Here you will find Michelin-starred cooking with a modern take on Galician traditional ingredients, an excellent wine list and lovely views.

Restaurante O Timón
Galicia 6, 36620 Vilanova de Arousa
Tel.: +34 986 555 083
If you are taking a boat from Cambados to Vilanova (or vice versa), then remember O Timón. It's just by where the boats depart and is full of every kind of fish and shellfish. The cooking is hearty and generous and the boat trip out into the ría is well worth it on a sunny day without too much wind.

Viñoteca Bagos
Rua Michelena 20, 36002 Pontevedra
www.vinotecabagos.com
Tucked away in a basement, this is a great find when it comes to hunting down small producers. As well as an interesting range of wines from beyond Rías Baixas there is a straightforward menu. Check out their tastings of wines from new wave producers.

Vinoteca Ribeira de Fefiñans
Rúa Ribeira de Fefiñans 24, 36630 Cambados
Tel.: +34 986 524 997
Here there is an excellent local and Galician wine list, and good food to match. Sit outside and enjoy the view of the water. No need to get a taxi home, it's a restaurant with rooms.

Yayo Daporta

Rúa do Hospital 7, 36630 Cambados
Tel.: +34 986 526 062
www.yayodaporta.com

In this Michelin-starred restaurant Yayo Daporta cooks local ingredients in a smart, polished, elegant and modern way. His sister Esther is the sommelier, a former best sommelier in Galicia.

FESTA DO ALBARIÑO

The first weekend in August sees the Festa do Albariño in Cambados. This jolly affair offers plenty of Albariño to drink from producers' stalls, fireworks and partying through the night. (If you are staying at the Parador de Cambados and want to go to sleep before 4 a.m., book a room that is far from the fair. I speak from bitter experience!)

Restaurante O Grelo

Campo de la Virgen s/n, 27400 Monforte de Lemos
Tel.: +34 982 404 701
www.resgrelo.com

This is an excellent place to discover wines from the DO and offers classic cooking with traditional local recipes.

VALDEORRAS

Pazo do Castro

Vila do Castro, 32317 O Barco de Valdeorras
Tel.: +34 988 347 423
www.pazodocastro.com

This hotel is convenient, especially in Valdeorras' hot summers, with its spa and swimming pool. The reliable restaurant features local cooking.

RIBERA DEL DUERO REGION

Abadía Retuerta Le Domaine
47195 Sardón de Duero
Tel.: +34 983 680 368

This exceptional hotel and spa is a destination in itself, quite apart from visiting the local wineries, and of course Le Domaine's own winery and surrounding vineyards. Established in a superbly restored twelfth-century abbey, with attentive service, including your own butler. The Michelin-starred restaurant is overseen by Andoni Luis Aduriz of Mugaritz. Breakfast is just as enticing, with plenty of local organically farmed produce.

La Bótica de Matapozuelos
Pza Mayor 2, 47230 Matapozuelos
Tel.: +34 983 832 942
www.laboticadematapozuelos.com

Michelin-starred cooking in a family restaurant in the centre of Matapozuelos. It is worth making the detour if you are visiting Rueda or La Seca, and only a little further from Valladolid.

La Cantina
Plaza Mayor 21, 47001 Valladolid
Tel.: +34 983 358 189

This centrally located establishment is very reliable for tapas. Wines are served by the glass from an Enomatic dispenser.

Dámaso
Club de Campo La Galera, Calle Corbeta s/n, 47009 Valladolid
Tel.: +34 983 405 372
www.restaurantedamaso.es

Dámaso Vergara himself recites the menu, which changes monthly and features local produce from Tudela. In a country club outside Valladolid, it is worth the detour to enjoy Ribera del Duero wines.

El Figón de Recoletos

Acera de Recoletos 3, 47004 Valladolid
Tel.: +34 983 396 043
www.figonderecoletos.com

The place for *lechazo*, milk-fed lamb, roasted the traditional way in a wood-fired clay oven. It's a wonderfully traditional place, with serious old-fashioned elegance and a classic menu.

Fuente de la Aceña

Calle del Molino s/n. 47350 Quintanilla de Onésimo
Tel.: +34 983 680 910
www.fuenteacena.es

In the heart of Ribera del Duero this stylish restaurant within an old mill has an equally stylish hotel attached. It's in a great site, overlooking the river.

Hotel Convento Las Claras

Pza Adolfo Muñoz Alonso, 47300 Peñafiel
Tel.: +34 983 878 168
www.hotelconventolasclaras.com

This period property right in the middle of Peñafiel is well placed for visiting the castle.

Landa

A-1 Km 235, 09001 Burgos
Tel.: +34 947 257 777
www.landa.as

The address says it all – Landa is on the motorway from Burgos to Madrid, making it super-convenient, but as a result the place can be super-crowded. Book ahead if you can. The rambling old property has plenty of rooms in which to eat – everything from a fairly quick selection of tapas if you are in a hurry home, to a leisurely lunch. The cooking is traditional Castilian, with excellent black pudding. Outside there is a delicatessen shop selling well-packaged foodie gifts, and there is also a hotel.

Posada Real Sitio de Ventosilla

Ctra Palencia-Aranda Km 64, 09443 Gumiel de Mercado
Tel.: +34 947 546 900

Isabella la Católica bought the estate in 1521, now you too have the opportunity to spend the night like royalty in the midst of vineyards.

Trigo

Calle de los Tintes 8, 47002 Valladolid
Tel.: +34 983 115 500
www.restaurantetrigo.com

In the heart of old Valladolid, very close to the cathedral, Victor Martín uses the produce of Castilla y León, but with a modern, delicate touch. There is a fine Sherry list, and a great selection of local producers, not just Ribera del Duero but also Arlanza, Arribes, Cigales and more. It won its Michelin star in 2017.

Villa Paramesa

Calixto Fernandez de la Torre 5, 47001 Valladolid
+34 983 357 936
www.villaparamesa.com

Just round the corner from the Plaza Mayor, this is very warmly recommended for its tapas. Wines are served by the glass from magnums.

CASTILLA Y LEÓN

León

The city of León was chosen as Spain's gastronomic capital for 2018. It is strongly recommended for tapas as well as eating out.

El Capricho

Paraje de la Vega s/n, 24767 Jiménez de Jamuz
Tel.: +34 987 664 224
www.bodegaelcapricho.com

A temple to beef. The quality is exceptional, with the best breeds, cooked over holm oak charcoal.

Cueva Miñambres

Cuevas 29, 24232 Valdevimbre
Tel.: +34 987 304 245
www.cuevaminambres.es

Another of the converted underground cellar/restaurants.

Cueva Restaurante Los Poinos

Canal de Rozas 81, 24230 Valdevimbre
Tel.: +34 987 304 018

Valdevimbre is famous for its underground *cuevas* or bodegas. Several of them have been converted into restaurants. Los Poinos (named after the wooden blocks on which barrels are rested), with straightforward traditional cooking, is one of the best.

RIOJA REGION

Asador Aker

Aguardienterias 0, 26214 Cuzcurrita de Río Tirón
Tel.: +34 941 301 799
www.asadoraker.com

If you are going to visit vineyards in Cuzcurrita, then Aker, just by the river, is the place for meat from the grill, and good honest cooking.

Calle Laurel

A Riojan institution, this street behind Espolón Square has 50 or more bars. Spend the evening visiting a few of them: try a different Crianza in each and a different tapa. The garlicky juicy mushrooms at Bar Ángel are classics, but there are plenty of others to try too. Be choosy, no need to linger if the wine isn't as fresh as it could be, it's served too warm or there's just no room to squeeze in. Visit between Thursday and Saturday when it is really buzzy, though touristy, and often filled with batches of journalists on press trips or coach parties on guided tours. When you are trying to get to the bar, remember that the crush, the partying three nights of the week, is the point. Just as you start to feel frustrated, you'll find a place that really charms and it will work its magic.

Dinastía Vivanco

Ctra Nacional 232, 26330 Briones
Tel.: +34 941 322 340
www.vivancoculturadevino.es

If you have spent the morning in the museum, or just want lunch and are near Briones, drop into the Vivanco museum tapas bar. To visit the restaurant you will need to book.

Echaurren

Padre José García 19, 26280 Ezcaray
Tel.: +34 941 354 047
www.echaurren.com

A lovely family hotel in the centre of Ezcaray, this is well placed for visiting the historic sites of San Millán and Santo Domingo de la Calzada. Stay for two nights and enjoy each of the hotel's two restaurants; one of which is Francis Paniego's double Michelin-starred El Portal.

Finca Los Arandinos Hotel

Ctra LR 137 Km 4.6, 26375 Entrena
Tel.: +34 941 446 126
www.fincalosarandinos.com

This contemporary boutique hotel with its own bodega is conveniently close if you have a booking at Venta Moncalvillo.

Hector Oribe

Gasteiz 8, 01309 Páganos
Tel.: +34 945 600 715
www.hectororibe.es

This very friendly, small dining room in the town centre is regularly filled with winemakers enjoying the good local cooking with a modern spin.

Hotel Marqués de Riscal

Torrea 1, Elciego 01340
Tel.: +34 945 180 880
www.hotel-marquesderiscal.com

This is a super-luxurious Starwood hotel. Architecture fans *must* book a room in the Gehry wing, ideally one with a view over the village rather than back over the spa wing. If you would rather look at the Gehry architecture then book a (slightly) cheaper room in the spa wing. There is Michelin-starred cooking in the restaurant.

Hotel Marqués de Vallejo

Marqués de Vallejo 8, 26001 Logroño
Tel.: +34 941 248 333
www.hotelmarquesdevallejo.com

A convenient, stylish business hotel in the centre of Logroño, just after the Paseo Espolón. There is an underground car park in the Paseo.

Hotel Viura

Herrerías s/n, 01307 Villabuena de Álava
Tel.: +34 945 609 000
www.hotelviura.com

Tucked into the heart of the town and surrounded by bodegas, Hotel Viura is the hotel that looks like a stack of boxes. Even if you are not staying, it is worth dropping in for a drink or a meal to explore the interior design.

El Lagar de Carlos y Elena

Huesca 13, 26002 Logroño
Tel.: +34 941 250 309

The Lagar was a classic name in Logroño, and it now has a classic wine family in charge. Carlos Martínez Bujanda and his wife Elena reopened it in 2014, taking the famous name of the old business and adding their own. In a relaxed atmosphere one can sample excellent local ingredients, typical traditional food and, of course, an excellent wine list. The well-priced list changes several times a year, and there are always wines available by the glass.

Terete

Lucrecia Arana 17, 26200 Haro
Tel.: +34 941 310 023
www.terete.es

A favourite in Haro for wood-fired lamb, this also serves the usual favourites of *pochas* – beans with chorizo – and *menestra* – vegetable stew. Just the thing with a bottle of Rioja.

Tondeluna

Muro de Francisco de la Mata 9, 26001 Logroño
Tel.: +34 941 236 425
www.tondeluna.com

This restaurant, well known for tapas, particularly its *croquetas* is just by Espolón Square, near the underground car park, and round the corner from the Central Market.

Venta Moncalvillo

Medrano 6, 26373 Daroca de Rioja
Tel.: +34 941 444 832

Carlos Echapresto (the sommelier) and his brother Ignacio (the chef) run this Michelin-starred family restaurant, which features some delightful playful cooking in addition to classics. Not dead centre in Rioja, it is worth a detour, in particular for the wine service: Carlos is an award-winning sommelier and a great guide to wines.

La Vieja Bodega

Avenida Rioja 17, 26230 Casalarreina
Tel.: +34 941 324 254

This lovely old restaurant in a seventeenth-century bodega has an equally traditional, classical wine list, ideal for exploring older vintages.

Wine Fandango

Vara de Rey 5, 26003 Logroño
Tel.: +34 941 243 910

This is run by the Arambarri brothers, who are owners of the Vintae group, producing Riojas, as well as being keen Garnachistas in other regions. A relaxed wine bar, it has a wide selection of bottles and some 20 wines by the glass. On the other side of the Espolón Square from Tondeluna.

THE NORTH AND THE BASQUE COUNTRY

Asturias

Casa Marcial

Salgar s/n, 33549 Arriondas
Tel.: +34 985 840 991
www.casamarcial.com

Nacho Manzano is the chef at this double Michelin-starred restaurant, cooking all of the Asturian classics, each one with a creative edge. He consults for the Iberica restaurants in London, but come to Arriondo for the real deal.

The Basque Country

Azurmendi

Barrio Legina s/n, 48195 Larrabetzu
Tel.: +34 944 558 359
www.azurmendi.es

This restaurant is just 20 minutes from Bilbao airport, and it is well worth flying in especially to eat here, if you are already in Europe. Eneko Atxa is the nephew of Gorka Izagirre, whose winery lies below the glassy restaurant. Diners begin upstairs, visiting the market garden of the restaurant, indulging in delicious treats specially placed for nibbling. You continue with a visit to the kitchen where you can watch the chefs at work and savour some more of the playful treats. Finally, lunch (or dinner) is a full 3-star Michelin experience with excellent wine service.

Bistró Prêt à Porter
Tel.: +34 944 558 866
The casual restaurant of Azurmendi.

Bodega Urbana
Gran Vía 66, 48011 Bilbao
Tel.: +34 944 416 181
www.bodegaurbanabilbao.com
Great concept: a winery, wine shop and café–bar. It is owned by the two leading wine consultants, Ana Martín and Pepe Hidalgo. There are regular tasting sessions and plenty of wines to try. They also have a branch in Madrid (Las Rozas).

Etxebarri
San Juan Plaza 1, 48291 Atxondo
Tel.: +34 946 583 042
www.asadoretxebarri.com
It is worth making a trip to Spain for this one (especially since it is only about 40 minutes by car from Bilbao airport, an easy flight from many European cities). It may be in the top 10 of the world's restaurants, but what is so very glorious is its unpretentiousness, tucked away as it is in a quiet valley. The restaurant more or less *is* the village, with the village bar on the ground floor. The cooking comes from the wood-fired grill and ingredients are exceptional and unshowy, though with clever elements. It is a great place to enjoy the finest wines.

San Sebastián
Restaurants in San Sebastian deserve a book in themselves and include the likes of Akelarre, Arzak, Martín Berasategui and Mugaritz. Probably my most exciting drink (not just wine) and food pairings have been at Mugaritz.

Essencia

Zabaleta 42, 20002 San Sebastián

If you want to drink rare sherries in San Sebastián then this venue, close to the Kursaal Auditorium, is the place to go – and you will find plenty more besides. In a city where it seems that all the tourists have come to eat *pintxos* – tapas – Essencia will give you those, but also a terrific wine list, full of adventures and surprises. Craft beer and cider also feature.

Rekondo

Paseo de Igueldo 57, 20008 San Sebastián

Tel.: +34 943 212 907

www.rekondo.com

The restaurant boasts excellent, straightforward cooking of the best ingredients but the real draw is the exceptional list of very well-priced top wines. It is best to visit with a group of friends so that you can sample a number of bottles; a great way to discover very old Riojas. There is a huge list and it's up to you to find the treasures, so it helps if one of you knows your way round the wine list.

GLOSSARY

Adega. Galician word for a winery.

Amphora/tinaja. Clay pot for fermenting or maturing wine. This traditional container for wine is now coming back into fashion, especially with the 'discovery' of traditional Georgian winemaking. They vary substantially in size. Today's versions can come with temperature controls. Some producers use small ones for maturing a portion of a blend; others use a large one for full fermentation. A philosophical choice, but also a stylistic one. Clay, concrete, stainless steel and oak each have different effects; clay can provide a more chalky character, without suppressing the fruit. I have used the words interchangeably.

Añada. Vintage.

Barrica. Barrel, usually a 225-litre Bordeaux-style barrel, the regulation size in Rioja.

Bodega. Winery.

Bota. Butt.

Carbonic maceration. Traditional winemaking method where whole bunches are packed into a vat, and the bottom layers, or the whole vat if masked with inert gas, start a fermentation within the individual grapes. Produces a juicy, young wine, best known in France as Beaujolais Nouveau. In Spain, often known as a *cosechero* or grower wine.

Cava. Denomination of Origin for traditional method sparkling wine, the majority of which is produced in Penedès.

Cepa. Vine.

Clarete. A dark pink/light red *rosado*, fermented with its skins like a red wine. Very widely found, usually a local wine for local consumption.

Consejo Regulador de la Denominación de Origen. Governing body supervising a wine region. Abbreviated to Consejo Regulador, CRDO, or CRDOCa in a Denominación de Origen Calificada, like Rioja.

Crianza. Ageing. Typically describing a red wine with one year's ageing in an oak barrel, and a minimum of six months in bottle.

Demi muid. French term for 600-litre barrel. Often chosen to lessen oak influence in a finished wine.

DO. Denominación de Origen. Defined production zone.

DOCa/DOQ. Denominación de Origen Calificada, Denominació d'Origen Qualificada. Applied only to Rioja and Priorat.

Finca. Estate.

Flor. Literally 'flower'. The layer of yeast cells that develops on the surface of a wine, in particular biologically aged Sherry and Montilla.

Foudre. Large oak vat, which may contain as much as 300 hectolitres, from the German 'fuder'. Oxygenates the wine slowly, without adding oak flavour.

Garnachista. A fan of Garnacha, whether grower, winemaker or consumer. One of the new generation of producers leading the revival of Garnacha, and seeking out abandoned bush vines. Working north of Madrid, Navarra, Rioja, Aragón. A pioneer has been Daniel Jiménez-Landi, and the team at Comando G.

Gran Reserva. The most venerable of ageing categories. In red wine in Rioja, this now means a minimum of five years; a minimum of two years in barrel and two in bottle before release.

IGP/PGI. Indicación Geografica Protegida is a quality category between Vino de Mesa (table wine) and Denominación de Origen. It's a useful category which often enables producers to be more adventurous, using different varieties and techniques.

Joven. 'Young'. Not barrel-aged; in its first or second year, for drinking now.

Lagar. A traditional container for pressing and fermenting grapes. In earliest times carved out of the rock, later made out of wood.

Lías. Lees. The post-fermentation deposits in wine: a combination of dead yeasts and other particles that will sink to the bottom of the vat in time. Lees-ageing the wine, with the fine lees, can develop richness and texture.

Malolactic or malolactic fermentation. Strictly known as the malolactic conversion. Often called 'the malolactic'. An optional choice after the alcoholic fermentation; a process where the crisp, 'appley' malic acid in the wine is transformed to the 'milky' lactic acid, a softening process. Commonly used in red winemaking, more of a stylistic choice in white winemaking.

Pago. A vineyard.

Parador. Government-run hotel, often in a castle or other historic palace.

Paraje. A specific plot or vineyard.

Parral. Galician word for pergola, a method of training vines on an overhead canopy.

Phylloxera. The louse that attacks the roots of *vitis vinifera* vines. Caused widespread international destruction at the end of the nineteenth century.

Reserva. An aged wine. Specifically in a region such as Rioja, for red wines, a wine with a minimum of three years; one year in barrel and six months in bottle before release.

Rosado. Pink wine, Rosé.

Socalcos. Walled vineyard terraces.

Tina. Large vat.

Vendimia. Harvest.

Vino de Autor. Also known as *Alta Expresión*. A term to describe a new wave in the late 1990s where producers turned away from Reserva categories to straightforward vintage-dated wines, often made with selected grapes, extended maceration and two years maturation in all new French oak barrels. These were part of the global trend at the time to produce dense, overextracted wines that would gain high scores from Robert Parker. Today, the style has calmed down, and often represents a more modern approach to wine in a traditional region.

Vino de Pago. Category introduced in 2003 to define single estate wine. Has been criticized since then for the variable quality of the wines.

Viñedo. Vineyard.

BIBLIOGRAPHY AND RESOURCES

Barquín, Jesús, Luis Gutiérrez, Víctor de la Serna, *The Finest Wines of Rioja and Northwest Spain*, Aurum, London 2011

Beevor, Antony, *The Battle for Spain*, Weidenfeld & Nicolson, London 2006

de Candamo, Luis G., *R. López de Heredia Viña Tondonia, Biografia del Rioja Supremo*, López de Heredia, Haro 1996

Consello Regulador da Denominación de Orixe Ribeiro, *O Ribeiro: Na Terra do vino*, 2010

Evans, Sarah Jane, *Seville*, Sinclair-Stevenson, London 1992

Fabiano, Ana, *The Wine Region of Rioja*, Sterling Epicure, New York 2012

Ford, Richard, *A Hand-book for Travellers in Spain and Readers at Home (1845)*, Centaur Press, Arundel and London 1966

Gibson, Ian, *Fire in the Blood: The New Spain*, BBC, London 1992

Gilmour, David, *The Transformation of Spain*, Quartet, London 1985

Gutiérrez, Luis, *Los Nuevos Viñadores*, Planeta Gastro, Madrid 2017

Hooper, John, *The Spaniards*, Penguin, London, 1987

Hopkins, Adam, *Spanish Journeys*, Viking, London 1992

Jacobs, Michael, *The Road to Santiago de Compostela*, Viking, London 1991

Jeffs, Julian, *The Wines of Spain*, Mitchell Beazley, London 2006

Kamen, Henry, *A Concise History of Spain*, Thames and Hudson, London 1973

Kurlansky, Mark, *The Basque History of the World*, Vintage, London 2000

La Rioja Alta S.A., *Three Centuries of La Rioja Alta S.A.*, Haro 2009

McNair, John M., *Education for a Changing Spain*, Manchester University Press, Manchester 1984

Preston, Paul, *The Spanish Holocaust*, Harper Press, London 2012

Pritchett, V.S., The Spanish Temper, Hogarth Press, London 1984

Radford, John, *The New Spain* (rev. edn), Mitchell Beazley, London 2004

Thomas, Hugh, *The Spanish Civil War*, Penguin, London 1971

Vega Sicilia, *1864–2014 Vega Sicilia 150 Anniversary*, Madrid 2014

www.labarranca.org

Wine guides

Guía Peñín, Madrid, annual

Guia Proensa, Madrid, annual

www.spanishwinelover.com

www.RobertParker.com

ACKNOWLEDGEMENTS

It is customary when writing Acknowledgements to thank your family last. I prefer to start with them. My husband, Richard, has been a terrific support throughout: fellow taster, car driver, enthusiast and critic, not just during the time of writing but across the years of our travels throughout Spain. This would have been a very different and lesser book without him. Very special thanks go to our daughters Consola and Seraphina who have been part of many of those travels and holidays. They have been very tolerant of endless vineyard visits and the occasional bottling line, as well as my late nights at the computer.

I first went to Spain to work during what is now called a gap year, before starting at Cambridge University. Since then I have returned on multiple occasions, practically every year. As a result there are so many people who have contributed to my knowledge and understanding over the years that I cannot name them all. Very many of them get special mentions in the book, and I thank them again here. However I'd like to highlight friends and colleagues in Spain who have made a real difference. Cristina Alcalá, wine writer and Galicia specialist; Pedro Ballesteros MW, a brilliant and remarkable ambassador for Spain; Ferran Centelles, sommelier–philosopher and a generous guide; and Amaya Cervera, creator with Yolanda Ortiz of the exceptional, independent Spanish–English website Spanish Wine Lover (www.spanishwinelover.com).

Special thanks go to Fernando Gurucharri and Miguel Berzosa of the Unión Española de Catadores. Hosts of the annual Bacchus wine-tasting, they have given me the chance to develop my ideas through wine-tastings and discussions with international colleagues in wine. There's a special category of wine professional who can make all the difference – sommeliers. Spain is blessed with some real stars, introducing consumers to new producers and new varieties, sharing excellence and originality. In addition to Ferran Centelles, I'd like to thank Audrey Doré and Josep Roca, José Godoy and Agustín Trapero.

Over the years I have been lucky enough to visit different areas of Spain under the auspices of ICEX, the Spanish Institute for Foreign Trade. Very often my host has been María José Sevilla, who could always be guaranteed to go a little further to make the visits more informative, as well as delicious. More recently, the Consejos Reguladores of DOs featured in this book have been a great help. I'd like to give personal thanks to some individuals within the CRDOs, who have given me specific assistance: Juan Gil de Araújo and Ramón Huidobro of Rías Baixas; José Ramón Calvo and J. Antonio Txapartegi of Txakoli de Bizkaya; the team at CRDOCa Rioja; as well as Xoan Cannas and the Instituto Galego do Vino.

Over recent years, with the generous assistance of the members of the Fundación para la Cultura del Vino (Marqués de Riscal, Muga, La Rioja Alta, Terras Gauda and Vega Sicilia), the Institute of Masters of Wine has been running Masterclasses in Haro for potential students. Today there's a new generation of MWs living and working in Spain, some of long standing, others recent passes, and all have helped me: Norrel Robertson MW, Fernando Mora MW, Andreas Kubach MW and some more very-soon-to-be MWs following up behind.

In the UK, I have really benefited from the assistance of specialist wine PRs. It is great to have a chance to thank them here: Charlotte Hey, whether she has been working for Spanish wine, or for Sherry or for individual producers, is a terrific friend and answerer of late night emails; equally Angeline Bayly of Bespoke Drinks Media; Rosamund Barton at R&R Teamwork; all the Rioja team, past and present, at Phipps PR; Emma and Ali at Emma Wellings; and Celine Bouteiller and Sue Glasgow, separately and together. Both in Spain and in the UK, a number of my fellow members of the Gran Orden de Caballeros de Vino have been valuable sources of information and advice.

I am very grateful to the team at *Decanter* magazine, and especially Amy Wislocki, Tina Gellie, and Christelle Guibert. They have given me the space to go deeply into some of the ideas I explore further here. I also feel very strongly about the importance of blind tasting – without being influenced by labels, bottle shapes and reputations. Working at *Decanter* and at the Decanter World Wine Awards I am able to taste Spain (and the rest of the world) blind. From that process, without preconceptions, you can make terrific discoveries. Some of those discoveries are mentioned in these pages. I'm grateful to fellow tasters for their expertise and for opening my eyes – especially Pierre Mansour and Christine Parkinson.

I owe a good deal to my predecessors as authors of books on Spain in the UK, Julian Jeffs and the late John Radford. It's been too long since their books appeared, so I am delighted that Richard Burton at Infinite Ideas relaunched The Classic Wine Library, and commissioned this title. Series Editor Richard Mayson has been full of great advice, and Rebecca Clare has been a marvellous editor. I'd like to thank also Elizabeth Hinks for proofreading and Catherine Hall for the index. Writing a book is a team effort; but the factual errors and inaccuracies are all mine.

INDEX

Note: Page numbers in *italic* refer to maps.

325